LANE

LANEGAN

By
Greg Prato

Written by Greg Prato
Printed and distributed by Greg Prato Writer, Corp
Published by Greg Prato Writer, Corp
Front cover photo by Charles Peterson
Back cover photo by Steven J. Messina
Copyright © 2023, Greg Prato Writer, Corp. All rights
reserved. First Edition, February 2023

ISBN: 9798376855645

INTRODUCTION

"Who is that mysterious man who just sauntered on stage mid-set, and started singing? Could it be…nah, it couldn't be. *Could it?*" It's fair to assume that this thought that entered my noggin on the evening of Thursday, May 30, 2002 would soon be shared with quite a few other fellow concert goers who attended a date on Queens of the Stone Age's tour in support of their breakthrough album, *Songs for the Deaf.*

But especially, early on in the tour, when it wasn't exactly widespread news that none other than *Mark Lanegan* was now a member of the Queens – and would sing lead on several tunes smack dab in the middle of the set each night (and eventually, returning towards the end for even further vocalizing).

At that point, I had only known Lanegan via his work with the Screaming Trees (and in particular, a CD I acquired back in the fall of '92, *Sweet Oblivion*). But when I eventually realized that some of my favorite Queens tunes featured Mark's vocals ("In the Fade," "Hanging Tree," "God Is in the Radio," part of "Song for the Deaf," etc.), it was time to dig a bit deeper. Beginning with *Bubblegum* and then going back to *The Winding Sheet*, I was finally introduced to the solo work of Mark Lanegan, and in turn – adequately familiarized myself with one of my favorite rock singers of all-time.

So…imagine my surprise (and delight) when I was asked by the *Heavy Consequence* site in December 2021 if I would be interested in conducting a phone interview with the man himself, to discuss his latest book, *Devil in a Coma*. Of course, I immediately said yes. And although I heard that he could be a bit of a prickly interviewee, I looked forward to the challenge.

Although his voice sounded a bit weak during our

chat, Mark was surprisingly nice and talkative – and sounded hopeful that his health had finally taken a turn for the better (after a horrible bout with Covid, which served as the basis for his aforementioned book). In fact, I recall ending the interview by telling him, "It was great speaking with you, because I've been such a fan of yours for so long, and personally, I'm just glad to hear that you're doing better as far as your health." His reply couldn't have been sweeter. "Thank you. That makes my day."

Having received his autobiography, *Sing Backwards and Weep*, from Old Saint Nick just a few weeks later, I looked forward to some stimulating reading. But what I wasn't prepared for was a book that I could not stop reading – despite it being an incredibly dark and difficult read in parts.

As a result, a thorough examination of Mark's past discography ensued (and discovering such outstanding solo efforts as *Whiskey for the Holy Ghost*, *Field Songs*, and *Blues Funeral*, as well as re-discovering *Bubblegum* and *The Winding Sheet*, among others) – which further cemented my appreciation of his music and singing, but this time, fully discovering his exceptional gift of lyric writing.

And then, just two months after our conversation…being absolutely *stunned* to learn that on February 22, 2022, Mark had passed away suddenly (after it appeared as though he was finally in the clear, health-wise). And while I thought *Sing Backwards and Weep* was outstanding, it ended abruptly (circa 2002) – so it failed to cover the Queens era, as well as his other projects of the next two decades. Additionally, his book was told solely from Mark's point of view, with no other voices adding their two cents.

Which, eventually led to the idea of paying tribute to Mark in book form – by interviewing as many of his musical partners, collaborators, and friends that I could, and having them share memories, recollections, and observations (as well as including my aforementioned chat with Mark). Plus, covering his career post-2002. The result? The book you are now holding in your hands – issued one year from his passing.

Live 'til you die,
Greg Prato

p.s. Questions? Comments? Feel free to email me at gregprato@yahoo.com.

p.p.s. If you haven't done so already, I wholeheartedly suggest that you also check out my earlier book, *Grunge Is Dead: The Oral History of Seattle Rock Music*, as the Screaming Trees' career is discussed in greater detail (as well as including quotes from exclusive interviews with both Van Conner and Mark Pickerel).

INTERVIEWS

JOHN AGNELLO – producer/mixer
SALLY BARRY – friend, singer
CHAD CHANNING – Nirvana drummer
GARY LEE CONNER – Screaming Trees guitarist
CHARLES R. CROSS – author/writer, editor of *The Rocket*
JEAN-PHILIPPE DE GHEEST – Mark Lanegan drummer
CLAY DECKER – friend, tattoo artist
JACK ENDINO – producer/mixer
JEFF FIELDER – Mark Lanegan guitarist
CHRIS GOSS – producer, Masters of Reality singer/guitarist
JONATHAN HISCHKE – Mark Lanegan bassist
JESSE HUGHES – Eagles of Death Metal singer/guitarist
MEGAN JASPER – Sub Pop Records CEO
ALAIN JOHANNES – producer, Eleven singer/guitarist
MIKE JOHNSON – Mark Lanegan guitarist, ex-Dinosaur Jr. bassist, solo artist
TRAVIS KELLER – friend, cameraman, photographer, Buddyhead founder
JOSH KLINGHOFFER – Mark Lanegan drummer, ex-Red Hot Chili Peppers guitarist
NICK OLIVERI – ex-Queens of the Stone Age singer/bassist
CHARLES PETERSON – photographer
MATT PINFIELD – friend, radio/TV personality
ROBERT ROTH – Truly singer/guitarist, Mark Lanegan guitarist
ALDO STRUYF – Mark Lanegan bassist
KIM THAYIL – Soundgarden guitarist
GREG WERCKMAN – Ipecac Records co-founder

CONTENTS

This book is dedicated to the memory and music of
Mark William Lanegan:
November 25, 1964–February 22, 2022

[Photo by Charles Peterson]

Chapter 1
MEETING

Memories of first crossing paths with Mark,
and initial impressions.

GARY LEE CONNER [Screaming Trees guitarist]: We
all lived in Ellensburg, and I was actually in the same grade
as his sister. Back in elementary school, we were both on the
"school patrol." That was a big deal back then – we'd put the
flag up and stuff – and she was the lieutenant. She would
always be like, "You're not walking fast enough." [Laughs]
She was kind of nasty, like before Mark was sometimes –
maybe it runs in the family, I don't know. Mark was about
two years younger than me. He seemed like a little kid,
because I was in high school band – I played trumpet – and
we were on a band trip up to Canada. His sister was in the
band, as well, and his mom was a chaperone, and he came
along because they didn't have anybody to watch him at
home. He was probably around twelve…he was probably
drinking by that point, because I know he started drinking
when he was twelve. He was this little redhaired kid – he
hadn't got tall yet. That was my first impression of him.

And then by the time I graduated, I started hearing
about him, because he was getting in trouble with the police
– drugs and alcohol and all sorts of stuff. He had a horrible
wreck driving out in the country – that was a big story around
town. He got hurt really bad. And, he sold drugs. He was
"the bad guy in town." He wasn't cool or anything. It wasn't
like, "Oh, that guy's into music" – at least *we* didn't know it.
I don't know when he started getting into music. And then,
Van [Conner, Gary Lee's brother] and Mark Pickerel, they
were in school at the same time. And they had classes
together and got to know him a little bit. I never went to
parties or anything around town, so I didn't meet up with

him at parties. But they did. I think Pickerel was a freshman, Van was a sophomore, and Lanegan was a senior – that's when they started going out and meeting up with him at parties. He was probably a bad influence. [Laughs]

Also, he used to live down the street from us. He walked by our house – I've heard this story, that he saw Van play with a bunch of toys out in the yard and was jealous. But he was one of those people around town that you know their name, and it got to be like, *"That guy's a real badass."* But then after, Van and Pickerel – this is in like, '83/'84 – Lanegan must have graduated in '82, because I graduated in '80, and Van graduated in '85. We had started cover bands – we had a band called Him and Those Guys, and another one called Explosive Generation. Pickerel was in the first one, and we did punk rock covers, Beatles covers, and heavy metal covers. Pretty much anything. Playing dances was the idea – we had no idea about original music, and how you did it.

Then one day, I heard Van talk about Lanegan. He said, "He's into all the same kind of stuff we're into." Because we'd been getting into a lot of new wave, punk, and other kinds of music – Black Flag, and stuff like that. He wanted to meet me, because he wanted to trade records. So, I went over to his house and went through some of his records, and he came over to my place. What did we trade…I think it was a Stranglers record, maybe Gang of Four. And this was in Ellensburg, where *nobody* listened to that kind of stuff. But there was this whole other bunch of people – Lanegan, his friend Matt Barnum who's an old friend of ours…he was in a band called King Crab later. So, we traded records, and I had his records for a while – this is probably early '85. I can't remember if we ever did trade back. So, that was our "pre-exposure to Mark."

And then Van and Mark Pickerel decided they were

going to start another band – without me – with Lanegan. Originally, he was going to play drums. He didn't really play drums very well, but that was what he was going to do. I don't know if Van was going to sing – because Van had been singing in the cover band. But they had to practice in our house – *in my room*, where we had practiced before. So, I kind of wormed my way into it. And I think my mom kind of had to tell them, "You have to let Lee play with you guys." So, I started playing bass. I always wanted to be a bass player – I was really into Chris Squire and Yes when I was in high school, before I got into punk. I was a total prog rock snob until I was about 20/21. So, Lanegan came over, and I played bass, Van played guitar – because he knew a lot of Black Flag covers. And we also did Hendrix and Who covers. It was like, old '60s psychedelic stuff or punk rock – which is really what the Screaming Trees started out as. A mix. Especially live, we were like punk rock doing psychedelic stuff.

So, Lanegan decided to sing – I don't know what Mark Pickerel was going to do originally. But anyway, he did that for a month two. This was in the summer of '85. Before that, I remember one time, Mark was still drinking, but the pivotal moment in his life was in the summer of '85, he was working at Twin City Foods – it was a big food processing place. And he was working in a pea field, and he got run over by some kind of truck or tractor. His legs…he didn't break them, but they were, like, swollen up black. And he couldn't walk – for a couple of months. And during that time, Van would go over and hang out with him and drink. One time I went over there, and it was like, five in the morning. I didn't really drink anything – I maybe drank one beer. But Lanegan and his girlfriend – who was living with him at the time – she was like, "*You guys get out of here!*" We were listening to music and stuff.

Van and Mark Pickerel were in high school, and they ran away to Spokane – which is the other way from Seattle. It's about 200,000 people. And there was a very small music scene there – like, a few punk rock bands. I never really heard about it until later. And we had no idea there was anything going on in Seattle. We went to Seattle to see shows – mostly big shows, at the time. Y'know, theater or arena shows. So, they went to Spokane and found out there was something going on. Van was telling Lanegan about this, and Lanegan is like, "*We're going to Spokane to start a band.*" We were all going to move to Spokane that night…probably the next day! It was like drunken, five in the morning talk.

And that was sort of the seed of the band. Where it was like. "OK. We're getting out of this town." And that was always the theme in a lot of our music. Especially on the first record [1986's *Clairvoyance*], the song "Strange Out Here" – Mark wrote all the lyrics to that one, and it's all about getting out of town. There's a couple of other tunes that didn't get on it, like one called "The Bath" – hopefully we'll release it one of these days – and the lyric was "Leaving tonight and I don't want to stay." So that was the idea – to get to Spokane and start a band. It didn't really take off.

But we kept rehearsing and I had been writing poetry for a long time. I always wanted to write songs – but I didn't really know how to do it. So, I was really into poetry, and then a few months before we got together, I got a four-track cassette recorder – and I had been actually writing some stuff. I played some of it for Lanegan, and he was like, "We should do some of these songs." That was the first idea – "Wait…*we can actually do original songs.*" This was pretty much par for the course for the next few years – I don't think we even practiced the songs too much, maybe a few times. And then we played live. Because I think I took the demos with a drum machine and had Lanegan sing, and we'd just give the tape to Pickerel and say, "Learn the song," then go to the studio and record it. But anyway, we made a demo tape – most of the stuff that would have been on the *Other Worlds* album. That was released in '88 on SST, but it was the very first thing we recorded, and it first came out on cassette in '85. You can tell it was like…"baby Lanegan."

That was the weird thing – he had only sang at a party once with some band. And he had no idea he could sing. We were recording these songs that I had written, and we wrote one song together – "Pictures in My Mind." That was probably the first song he ever wrote – I think he wrote most of the lyrics. We sat down in my room with a four-track and two chairs, and I was telling him how to sing. [Laughs] So, he did that. And then at the same time, we heard about this studio in town – Velvetone. It wasn't really called "Velvetone" – that came later, that was the record company name. And Steve Fisk was around town and he was the engineer. To us, he was kind of famous – because he had a single out and Pickerel heard of him. But he was the engineer down there, and we went down there and booked a weekend…and it kind of clicked. Especially with Steve – he thought we were pretty interesting, being from Ellensburg.

Right after that was when Steve and Sam Albright – who owned the studio [Creative Fire in Ellensburg] – they had a record label, and they didn't have much on it. They had Twangbabies – which was kind of a comedy/country band. That was the only record they'd put out. And they were like, "We should do a record." We had to pay for most of it – but they helped us a lot. We didn't play live until after *Clairvoyance* was done. It was kind of the opposite of most bands – we did a record and *then* played live. Then we found out Mark could sing. We spent several months working on the *Clairvoyance* record – started in late 1985, and through the spring.

On that record, some of the songs we wrote together – which was not what happened later, except for on [1992's] *Sweet Oblivion.* And Mark found his voice all of a sudden. You listen to stuff like "Strange Out Here" – he wrote the lyrics to that and I wrote the music. He played violin. He didn't know how to play, but he played this funky violin part – which Steve put on this weird, backwards, atmospheric sort of sound. It kind of sucks because later, he stopped really writing stuff in the Trees – I guess he didn't think he could write. Because after *Clairvoyance*, it pretty much turned into me writing songs all the time and I'd give it to Mark, and he'd be like, "We should do this one, we should do that one." And some of them were *way* too psychedelic – so he'd change the lyrics since he was going to sing it. And at first, there was probably some controversy between us about that. But after a couple of records, I was like, "OK. He knows what he's doing." Because he loved music and had a real feel for what was good and what was not.

Also, the thing was the other three guys in the band didn't want to be a psychedelic band, and I wanted to be like a psychedelic revival band. If you look at the cover of *Clairvoyance*, the way everyone is dressed, I have the Beatle hairdo and round glasses, psychedelic tie – that was what I was really into. Because right before, I really got into the whole *Pebbles* compilations – '60s garage rock, and a lot of the '80s paisley underground and garage rock revival. That was what I thought we were doing, so, that was what I was writing. And I loved psychedelic music from way back – the Beatles were one of the first bands that I really listened to.

After we finished the record, we finally got to play a couple of shows. The first show we played, I don't know if you would consider it "a show" – because it was at a group home for mentally disabled people called Elmview, in Ellensburg. Someone we knew worked there, and said,

"We'd love to have some entertainment." There was a video, but it disappeared – I remember seeing it years ago. I was just standing there and Mark was singing, and all these people were having fun. It wasn't a lot of people – probably ten or twenty people, in various stages of mental disability.

Our *official* first show, we got hooked up with Calvin Johnson from Beat Happening, and K Cassettes. He helped us distribute our cassette. And then I realized, "Calvin Johnson...that sounds familiar." It turned out that Calvin lived in Ellensburg when he was in the seventh and eighth grade, and was in my class in junior high. I remembered him, but he was just this little, geeky guy. I remember one time, I think he pulled the fire alarm – supposedly. Calvin was great. A lot of the early days of Screaming Trees were tied in with Beat Happening and Girl Trouble. We did a lot of shows together.

Our very first show was in Olympia, at a place called GESCO – it was just in an old garage downtown. We opened for a band called 28th Day – it had Barbara Manning, who later did solo stuff, and the SF Seals. And something clicked at that show. I had played live, but I didn't go nuts though – when we did the cover band thing. But for some reason, at that show, I was jumping all over. I don't know if I was doing windmills yet or not. [Laughs] It took a while to figure out doing that without killing myself. I remember after the show, everyone was like, "You're a wild man!" I'm like, *"Really?"* It was funny, because I was wearing these horrible Beatle boots – with the big heels. I don't know how I did it with those. I got rid of those pretty quick. It was like, "Whoa. People actually like us?" It was either that show or the next one, that Buzz Osborne was there from Melvins, and a lot of people we got to know later from Olympia. So, that was a real formative experience of, "There is something going on over here."

Still, Seattle to us was like, a million miles away. We heard Green River and had one of their albums, and maybe Skin Yard. But there really wasn't much of a scene there. It was real, real underground at the time. And Green River was probably the only band anyone ever heard of outside of Seattle. One of their albums was on Homestead, so it was a little bit national. Then, a month later, we went and played in Olympia and we opened for the Wipers. I can't remember if we listened to them before or not, but that was amazing to see the Wipers and Greg Sage. That was the second show we played, and there were more people at that one, because the Wipers were playing. And then, the album came out. We did a tour of the west coast – just about six or seven shows. And that's when…see, Steve Fisk knew Ray Farrell, who worked at SST, and got some people to come down and see us – we played a record store show, at Texas Records in Santa Monica. I think he really liked Mark's voice, because that was one of the first times someone went, "Man, *he can really sing*." And we found a little bit of ourselves live. Even when there were a couple of people there, we still tried to put on a good show and do all the crazy antics. So, that was the first time we ever got out of Washington and played shows.

The first year we were together, we hung out a lot and everyone worked in the video store. My family started it in 1984. Lanegan worked in the video store, Mark Pickerel worked in the video store. And there was this huge back room. That was another main thing that helped the band – we decided that we would move the stuff out of my room at home to the back of the video store. And it was 50 or 75 feet by 50 feet. It was *huge*. A giant room. Empty. In the back alley, downtown – so we could be loud. Although, in the video store you could hear it, but nobody was going to say anything – because my mom and dad were always really supportive of the band, so they didn't care. And later, people were like, "The Screaming Trees are practicing back there! Oh my God!" [Laughs] So, that was a great thing to have. And that's where I wrote – I had my four-track back there, finally.

JACK ENDINO [producer/mixer, Skin Yard guitarist]: I started hearing about them in '85/'86. I was in Skin Yard and I was working in Reciprocal Recording as of '86. Skin Yard had been around since '85. I was good buddies with Soundgarden, Green River, and all those other guys that I'd been recording. And people just started talking about the Screaming Trees. At that point, I think they had put out a couple of records on SST. They lived in Ellensburg – I don't remember seeing them right away…I don't even know the first time I saw the Screaming Trees play a live show. It would have been very typical in those days for me to have been recording them before ever seeing them – because I was so busy in the studio. But I probably saw them at some point, and I wound up recording the *Buzz Factory* album.

KIM THAYIL [Soundgarden guitarist]: We played a show at Central Washington University, in Ellensburg – sometime in '86 or '87. We were opening for Faith No More. We played a few shows in the northwest – when Chuck Mosley was still in Faith No More. The first one was in Ellensburg. At that show, we met all the guys in Faith No More, which figured prominently in the rest of our career and we toured with them a number of times. We also met Steve Fisk – who was a producer who did Screaming Trees records on Velvetone, and then later, SST. Also, we met Eric Johnson, who ended up becoming our very first tour manager – in Hiro Yamamoto's green van, with no windows on the sides or the back! We gave him the nickname "Gunny Junk." He worked for Soundgarden for years, he went on to work with Pearl Jam, Rage Against the Machine, Neil Young for 15 years, and is currently the tour manager for Metallica.

And we met Damon Stewart – who was a DJ at a college radio station, who went on to become a commercial DJ in Seattle at KISW. And he played a lot of Soundgarden, Nirvana, Mother Love Bone, and...he played a lot of Screaming Trees, who we met *also* at that show – we meet Lanegan, the Conner brothers, and Mark Pickerel. I would regularly talk to Mark Pickerel after that, and occasionally I would talk to Lanegan. I didn't talk to Gary or Van as much – unless I saw them out at a show. But Mark Pickerel was very forward about exchanging numbers and staying in contact.

The Screaming Trees played a very important part in the advancement of our career, because they went from Velvetone Records to SST Records. And when they were at SST, they talked to Greg Ginn and Chuck Dukowski of Black Flag fame, who also, ran SST at the time. Mark Pickerel, Lanegan, and Gary spoke highly of us – "There's a band in Seattle that would be perfect for SST." They talked us up, as well as a few other SST bands – Saint Vitus, Das Damen, and the Meat Puppets might have thrown a word in for us, as well. We were on Sub Pop at the time, but we didn't have a record deal. We were planning on making future records with Sub Pop, but due to cash flow problems, we took the great opportunity that was presented to us by SST and made a record for them [1988's *Ultramega OK*]. And off we went.

CHARLES R. CROSS [author/writer, editor of *The Rocket*]: I saw the Screaming Trees *a ton* – they were one of my favorite bands. The Conner brothers, the way they moved around – Mark didn't move as much – they were something to watch. Physically, there's not a lot of bands that looked like that on stage. But what was most distinct about the band since day one was two things: their guitar sound, which wasn't quite like any of the other bands; and then additionally, Mark's voice. Not that the drumming wasn't great as well, it was – Mark Pickerel is one of my favorite drummers.

Whether the Screaming Trees really qualify under the typical "grunge narrative"…or does anybody, other than Blood Circus, the Fluid, and a couple other bands? I'd already been hip to bands like the Three O'Clock and some of those other LA [paisley underground] bands, and the Trees definitely had some of that sound to their sound. I liked that. They also had more pop elements than Mudhoney, and some of the other bands.

MIKE JOHNSON [Mark Lanegan guitarist, ex-Dinosaur Jr. bassist, solo artist]: I think it was probably in 1987 – right after the first Screaming Trees record came out. Those guys came through Eugene, Oregon, where I lived and had a band, Snakepit, and they had a show set up with Beat Happening. It was supposed to be Beat Happening, Girl Trouble, and Screaming Trees, and Girl Trouble opted out, so my band wormed our way on the gig – and we wound up meeting those guys. Mark and I became friends after that.

CHAD CHANNING [Nirvana drummer]: I think the first time I met him might have been in Ellensburg. My girlfriend, Justine, just read Mark Lanegan's book [2020's *Sing Backwards and Weep: A Memoir*], and in there, he talks about seeing Nirvana for the first time. There was something in there about how originally he wasn't going to go to the show, but he ended up going to the show and he really liked it. He seemed really nice. Kind of a quiet demeanor.

GARY LEE CONNER: We were working on another record for Velvetone. After the California tour, in '87, Steve Fisk was helping us try and get an actual label. And we had a little bit of interest from Pink Dust – who I think was part of Restless and Enigma. It was like, the more indie part of Enigma. The first couple of Flaming Lips albums were on Pink Dust, so we were like, "Well, maybe we should be on that label." But then right when we were thinking about going with those guys, all of a sudden, we were at the video store working, and a call came in – I think it was just an out-of-the-blue call – from Greg Ginn from SST, and talked to Lanegan. He talked to him for a while. He was not saying, "Oh, we want to sign you guys." But then Mark said, "Do you want to sign us?" And Greg was like, "Yeah!" He really liked *Other Worlds.*

     I don't know about Mark, but for me, that was probably one of the coolest things – other than getting married and having kids. Getting signed to SST was just a dream come true. When we started the band, we weren't like, "Oh, we want to be famous." I was just like, "We want to be a band. *A real band.* And put out records…maybe two." We didn't think too much about touring. But we were so lucky, because once we got on SST, they also had a booking agency that was part of SST – and they'd done all the Black Flag tours in the early '80s. They had a whole network of clubs that we could play in. It was one thing going to California – that was kind of short. But all of a sudden, we're off for a whole month at a time. And I'm sure a lot of the tension probably started on tour. Because when you're sitting in a van with everybody for an entire month…at first, you'd only get one hotel room. Then after we could afford it, we got two hotel rooms – one for Mark and the other one for everybody else. [Laughs]

CHARLES PETERSON [photographer]: The very first time I met Mark was when Bruce Pavitt and I drove out to Ellensburg to photograph the Screaming Trees for the *Sub Pop 200* compilation booklet [circa 1988]. It was just Mark and the band in an alley on a summer day. When you first met the band, it's always the brothers that strike you first. But Mark seemed quiet. I don't really recall him much from that visit, per se.

I don't think he'd quite grown into his "persona" yet. I mean, it was pretty early days for the band. I remember him being a little camera shy. And then the next time we properly met was when he was in Seattle, and he came over to the house to shoot some promo solo pix for the seven-inch that Sub Pop was going to be doing. He came over, and he was always concerned about the way he looked in photographs. Even more so at that age probably than later on.

MEGAN JASPER [Sub Pop Records CEO]: The first time I met Mark was at a Dinosaur Jr. show – where the Screaming Trees were opening [circa 1988]. Both were signed to SST Records. I want to say it was in New London, Connecticut. I thought the Screaming Trees were amazing and I loved them, and Mark did the thing that Mark always did – showed up on stage, played a killer set, and then I don't think I saw him again until the next show. I will say that my first impression was that he was really shy. But he was kind – he said hello. I moved to Seattle in '89, so I met those guys before I came out here. When I met Mark, I don't think he was drinking – I think he was totally sober. And I remember – and I think it's in the book [*Sing Backwards and Weep*] – that he'd been told by a doctor, he wouldn't live much longer if he kept drinking the way he had been.

SALLY BARRY [friend, singer]: I met Mark in 1989 – in New York City at the Pyramid Club. I lived in New York at the time, and I was playing drums with a band called the Honeymoon Killers. The Pyramid had booked a Halloween show with us, Gwar, and Screaming Trees – who were on tour at the time. How I met Mark was the Trees came in and Mark asked which "one" I was. He was like, "Are you Sally?" I said, "Yeah," and he delivered a hug from his friend, Justin, who was another musician that I'd met and hung out with on one of the previous Killers tours. So, he was passing regards. Then a couple of years later, Justin moved to New York and we were living together. So, anytime the Trees came through, we would hang out and Mark would come downtown – and sometimes stay at our apartment.

JACK ENDINO: I ended up recording a solo record for Van, which was called Solomon Grundy – which came out on New Alliance, which was a sub-label of SST, really. And then Sub Pop had me do Mark's first solo record not very long after that – [1990's] *The Winding Sheet*. And I ended up working on [1994's] *Whiskey for the Holy Ghost*...well, in between there, Sub Pop finally got in on the Screaming Trees action – even as they were already talking to a major label. And they did *Change Has Come*...it was a double seven-inch, if I remember right.

I think there were two songs that I recorded and two songs that Steve Fisk recorded, and Glitterhouse released it as a CD EP and stuck an extra Steve Fisk recording on there – so it became a five-song CD EP or a four-song double seven-inch. And that was the one-and-only thing that Sub Pop ever did for the Screaming Trees. The Screaming Trees ended up recording with Terry Date and Chris Cornell – to do *Uncle Anesthesia*. And then in spring and summer 1991

– Reciprocal closed around July of 1991, so it was in the last couple of weeks of Reciprocal Recording's existence as a business – that I was working on Mark Lanegan's second solo record, *Whiskey for the Holy Ghost*. And that record I think took four different producers to bring it over the finish line.

ROBERT ROTH [Truly singer/guitarist, Mark Lanegan guitarist]: At one point, after my only band before Truly [called Storybook Krooks] broke up, I tried out for Nirvana, and there was sort of a two or three month period where I was waiting to hear back from them. And Lanegan was the one who delivered the tape of my band to Kurt Cobain. This was August of '89. My friend was Justin Williams, and he ended up playing violin on *The Winding Sheet*.

As it turns out, a bunch of Seattle folks worked at a record store called Peaches, and they were selling a ton of the Storybook Krooks tape out of there. We kind of started a buzz. But, the band broke up. I ran into Jonathan Poneman on the bus, and I gave my tape to Justin – who worked with Mark. Mark loved the tape, and in the interim, wanted to start a band with Justin and I. He was just starting on *The Winding Sheet*, and then, the Trees got signed to Epic. So, that never happened.

Then, Truly started not long after. We were in the studio working on what would become *Fast Stories from Kid Coma*, and Mark came out to the studio – just to hang out and listen. He was one of the first people to hear tracks like "Strangling" and "Chlorine," and really loved it. We just always got along with him – he was a nice, mellow dude…aside from his reputation. We got asked many times to open for the Trees, and Pickerel [who left the Trees and joined Robert and Hiro Yamamoto in Truly] was hesitant for some reason. The same with Hiro and Soundgarden [Hiro left Soundgarden shortly before Truly's formation] – at first we got asked to open for them a bunch.

Eventually, we did play with the Trees – it was for a thing called Endfest. It was Truly, the Trees, Dramarama, and…Barenaked Ladies. [Laughs] So, Mark and I would run into each other and drink, shoot the shit, hit on girls together, and whatever – just part of the late night Seattle drinking scene. That was sorta early '90s.

MATT PINFIELD [friend, radio/TV personality]: I first met Mark at the radio station that I was the music director and programmer of, WHTG in Asbury Park, New Jersey – back when *Uncle Anesthesia* came out, in 1991. He came through the radio station and sat in with me for an hour and hung out. And that's where our friendship began, because we talked about music – "Bed of Roses" was their brand new single and *Uncle Anesthesia* was their first release on a major label [Epic].

They had almost an indie, post-punk, Joy Division, Cure, "dark wave" kind of feel in their earlier music. You could tell there was some inspiration from some of the stuff that was coming over from the UK. Their sound changed if you listen to some of the early independent records – even the artwork was very reminiscent of some of the stuff that was happening over there at that period of time. Which is really interesting, because it kind of informs the way Mark had done so many different styles of music as a solo artist and experimented so much.

JOHN AGNELLO [producer/mixer]: It was around 1990 that my whole life took a dramatic turn for the better. I was invited to a meeting at Columbia Records, who wanted to sign Dinosaur Jr. They brought me up as the "young, hip, new engineer," who they would put in the room to make the

Dinosaur Jr. record. And I got to meet J Mascis, and there was another person at the meeting, Don Fleming, who was basically in the band at the time, and they had done a single for the song "The Wagon," which they re-did for the *Green Mind* record. Columbia did not sign them, but I made a good impression on both of those guys. And Don went on to produce records like Teenage Fanclub's *Bandwagonesque* and the Screaming Trees' *Sweet Oblivion*.

And Don hired me as his engineer – in New York, at a studio named Baby Monster on 14th Street. And that's where we recorded *Sweet Oblivion*. And that's when I met Mark. Me and Mark hit it off really well. To the point of Don kind of bequeathed the role of watching or looking after Lanegan – I was kind of "in charge" of him. And *that's* when we became friends. In his book, when I walk into the scene for his second solo record, he talks very glowingly about me. I know he trashes a lot of people in that book, but there's a couple of us that make it out scot-free. We got along really great. *Sweet Oblivion* did great, and the *Singles Soundtrack* and "I Nearly Lost You" was the big hit for them.

SALLY BARRY: When he was in town doing *Whiskey*, he was hanging out with us a lot. And Justin was going to do a little keyboard part on *Whiskey*. Mark and I really liked to go out drinking together. We had become fast friends – we got along great. And I could keep up with him, drinking. [Laughs] I was a prodigious drinker at the time. Justin was not so much of a drinker and he had a regular day job – I was self-employed, making my own hours. So, Mark and I would just go out on our own in the city, and do a lot of drinking.

We were in Max Fish or someplace like that, and we were sitting there and many drinks in, and we both started spontaneously singing along with the jukebox. He didn't know I sang – he just knew I was a drummer, and we started singing together and it sounded great. He was like, "Oh shit! Come and sing on my record!" So, I hung out during the *Whiskey* sessions. We hung out together a lot during that. A couple of years later, Justin wanted to go back to Seattle, so I moved to Seattle and things just went from there. I was good friends with the Trees and with Mark, and we all just hung out a lot.

CHRIS GOSS [producer, Masters of Reality singer/guitarist]: It would have been when he was recording the *Dust* record with George Drakoulias with the Screaming Trees [circa 1995/'96]. George had called and asked if I wanted to do some backing vocals for the album, and being a Trees fan at the time, I said "Of course." And that's when I met him. At the time, he was still a heavy heroin user, and when he was in that condition, he was very shy. I think he respected me a bit from the work I had done previously.

In any case, he was kind of shy and quiet. I don't want to say "ashamed," but not too proud of the condition he was in. A lot of junkies – especially when they're new at it, which he wasn't – kind of wear their heart on their sleeve, and are almost like, *proud* of the fact. Kind of hip. Like, they think they're "hip junkies." And that wasn't his case at all – you could tell he did not like the condition he was in.

JOSH KLINGHOFFER [Mark Lanegan drummer, ex-Red Hot Chili Peppers guitarist]: It must have been around the early '90s [that Josh first heard Mark's music]. I think I turned twelve in 1991, so I probably first heard of them in '92 – by the time the *Singles Soundtrack* came out, I knew of them already. But I have a friend who was a huge fan of the SST records. So, I was listening to them a bit back then through him. And I remember the Screaming Trees,

Soul Asylum, and the Spin Doctors all toured together in '93 – but I didn't go for some reason, but my friend went. And he said that they didn't really play anything off those early records. I kind of listened to them in and amongst all the other bands of that time. But through my friend, I would gravitate more towards some of those earlier records.

Which wasn't really by any stretch a functioning band – if I listened to those early SST records, or even *Uncle Anesthesia*, it didn't seem like the band that was continuing to tour and make records like *Sweet Oblivion* and *Dust*, and Barrett [Martin, Mark Pickerel's replacement] being the drummer. It seemed like a very different band. And in '96, I had a strange intern-type job at Ted Gardner's office – he was one of the founders of Lollapalooza. So, I was kind of running around at that Lollapalooza like a runner. Like a little assistant. Definitely once – if not more than once – I kind of ran into Lanegan, running an errand from here to there as a 16-year-old. And he was wearing all black, looking very...*unapproachable*. [Laughs] I saw the Screaming Trees at that Lollapalooza, and they seemed very unexcited to be there. Or least *he* did.

GREG WERCKMAN [Ipecac Records co-founder]: I was a fan of the Screaming Trees and any time they'd come to San Francisco, I'd go see them play. I met Mark a long time ago. One time, he came to town and he wasn't feeling great – I think he had just gotten out of rehab – and he was doing an interview at the college radio station. He called and asked if I wanted to go to lunch. Basically, he was like, "I'm in a weird place right now. I need to get my feet back on the ground with my solo career." And he asked if I would manage him. So, I did that. I told him I was really busy with my own stuff, but I would help him get his feet on the ground. I worked with him in that capacity during the time he was making the record *I'll Take Care of You* [an all-covers release, from 1999].

I helped him put some stuff together – get a little money for publishing stuff – and we stayed really good friends. At a certain point, my life with my label got really busy, and he needed more and more time, so I helped him find a real full-time manager. And through the years, he found little loopholes in his deals – he really liked my label, so he'd be like, "I'd really like to do things with Ipecac from time to time." Which I was more than happy to have – and it also helped him financially. At Ipecac, we don't offer real huge advances, so he went to some labels that gave him a lot of upfront money – to help him live – but kept it open so every once in a while, he could do something with us.

ALAIN JOHANNES [producer, Eleven singer/guitarist]: I think the first time I actually saw him in person was when we were on the *Euphoria Morning* tour, and Chris [Cornell], Natasha [Shneider], and I ended up at the same airport as the Screaming Trees – getting on a flight. And then I didn't really see him until the Desert Sessions. My band, Eleven, became labelmates with Queens of the Stone Age when A&M folded and became part of Interscope. And then we ended up befriending and touring with Queens of the Stone Age, and eventually, I joined. We toured and became friends – I recorded some b-sides for Queens, and then Josh goes, "I do this thing, Desert Sessions – at Joshua Tree in Rancho de la Luna. I'd love for you to be a part of it."

So, I drove out there [for recordings that would eventually comprise 2001's *Desert Sessions 7 & 8*]. And Josh goes, "*This is Mark Lanegan.*" I scan the room, and didn't see anyone. And then I turn back around slowly, and I see somebody's half-face at the opened door – kind of hiding, staring at me with one eye. [Laughs] And he goes,

"*Hey bro.*" And within 20 minutes, I was conducting him on "Hanging Tree," because I had written that song that morning. Because the Desert Sessions is you get up, write, and record – and that's it. *There and then*. So, the song's pulse and meter is in five. Mark's like, "I don't know about this. You'd better get in there and show me." So, we were both in there cracking up, because there was such a funny visual – of me seriously in front of him, waving my hand in the air for him to feel the one. We got along immediately great – we knew we had a connection.

NICK OLIVERI [ex-Queens of the Stone Age singer/bassist]: I first met Mark when we were working on *Rated R* [Queens of the Stone Age's 2000 album]. I went to visit Josh [Homme] once to see him play with the Screaming Trees, but when I went back after the show, Mark was already gone. But I did meet him when he was making [2001's] *Field Songs* and we were making *Rated R* – he came in to sing "In the Fade." I didn't really get to know him until we were out on tour. He was pretty "to himself" a lot – when I first started playing with him. It took him a while to warm up to me.

For a while, I didn't think he liked me. He'd be in the back lounge of the bus, chilling out. He kind of took over the back lounge, because he'd smoke cigarettes pretty much non-stop [Oliveri recalls at the time, Mark preferred "Pall Mall non-filters – the red pack"]. I'd go back in there, and he'd put his hood down over his eyes, like, "I don't want to talk to anybody." So, six months into the thing, I'm like, "Josh, I don't know if this guy likes me." And he goes, "It just takes a while for him to warm up." So anyway, one day he told me a joke, I laughed my ass off about it, and we kind of opened up to each other from that point on.

TRAVIS KELLER [friend, cameraman, photographer, Buddyhead founder]: The first time I met Mark was around 2001. The guy that was managing him in that era had invited me over – because I run a label, and that would happen often. The whole office was the guy who managed Stone Temple Pilots, but the guy that managed Mark I believe was under that guy. I showed up, and right as I was getting there, Mark was there too. He's a big dude – he's kind of an intimidating guy. He's so tall and mean looking. His manager introduced me – "This is Travis, he runs Buddyhead." Buddyhead was one of the first internet magazines. And Mark cut him off, and asks me, *"Can you go get me a coffee down the street?"* Brian said to me, "You don't have to do that, we'll get someone to go."

I think after that, it was when he was in Queens of the Stone Age, because I was kind of orbiting around that camp at the time. And Icarus Line – which is Joe Cardamone's original band, and I put out their first record [2001's *Mono*] – they opened a string of shows…I guess it would be for the *Songs for the Deaf* tour. It was up the west coast – so we saw them a lot on that. That was probably the first time having real conversations with him. And then I just kind of orbited that world, and I would see him from time to time. But I didn't really get to know him until these past few years – through Joe again, because Joe had connected with him. That would probably be 2015/2016.

ALDO STRUYF [Mark Lanegan bassist]: It was around 2002, when he was playing with Queens of the Stone Age. Josh from Queens was playing with Chris Goss in Masters of Reality, and we supported them – a band called Millionaire. And Josh asked us to go tour with them. So, we did a couple of tours with Queens of the Stone Age. From the first day on, I was in contact with Mark – because he was also on the *Songs for the Deaf* tour and he was singing a few songs with them. We became friends right away on that tour.

He's always pretty imposing if you see him for the first time. The first thing he said to me, "We know each other from somewhere. Where do I know you from?" And I didn't know him – only from the audience. But we talked the whole day about music and we had the same record collection – the same interest in music. And I knew quite a lot about it, because I worked in a record store back then. He was pretty amazed with all the knowledge I had of the same stuff he knew about. We became friends quite quickly.

CLAY DECKER [friend, tattoo artist]: I first met Mark in Japan [while Queens of the Stone Age were on tour in support of *Songs for the Deaf*]. The first thing he said to me was, "Hey. *Can you get me some drugs while we're here?*" So, I went and got him some, came back, and he was disgruntled with the amount of drugs I got him for the amount of money he gave me. I said, "Man…we're in Japan. You're lucky I was able to even get you anything! What the fuck?"

My first impression of him was exactly what I expected from what everyone had told me about him – being kind of demanding and grumpy. But by the following morning, he had totally opened up to me. And when we realized what time it was, I had a tattoo appointment I had to go to in an hour, and he was like, "Oh my God…I've got press!" And he looks at me and goes, "You're coming with us to Australia, right?" And I was like, "No, dude. I'm here on my own trip to Japan!" So, we had to finish the conversation two weeks later back in LA – which we did, as we carpooled to Coachella.

JESSE HUGHES [Eagles of Death Metal singer/ guitarist]: The first time I ever met Mark was the day Joshua Homme drove me – in my mother's car – to Hollywood, to begin recording *Peace, Love, Death Metal* [Eagles of Death Metal's 2004 debut]. And Mark was sleeping on Josh's couch at the time. My first day in Hollywood – literally – and I'm just coming off of a divorce and being a square, so I'm like shits and giggles every second. And I remember right before Josh opened the door, he went, "Oh. Mark's on the couch. *Be careful.*"

As soon as I walked in, I looked to the right, and there he was on the couch. He sat up, and he said to Josh, "Who's this guy?" And Josh goes, "That's Jesse." And Mark says, *"He looks like a pussy."* I couldn't help it, I just said, "Well…I'M NOT!" And he went, "OK then. Have a seat." That was my first impression of him – he's gruff, at that time he was not coming from a bad place. I *did* look like a pussy, quite frankly.

And then I sat down next to him, and I asked if I could put on some music, and he said, "Yeah. That would be the best way to get to know you." And I sat down and played music for him – for about 30 or 40 minutes. And when I was done with my playlist, he goes, "I think I like you." It was "Shot Down" by the Sonics, and then I did Lindsey Buckingham's "Trouble" – and I remember we bonded on Lindsey Buckingham. That's where I became really interested in the man, because he's got this reputation for being so gruff, but Lindsey Buckingham songs are very sweet, very melodic, very nuanced. They can be very touching. And he was zeroing in on every element of that. And I was instantly intrigued. I kind of marveled at that. What he seemed to be able to focus in on immediately were the things that you wouldn't expect for a person like him to cherish, or to covet.

25 LANEGAN

JEFF FIELDER [Mark Lanegan guitarist]: I met Mark Lanegan through Isobel Campbell. How that happened was this is back in 2009. A friend of mine, Phil Hurley, is a great guitar player, and he was playing in a band that was at the Folk Alliance Festival. Isobel had just finished the second Isobel/Mark record [2008's *Sunday at Devil Dirt*], and she had come to America to meet some American musicians – she wanted to broaden her horizons, I think. So, she went to the festival – just as an audience member. She bopped around until she found Phil's band, and he's a pretty hot guitar player.

So, they got to talking after the gig – and I think Phil lived in LA at the time, but I knew him when he lived here in Seattle – and she asked him straight out, "Would you fancy being in my band?" And he's like, "Nah, I'm pretty into this thing. But...there is a guy in Seattle that I think would be great." He told me about it, and at the time, I was working in this restaurant. I *hated* my job – this one in particular. And I had been plugging away for years and years – kind of going nowhere. And I had the first Mark/Isobel record [2006's *Ballad of Broken Seas*], so I was fully aware of all this.

It was about a month and a half later, I got a phone call from Isobel from way overseas. I was blown away. And then she came to the States a couple of months later – it was all very slow – and we met in Tucson, Arizona. That's kind of where our relationship started. She had met all these people on her trip to America, and kind of got into this scene – there was this whole scene in Tucson, which was great – Giant Sand, Neko Case, the New Pornographers. And they're a really tightly knit. This was all in 2009. We started recording in LA – what turned out to be [2010's] *Hawk*. And it was just the two of us and an engineer. We'd stay up all night just doing these guitar parts and these arrangements for all the songs. And it was just me and her.

And about on the fifth day or so, Mark came in to sing – and that was my first encounter with him. I remember it really well – it was really dark, I think he requests the lights down. And I was bubbly and happy to be there. I wanted to make a good impression. I didn't know him *at all* – I just knew his music. And he came in, and I go, "Hi! My name is Jeff!" I put my hand out…and he gave me this limp, dead fish handshake. And he just looks at me, "Hrrmmmm." And goes, "*Come here*" to Isobel, and took her to the backroom.

I could totally hear them talking, and he goes, "Who is this joker? Where are your normal guys?" And she's like, "This is Jeff. He's good – we've been working all week." "Hrrmmmm." He was just *not* into it. And she told me before, "Don't tell him you're from Seattle. He doesn't like to talk about Seattle." But of course, it came up really quickly. I was like, "Yeah, I'm from Seattle!" He's like, "Hrrmmmm." So, it was very uncomfortable. But we ended up recording probably three songs that night – with just the three of us in a circle. And that was *extraordinary.*

JEAN-PHILIPPE DE GHEEST [Mark Lanegan drummer]: The first time I met Mark was in 2011 – after Aldo asked me to play in the band, because Mark asked him to put the band together. I met him first in Antwerp at the rehearsal space. Aldo already told everyone in the band how Mark was – his character, and that he would get crazy in the tour bus, and smash everything apart. So, I already had this impression before I met him. But my impression was he was very reserved. Shy. But he made a big impression on everyone – he's very tall and he had this power, this energy that would fill the whole space you would be in.

JOSH KLINGHOFFER: He did one song at this event I

was at in London – it was an UNKLE performance at the Royal Festival Hall [in 2014], where they were doing UNKLE music. And I heard right before the show that Lanegan was going to sing a song. I was there with a friend who was involved with the show, so we were just puttering around backstage, and we open a door just to find somewhere to sit down, and Mark is in there by himself – staring at the ground! We just quietly backed up and left.

And then another time, he sang the Joy Division song "Atmosphere" with Peter Hook and his band – on the anniversary of Ian Curtis' death. May 18th, a few years ago. I'm friends with [Jane's Addiction bassist] Eric Avery, and he was going to do a song as well. So, I'm there early with Eric, and Mark's outside on the street smoking. That was my third experience in person. I think I just sat there quietly, and he was like, "So…what time is this going to be?" It seemed like he didn't want to be there, but I don't think that's true – it's just his demeanor. And he sang that song, "Atmosphere," *amazingly.* It was the finale of that performance.

JONATHAN HISCHKE [Mark Lanegan bassist]: I had been working quite a bit with musicians around the Rancho de la Luna studio. Your Dave Catchings…all of that crew. I played in a band called Earthlings, and I played in a band called Mojave Lords, and had gotten to know everyone in that orbit – which is a pretty cool little scene they have out there. Something came up where a friend of all of ours, Brian O'Conner – who is in the Eagles of Death Metal, and is just kind of a staple out here – he's been sick for a long time. He's had cancer for a decade now, and he keeps rebounding and getting through it. He's just a survivor. Everyone jumps to his aid when he's having problems – either with not being able to work, running short, or bills mounting up for treatments. So, there's been many benefits over the years –

in LA and out here. One came up, and I was asked if I would like to play with Mark – because Mark was going to be headlining it.

First of all, that was like the greatest call. I mean, I was *so* honored to be asked to do that. And what was even more of an honor was that the rest of the band – I was the newcomer – had worked with him extensively. And I was shocked that they asked me to do it. The band for this one show was David Catching, Chris Goss, Shelley [Brien, Mark's second wife], Duke Garwood, Joey Castillo, and myself. So, it was kind of this all-star crew of people who had worked with Mark – in different capacities. And I was the new guy. It was one of the honors of my life – to be asked to do that with those people, and backing up Mark.

The band rehearsed the music before Mark showed up. We had a few days of going over things, getting it together. It was mostly material from the albums he'd done with those people in the past – it was a lot of *Bubblegum* stuff, which I love. Which I think is one of unsung classic records that this crew out there has made over the years – along with some of the Desert Sessions stuff, some of the Queens of the Stone Age stuff. All great stuff...but that record I think is *exquisite*. So, it was doing a lot of that material, which was exciting.

I remember we worked on the stuff, and then Mark showed up – the afternoon before and the day of the show I think we did run-throughs. I just remember when he walked into the room, it was like the air changed, or something. He was such a presence – even though he didn't say much, he just had this presence to him. It was like an outlaw walking in. I just remember meeting him, him being nice enough. He didn't make me feel like an ass or anything – he just didn't say much.

And he was looking *really* crazy at that point – he

had a gold grill, his hair was different colors, big thick glasses. He looked like a pirate. A modern version of a pirate. It was one of those things where I was like, "Well, OK...*let's see how this goes.*" I was nervous. And then we started playing something and he started singing, and it was just like I could not believe I was watching that voice in front of me, being itself. It was one of those things that I'll never forget. And there's not many of those – where someone opens their mouth and you feel it in your bones. He did that to me. It was incredible.

He doesn't like to rehearse much, so we went through it a couple of times maybe, then went through it the next day, and we played the show – it was great. It was a very special night. I just remember afterwards, he was very excited. He hadn't played with those people much up until that point. And I don't think he'd played much of that music in quite a while, either – he had a real good time doing it. I remember he gave me a hug afterwards and he said he's excited to work with me again.

Chapter 2
PERSONALITY

Mark's multifaceted and complex character.

SALLY BARRY: He was crunchy on the outside, chewy on the inside. He really was just like that. That's part of the reason that he and I got along. We both had these strident, outside personalities when we were out and around other people. But inside, he was kind of quiet. I think he thought about deep stuff. And you always felt safe around him. I hung around the whole band a lot – the Trees – and you always felt like, magically, nothing bad could happen.

CHAD CHANNING: He appeared kind of quiet and reserved. Very soft-spoken.

KIM THAYIL: It was not an affectation or an act – as you might see him on-stage, he would be very similar to off-stage. Occasionally, you could get him to smile. But there were certain singers that didn't like to talk when they got off-stage. I suppose if your style of singing is to talk or to yell, then you might be more of a "bounce around monkey" after a show. But if you're actually singing and performing – which requires listening while you're singing to the pitch and you perform well – that takes a strength, not just to push air, but to push air in the right place that you're pitching. That requires some degree of focus. And that kind of energy can be draining.

It makes your vocal cords sore, and the last thing you want to do when you walk off stage is get into a conversation with some fan. So, there were a lot of Seattle singers – because they had that ability and strength in their vocals – that tended to be much more quiet after a show. Chris was one of them, Lanegan was one of them, I think Eddie's one of them. Just like being a pitcher – imagine someone like Randy Johnson throwing a hundred-plus pitches, and he leaves the game and ices his arm or wraps it up…you don't go to him and say, "Hey, toss me one of those beers." And I think because these singers were so good and had a particular talent they would utilize, they would kind of withdraw and give their throats time to wind down and chill.

JEFF FIELDER: When I first met Mark, I remember it was his birthday, and I said, "Hey man, how old are you?" And he goes, *"You don't get to ask me that."*

GREG WERCKMAN: Mark had a wicked sense of humor – very self-effacing. I would say even very low self-esteem. Whenever he was around other artists, he tended to shrink. I remember at one point, I told him, "Hey, Mike Patton [who co-founded Ipecac Records with Greg] wants to work with you. Mike is trying to find a project, because he would *really* like to do something with you." And Mark would always be like, "Oh my God. Why would he want to waste his time with *me?* He's so talented." So, it seemed like he never took ownership really of his talent. I'm sure that has to do with how he was brought up and some of the ups and downs of his life that he experienced.

JEFF FIELDER: Mark was very self-aware of how he comes across. I never saw him be cross with anybody who wanted to get to know him – as far as some sort of interview. He was reluctant to do them, but once he was there, he was super-funny. He had an amazing sense of humor. And taking himself seriously wasn't part of the make-up – at all.

He didn't understand why people would want to hear him do anything. He'd take things off the setlist, and I'd be like, "Why are you doing that?" And he'd say, "Nobody wants to hear this shit, man." It was constantly like that. I was like, "Believe me dude…*they want to hear it.*" "Ah fuck it…whatever." Really self-deprecating, all the time. But he was just ridiculously funny.

ALAIN JOHANNES: There are few people I've heard laugh so heartily and fully.

NICK OLIVERI: He liked to laugh and keep you laughing – even though he had this dark persona that everybody sees him as. When he did open up to you, he was quite a funny guy. And a very infectious laugh. He'd come up with these words, and you'd be like, "What does *that* mean?"

CLAY DECKER: I love wordplay, and so does he. We'd sit around and every now and then I'd say something, and he'd say, "Hey man, do you mind if I write that down?" And I'm like, "Of course not. Anything I say Mark is for you. You can do whatever you want with it." But when we took that road trip to Coachella, we had some inside jokes that lasted our entire friendship. Somehow, we came up with a term, "infantscatsy" – a fetish for baby shit. [Laughs] And when Mark got out of the hospital in Ireland, he sent me a text. "Hey, I just got out of the hospital. I met some nurses in there that specialized in…*infantscatsy.*"

JOHN AGNELLO: He was hilarious. In his book, he talks about that session where I made him come over to the studio immediately, because I was done and I wanted to print the mix [for *Whiskey for the Holy Ghost*], and he had no clothes – because his friend Sally was doing laundry. So, he showed up in her kimono! This is him – he was fucking hilarious at times. Obviously, he had burdens and troubles and shit like that. But he was *so* funny – we laughed our asses off.

I'll tell you another funny story with him – I recorded the Dinosaur Jr. record, *Where You Been*. That was around the same time I worked with Screaming Trees. They had Andy Wallace mix *Where You Been*, and I got sent a CD reference from the mastering facility. I didn't mix it – I recorded it. But it sounded not great – to the point where I had to call a bunch of people and say, "This is really not great. I can't believe this is the record I recorded."

When we listened to the CD, I was shocked and nervous and freaking out about my career and how bad it sounded...and Mark was just laughing! He was laughing at J, that the record was *so* bad – he thought it was hilarious. And I looked at him like, "You motherfucker...*this is my career.*" And he's like, "I don't care! He really fucked up your record!" They were really good friends, but Mark had that devilish thing. He was hilarious – but he was also kind of sardonic.

GREG WERCKMAN: My favorite Lanegan story is about his sense of humor. There was one time he came into San Francisco and he was playing with his solo band at Slim's. And he had had really crazy experiences throughout his career playing in San Francisco. One show, he ended up getting arrested! But this one particular time, he was like, "Hey, I just got in town. Let's meet for dinner before the show."

I met him and it was one of those times where every once in a while you'd get Mark, and he was just absolutely goofy and funny. And this was one of those times. We went to dinner and we were talking about baseball or basketball – which he loved to talk about. Or Shepherd's pies. Maybe even a little about music, but nothing about career or business. It was really light. And I was really happy, because I was thinking, "Wow. This is going to be a different

Lanegan show." *But it wasn't.*

He got on stage, and maybe after two songs, he hadn't said anything to the crowd. After about the third song, he says, "Thanks for coming out. I'm having a tough day...I found out just before the show that my mom died." The air went out of the room. Later, the show ended and I go downstairs, and I go, "Dude...*what's going on?* You didn't tell me about your mom." And he goes, "Oh, it's not true. *I never know what to say in between songs.*"

MEGAN JASPER: One of the best storytellers I've ever known. I would also say that he could be moody. Supersmart. And really particular – especially with music. The times I would hang out with him just as a friend, I feel like the side that I always saw of him was the funny side – and that was stories and jokes. I would also say when he would tell stories, he would have me cracking up – and just because sometimes of one word he would use, or one line.

Working with him I would describe him as a total perfectionist. And *very* particular. So, it would take him a long time to finish or hand in a record. And when he handed it in though, it was fantastic, it was perfect, and it was ready. But, in that process, it was not uncommon for him to have a record mastered *four times* – and sweat over each one, because each one was not perfect.

There were so many moments that I had the good fortune of enjoying with him – when he really was not fucked up and he was totally straight and incredibly kind, funny, generous, and charming. I got to spend so much time with him, even on the phone – because every time back in the day when he needed to talk to Bruce or Jon and they were not available, I would keep him on the phone until they were off the phone and available [Megan was Sub Pop's receptionist at the time]. I got to hear *so many* of his funny stories, or him talking about his family – those moments where you're just killing time, but they're wonderful moments…because you get to learn who someone is.

MIKE JOHNSON: He was a friendly, funny, nice guy. Like, a regular dude. I think the reason why he and I became friends quickly was – at least from my perspective – he reminded me of people I knew from the small town that I came from in Oregon. He had a little bit of an intimidating air to him…not quite so much when I met him, but later, he was more imposing.

CHARLES PETERSON: I think at the time that I met him, he was sober. I found him to have a really great sense of humor – that fit in line with the other caustic, cutting, semi-self-deprecatory humor that the Seattle music scene grew. His sense of humor struck me…but he could get quite serious about things, and he was pretty sure about what he wanted – to a degree. Yet, at the same time…he knew what he didn't want, but he wasn't sure what he actually wanted – if that makes any sense. He just seemed like kind of a "dude" – just one of us.

I mean, Chris Cornell was probably one of the shiest of them all. But it's sort of that "lead man kind of thing" – where in their real life they're somewhat reserved, and then when they hit the stage…but Mark was pretty reserved on stage, as well. He was not the person that struck me as one that would go down that totally destructive junkie path. We were all being somewhat destructive in our own ways at that time. He was just like Kurt in a way – he was an outsider who quickly became an insider, for better or worse.

CHRIS GOSS: Even though it seems like it was on or off, or changing, looking back it was consistent – even with the ups and downs of heavy drug use – there was a consistency to it. And I think that one riding consistency was dedication to his artform. I'll always think of Mark as an artist and a poet. That was it. It seemed like his only concern. And God bless him for it. I told him that he needed a hobby, and someone else had said the same exact thing to him – because he doesn't go to anything for relief from music and art. And he doesn't snap off from it. Which I think is necessary.

But there are artists, like David Bowie for example, who is interested in everything and then apply it to his art. So, that's one way of looking at it. But Mark was a one-track mind – just what's next on his plate, as far as music goes. And that's why he does so many co-projects with so many artists. His occupation is his respite, and his respite is his occupation – it kind of never ends. So, he definitely filled in the time of his life – the brief few seconds we have here – with prolific work. "Prolific" is the word.

ROBERT ROTH: Just absolutely friendly to us. An ally. I felt like we were all on the same page. So, I didn't feel there was a sense of competition. He told me he listened to "Hit Ignition" from our second Sub Pop single [1993's "Leslie's Coughing Up Blood"], and that he listened to it three times in a row earlier that day. We were mutually supportive. But nothing antagonistic. I remember we went to see a movie together – me, him, and Pickerel.

NICK OLIVERI: I remember a funny story I'll tell you – he had maybe fallen off the wagon, and he comes downstairs in a hotel. I'm in the downstairs lobby, and we're waiting for Josh. I look at Mark's feet, and his boots are on backwards – left on his right, right on his left!

JACK ENDINO: I'm sure I heard his whole life story a

couple of times in the studio, because he would get very introspective and start telling me stories about how he was on a first-name basis with the local cops in Ellensburg when he was a teenager. All these "youthful misadventures" that he'd had by himself and with the Conner brothers and other delinquents of Ellensburg – growing up there.

Y'know, I don't think he went back and played Ellensburg until…it wasn't very long ago. He just didn't want to go back to that town. But how would I describe his personality? Pretty serious – took himself very seriously. Had a very dark sense of humor. Extremely self-critical, kinda grouchy, kinda easy to upset – we're talking in the studio, really.

CHARLES R. CROSS: Mark young was very shy – not very active really as a singer on stage. His acne was still pretty apparent at that point, and his hair was in his face. Women always liked Mark – he had an appeal to women who liked "dark bad boys." Bless Mark's soul – wherever he remains – but I think it's safe to say that there was never a point where Mark was the most attractive guy in the Screaming Trees. And I think that bugged him, too – that maybe led up to some of his being a dick with other people's girlfriends.

TRAVIS KELLER: One of the most solid friends. He was kind of like an older brother to us – and when I say "us," I mean Joe [Cardamone] and our little crew. He would have helped us hide a body if we asked him to – you know what I mean? He was just a great friend. Funny, but also stoic. Just cool. I would say he's funnier than most people know. And just really well-read.

I loved talking to him, because he was a great storyteller. He lived like a million years. We had a lot of similar friends through music, so when he would tell me stories, I would know a lot of the people. But just a really good dude, solid friend, great storyteller, and someone who's just seen a lot of shit. It was always like he was dropping wisdom on you – even if you really didn't know he was.

JEAN-PHILIPPE DE GHEEST: I remember the first discussion I had with him – it was after the first rehearsal in Antwerp – at that point, I just broke up with my girlfriend at the time. And he said, "If I can give you one piece of advice...*never go back."* And I did go back. And two years after, we broke up again.

NICK OLIVERI: One time, Josh and I did a tour with Masters of Reality, and we opened a tour for the Mark Lanegan Band in England. We did a few shows with them. And the first show, he came backstage after his band was done playing, and I just got done congratulating these guys, like, "You guys killed it. It was *so* good!" Mark comes back, throws his cigarette on the ground, and goes, "WHAT THE FUCK WAS THAT?! You guys all got your jobs at McDonald's when you go home...*but this is my job!* And if we play like that, I ain't going to have a job anymore!" I'd never seen him do that – he was just going off.

GARY LEE CONNER: He could be the nicest guy in the world, the funniest guy, or, he could be the meanest and the most horrible, nasty guy in the world. He ran the whole gamut of good and evil. I think he's got more of a reputation for being a mean guy. And I think drugs didn't help with "the mean guy" – it made it worse. Or even worse, sometimes just disinterested. That was some of the trouble we were dealing with – "disinterested but in control" is a very difficult situation.

Like, in the mid '90s, he did not want to quit the band or break the band up. He was adamant about that. Because we even approached him one time – this was in between *Sweet Oblivion* and *Dust* – and Van and I were going to quit and try to get a different singer and have a new name. And he's like, "NO WAY!" But, at the same time, he didn't want to be involved in anything – except for listening to the songs and saying whether or not we should do it. And, forcing me to write songs for like, two years straight, every day of my life – and I'm not having any other life whatsoever. We'd laugh about stuff all the time, but then, we'd have problems, too.

CHARLES R. CROSS: In some ways, you admire Mark for just how unrepentant he was. If he disliked somebody, he disliked them *forever*. If he liked them, he trusted them and he respected them. He didn't shift allegiances.

ALDO STRUYF: There's two Marks. One, the way he is to his friends, and the other one, the way he is to the outside world. Everybody knows that second one, but to his friends, he was very, very funny. Also sometimes he would get really mad, but after thinking about it after a couple of hours, he would say sorry. He was a warm person. He invited me to his house all the time. He made dinner for me. He was always ready if I wanted to go and buy some records, let's say – he would drive me to the record store in LA. I think he liked being on his own, but to his close friends, he was really nice.

JEAN-PHILIPPE DE GHEEST: He would be not speaking that much and isolate himself on the back of the tour bus – listening to some music or working on things.

Especially since he quit drugs, alcohol, and smoking, so he wouldn't be too much in the front of the bus – where everyone would drink a beer or whiskey, or have a smoke. He would be very apart. But then, all of a sudden, he would be this funny guy telling you stories – and we'd be laughing like hell.

But most of the time, we didn't really have this strong relationship as I would expect of a band. He was "the boss" – he knew what he wanted, and we were the guys who had to do the job. I think it was his way to stay focused on his work. Maybe it was some kind of control – just to keep control of everything. There was this kind of separation. But then he would make this effort to get to us and to have a chat.

Also, the big thing was we had these really different cultural backgrounds. Especially Belgium – compared to other European countries – we have a special kind of humor. Belgium is such a small country – we don't have this "patriotic thing." So, as soon as I would try to break the ice and tell a joke or something, often, it would just not work – because he would not understand. The same with Jeff Fielder – he'd be like, "What's so funny about this joke?" It was Belgium humor. And also, the language – especially for me being shy, I don't speak that much. So, it's even more difficult when you have to express yourself in a different kind of language and to express the feelings you have.

TRAVIS KELLER: I remember when we did the photo shoots, he'd just ask me to do them and we didn't work out a price. At the end of the day, he handed me 900 bucks in cash. It was like a drug deal! At the time, it was so much money to me. It saved my life – it felt like ten grand to me. It was just really a sweet gesture, but also...*it kind of felt like a drug deal.*

JACK ENDINO: Even though he was a cranky son of a bitch and he was nobody's ray of sunshine, he had a lot of fans. A lot of people were big, big fans of his singing. As well as his artistic integrity – he never attempted to do anything *truly* commercial. He just had no interest in it. I can only compare him to Nick Cave – as far as just having his own deal, his own thing. Directing his own career, only doing what he wants to do/when he wants to do it. And fuck anybody who thinks differently. As far as I can see, he was completely in control of what he was doing and didn't do things that he didn't want to do. You couldn't tell him to do anything that he didn't want to do.

I remember something really indicative was I went to see Queens of the Stone Age at one point. There were a few pretty well-known Queens of the Stone Age tunes that had Mark's vocal on them. At the show, there were some people in the audience calling for a couple of those tunes. And Josh had to point out to the audience, "Look, I'm not Mark Lanegan. I can't sing these tunes." But he went on to talk about Mark, and he said – and I don't remember the exact wording, but it was somewhere along the lines of – "I love Mark, he's a dear friend…he's the meanest son of a bitch that I call a friend." Those of us who knew Mark were dying of laughter at that point – because Mark could be pretty edgy sometimes, and quite moody and quite hard to get along with, if that's how he decided he was going to roll. He made his opinion known – like it or not, take it or leave it.

ALAIN JOHANNES: He would come off as grumpy, but he had a super-huge heart. Amazingly caring person. And extremely artistic. Impeccable taste. We had a great friendship and connection – where we could lean on each other for advice in a very fun but also mature way. I could always count on him.

He got me through my latest record [2020's *Hum*], when I was barely surviving, being in bed three months – when they didn't know I had Covid. I was in a hospital, and when I came out of that, right after that is when they figured out what was going on all over the world. I had been in Italy in November of 2019.

But I made this solo record that was written and recorded in twelve days – and it was Mark that made it possible, because he was always there. I'd be like, "What do you think of this?" I'd send him a little thing, and he'd go, "Oh, it's amazing! But it needs to have this, and that…"

JEFF FIELDER: He knew what his "character" kind of was. I remember we were backstage and we were fucking around, telling some jokes – we were laughing. And somebody came backstage, and Mark hits me on the shoulder. So I was like, "OK, I get it." We'd be talking about movies or something, and if it got too close to showtime, he'd be like, "Alright…shut it down, dude. *Gotta get in character*."

His friends that he had in certain towns, he was just *so* loyal to them. And maybe he knew them through the old days and all that, and they just stuck with him – but he was so loyal to those people. He had a really hard time letting new people in. So, when I sort of broke through that barrier and we were able to have a normal conversation – prolonged, like through a dinner or something like that – I felt really special about that. Because you don't "get in." And if you do, it's pretty rare.

ALAIN JOHANNES: There's always been a guy that is there for everyone and can take the punches. And the few times I fell down hard – he was there for me. He was there in a very gentle and intelligent kind of way.

JESSE HUGHES: That motherfucker is the real deal. A dark individual with dark appetites. The sort of appetites where he would inform girls sometimes in advance, "*My love is death*." His love is a commitment.

CHARLES R. CROSS: I have no musical talent like that, I wish I had that voice – but not in a thousand, million years would I want that life. That life was pretty dark.

Chapter 3
VOCALIST

What made Mark so unique as a singer?

CHARLES R. CROSS: The timbre of his voice – which was really unlike any other singer – and no matter how many cigarettes or drugs he did, it really didn't shift a lot over the years. He had this very unique voice. A deep voice. To be honest, it didn't work on every song. But particularly on a ballad, he was able to bring a deep darkness to his voice. He could have sang "Mother Goose," and it would have sounded like a murder ballad. He just had one of those very unique voices.

JOSH KLINGHOFFER: His voice is pretty particular. The life he had led, he was able to channel that into one of his voices. He could sing louder and high – he could still get out of the low, guttural thing if he wanted to. But I think he just had this voice that was so honest, and so reflective of the person he was. Probably much like what people were saying at the memorial service – he seemed to be the kind of person who tried to hide the fact that he had such a big heart, and was such a sensitive, feeling person. I think similarly with his voice, he just couldn't not be incredibly emotional with his voice. I think people can sing all different ways and know how to sing or don't know how to sing, but just have a voice – they're trained, they're not trained.

Mark Lanegan just opened his mouth, and sang whatever words – his own words, someone else's words – and you're probably going to feel something or it's going to grab your attention. And whether you like it or not, or connect to it or you don't, his voice *commands* attention. It's totally what I want to listen to these days – it's honesty, no pretense. I basically want to hear the person's emotional life.

And I feel like he couldn't help but do that. In a way, he was probably singing to live – I don't know if he could consciously say that's what he was doing. But to me, it sounded like he was showing us all through his singing and his music and his songwriting who he was as a person, emotionally. And it probably worked on many levels, because a lot of people got to know him in a way that probably don't know other artists that they listen to.

KIM THAYIL: There seemed to be an earnest sincerity to his brooding. There was something with the way he sang that was very much as his temperament was. He tended to not emote very heavily – not wear his emotions on his sleeve. He didn't laugh a lot or cry a lot – he wasn't super-expressive in his demeanor if you were around him. But more so certainly when he sang. But as he sang, it was very much an earnest interpretation of his demeanor and temper. It seemed to certainly capture the introspective, wounded, brooding, contemplative aspect of his personality. I suppose you've heard the nickname "Dark Mark," as people occasionally refer to him as...

MIKE JOHNSON: He had an incredibly great voice to begin with – he had a gift. But he was also a great *singer*. He had that gift that very few people have – where he sounded like he was "inside the song." He wasn't just a guy singing a song, there's a real genuine power to it – whether he's singing loudly or quietly. It was not like any other people I've ever been around.

MATT PINFIELD: He's one of those vocalists that just had this soulful, guttural honesty...darkness and beauty at the same time.

JOHN AGNELLO: His voice was just so powerful and gravelly. He had wonderful pitch – his delivery was great. He was soulful. Listen, the troubles in his mind or the troubles he had all contributed to what came out of his mouth. I think that was a big factor. I really do. I think the burdens he lived with, his demons…when he sang, he channeled that stuff through. And it gave me chicken skin. But once again, there's two sides of the "Mark Lanegan coin" – he's in the vocal booth, and he knocks over his spit cup, because he's chewing tobacco. And I'm like, "Mark, you're a fucking idiot. Now the vocal booth smells like chewing tobacco." That was a difficult day with him – he sings the shit out of a song and then does something really dumb because he's not paying attention…and I get to yell at him and he doesn't care.

JEFF FIELDER: I've heard people say, "You're not really born with anything. You just learn and you practice and you get good." But I couldn't disagree with that more. And Mark is a good example of that, because you can't *learn* your voice to sound like that. I mean, you can practice and get good at mic control, and know how to fill a room with it and be on key and things like that. But you can't learn that – you're born with that. And that becomes otherworldly. Because if you were at one of the shows – in particular, the church shows…we would play these cathedrals all over Europe and with very simple instrumentation. If it wasn't just me, it would be me and a cello. Something really stark. And there would be all these crucifixes and everything was backlit and uplit, so we always played in the dark.

That's one thing I miss – playing in the dark. We could barely see our instruments. But it was part of the whole thing. And it was theater…but it wasn't contrived. That's a hard thing to pull off – when something is so stylized like that, and it doesn't come across as disingenuous or put-on. That's a hard thing to pull off – and that was his whole deal. When his voice would fill that room...there was nothing else. That's the honor that I have. He was hard to get along with or whatever – who gives a shit. That doesn't bother me. It doesn't give me bad feelings about the guy or anything like that. It's just the way he was, and that's OK. He was difficult a lot, but it didn't really matter to me. I'd be pissed off at him or whatever – we had some bad days. It was definitely never easy...and it was rarely fun, actually. Gigs to me can be really a blast. And his shows were fulfilling in many ways – but they weren't fun to do. Because I felt like it was *such* a responsibility.

And it took so much discipline to keep it all in this particular situation. And I took it really seriously – I didn't just blow it off. I put a lot on myself – so it was really taxing. But it was all worth it – just to hear the music and being part of it. And if it was just the two of us, we could fill the room up with this kind of...*atmosphere.* It wasn't just music, it was a whole *atmosphere.* And his voice was intense, man. And what he sung about and the way he sang it. It was so artful and personal at the same time. I remember one time, we put together a setlist – he would have me write the setlist sometimes – and he'd say, "We can't put these together." Like, four songs in a row. I'm like, "They're totally different." He said, "It's all about the same shit. It's all about death, man...fuck, I guess they're *all* about death."

ALDO STRUYF: A voice that you can't imitate. I've recorded lots of albums with him, and if it wasn't the first take, it would have been the second or third take that was the right one. I know a lot of people who try 20 times or 50 times to sing a song on an album. But he did it mostly one or two times, and then it was recorded. So technically, he was really good. He was always listening to singers who did something different than the usual – like the Carpenters, Johnny Cash, or whoever.

He was always interested in people like Rob Younger from Radio Birdman – who would phrase differently. The same with Simon Bonney from Crime & the City Solution. And also, he was really quick in writing lyrics and finding a melody of a song – he would do it in a couple of hours, which was really amazing, because I think a lot of people spend days, weeks, or months trying to find a nice vocal part for a song.

JONATHAN HISCHKE: I think there was some quote I read from Isobel Campbell, where she said he had an "effortless Americana"…like, an effortless soulfulness. He wasn't putting it on. It wasn't like somebody trying to be a soul singer or trying to be a rough and tumble country singer or trying to be *anything*. He just had that soul in his voice – and it didn't matter what he sang. He could be singing his own lyrics, he could be singing a Christmas song. Like, I loved his Christmas record that he made with Alain Johannes [2012's *Dark Mark Does Christmas*]. He does "O Holy Night" – which is my favorite Christmas song, and he does it great. It's beautiful, raw, and soulful…and not perfect – in all the right ways. And it doesn't sound like he was ever working too hard to be intense.

And you can see it in his stage presence, too – he wasn't performing in that sense. He just was there, a microphone was in front of him, people were playing music behind him, and he was just floating on the music – with this dirty, muddy, gravelly, soulful voice of his. As a singer, he could make anything sound great and meaningful. But when he was singing his own lyrics and telling his own stories, it's like "next level amazing." I don't know of anybody else –

especially where he came from. Maybe Kurt Cobain was close. But of that scene, of his peers that he was coming up with, I can't think of anybody else who has *that*.

There was a lot of soul up there and a lot of turmoil – a lot of hardship in a lot of those people's lives. But I just don't hear that same weariness…just soul. And that's not me bagging on Chris Cornell – it's just a different way of expressing one's self. Mark didn't give me the impression like he was trying to be anything – besides just what came naturally to him, after years of whatever he'd gone through in his life. It was a really special thing – not too many people tap into that the way he did. I can only think of black blues singers and soul singers of a bygone era that could get there. Maybe there's a few singer-songwriters here and there who can get there at some points. But Mark just seemed to be in it all the time – no matter what he was doing.

ROBERT ROTH: Probably the amount of cigarettes he smoked! But honestly, I think that he really dug down into his soul. It was deeply at the core of his spiritual/emotional center – is what he sang from. I think that a lot of singers…a lot of people think that the person who can sing the highest note is the best singer – at least that's kind of how it seemed like when I was a younger musician.

It took me a while until I started to realize I was a baritone – not as deep as Mark, but that's sort of where my voice lived. And I think Mark very boldly embraced his "baritone-ness," and having a deeper sound than Chris Cornell. Most singers in rock going back to the '60s, it's "Who can sing the highest note?" Like Johnny Cash and Nick Cave, *those things* were probably more where Mark was coming from.

MEGAN JASPER: There was a moment when Mark was

to the best of my knowledge clean – he even quit smoking – and it's like his voice totally "warmed up" and softened. I feel like there was just a smoothness in his voice that you can hear. And it was around the time that he was working with Greg Dulli a lot – and they were recording Gutter Twins songs and probably even just demos that they scrapped. But that period of time was something that was really special for Mark Lanegan's voice. I remember hearing it and going, "Oh my God. His voice sounds *really* beautiful."

GARY LEE CONNER: The other day I just heard that song "Hurt" by Johnny Cash. It's this really sad song – he's not in his best voice. But I suddenly realized how much Lanegan sounds like Johnny Cash. I never thought of that before. But, at the same time, he had this tone that was not like anyone else. And also, one of the best things about his voice was the high register – he did that kind of shit that Kurt Cobain would do *before* Kurt.

Like, on a lot of our early SST albums, he would sing the higher stuff – but he had the low-end to back it up. It's like something that David Bowie had – where he did that weird whiny thing, but he had the low-end to back it up. For instance, Billy Corgan – he tries to do that, but he doesn't have the low-end to back it up. So, it just sounds whiny. Lanegan never did the whiny thing. I had that same "Billy Corgan problem" – I'd try to do the whiny voice like Bob Dylan, the Seeds, and Roky Erickson. And Mark had to listen to demos of it! If you want to hear an example of it, on YouTube, I posted an original demo of "End of the Universe" from *Buzz Factory*.

Besides having the strong voice, it's very, very unique, too. He doesn't sound like anybody else. Some singers you hear, like people will say Steve Perry from Journey is a great singer, or Phil Collins. It's like, *this generic voice that can be on a Disney soundtrack.* [Laughs] We used to joke about how Mark could sing an old ad in the '80s about eggs – "Have some eggs now, morning, noon, and night!" And we'd be like, "Mark, you should sing that!" But even if he did, he'd sound way better – because he had such an original voice.

There's an old cliché about singing the phonebook, and I remember somebody said something like that one time. That low, smokey thing. And also, being able to hit the high stuff. And he always had a really mellow high voice that only a couple of songs he used it on. One was the cover of "Darkness Darkness" that we did in the mid '90s for the Schwarzenegger film, *True Lies.* That was one of his best performances I think, ever. But it's so different for him – he's not pushing the high end, he's singing high, but real kind of mellow. But strong, still. I always loved his voice.

If you listen to *Clairvoyance,* there's a few songs where he doesn't sound quite like he did later. A while back, I put on the first song from *Other Worlds,* "Barriers," and his voice is higher. He sounds like a baby. There's really no evidence of "This guy's a great singer." But I think if you listen to *Clairvoyance,* you hear a lot of moments of, "Wow. That's really some great singing." *Clairvoyance* is kind of interesting, too, because on that record, he did some things like singing with himself – like the Doors. Because he would deny it, but he was *way* into the Doors.

In fact, here's another story about the early days working at the video store – we would listen to records all the time. And I would play the records and sit there, and we had to listen to "Hyacinth House" and whatever the song is after on *LA Woman* ["Crawling King Snake"] over and over again. Every time I hear that song, it always reminds me of him. It's a really great song. But yeah, he was *way* into the Doors. Because when people started saying he sounded kinda like Morrison, he would kind of get "that look" – he wanted to deny it.

So, by probably six months after we recorded the *Other Worlds* stuff, he started to find his voice. And all through the SST stuff, there's all sorts of amazing things, like "Ivy" – the first song on *Invisible Lantern*. Or "Grey Diamond Desert" – that's where he's doing the low stuff. He used to have so much trouble – especially live – with sound engineers getting his voice the way he wanted it. Especially the low stuff – because it's not easy to get it to come through.

CHARLES PETERSON: He was able to combine that Tom Waits kind of gruffness and folkiness, with that sort of more traditional, stadium rock singer in a way. He really cut through both worlds with that, and made it work – and unique. There's plenty of singers that could do what he did on one end of the scale or the other, but I think Mark was able to successfully bring those two together.

CHRIS GOSS: I really learned on [2004's] *Bubblegum* that his range is a lot higher than most people could even imagine. I was really surprised. He doesn't like to just show the high side of his voice for some reason – maybe he prefers being a baritone all the time. But he was singing falsetto on some stuff when we were recording *Bubblegum* that blew my mind, that I never imagined that he could sing like that. He's one of the kind of writers, and I don't think I get next to Mark poetically, but I do share this factor that I'm a writer and Mark was a writer who could write great songs, but they're for himself. And they're hard to cover. I think that's why Mark isn't covered by a lot of people. He wrote music for himself and it seems that it can only be done by him. And that's what I think made him unique – and will always make him unique.

SALLY BARRY: You either have that kind of gift in your voice or you don't. I know that in the beginning, he said he really didn't know how to sing, and that Van and Lee kind of taught him how to sing. But beyond that, that's what they call a "God given voice." *It's just there.* There's a thing beyond a technical voice – which is soul and artistry. And there are a lot of really technically proficient musicians, that the emotion is just not there. There was no disconnect between him opening his mouth and the emotion coming out. And that's a gift – that's really special. I mean, some people are terrific musicians, but it's cold. And then you have *the artists.* I think Mark was a true artist. And a true poet – despite the fact that he thought he couldn't write poetry.

NICK OLIVERI: One of the best voices I ever had the pleasure of working with or see play live. The natural vibrato thing he has was incredible.

MIKE JOHNSON: He had that power that I'd never seen anybody have – where he could just stand there, and what came out of him…I don't even think *he* knew. One of the most powerful musical experiences of my life was one day at he and his ex-wife Wendy's house, we were just sitting around. I was playing guitar and he was standing there, and he was like, "'Play 'On Jesus' Program'." So, I started playing it, he sang it, and the acoustics in his house…it was absolutely like nothing I'd ever heard anybody do. I didn't say anything, but it was like, *"Oh my God."* It was incredible. I'd played music with the guy for a decade at that point at least. There was nobody like him. He was the greatest.

JOHN AGNELLO: On maybe *Field Songs*, we were working in Seattle, and I said, "Mark, I've got this idea for this background part." I sang it to him, and he goes, "Oh...go sing it yourself." And I was like, "No...you! It's *your* record." And he would refuse to sing it. So, I had to go out and do it. And I was like, "*You're Mark-motherfucking-Lanegan*. You've got the greatest voice in rock history. Go sing!" And he would just refuse. *I* would actually do backgrounds on the record – which was insane. But that's how he was – he didn't care. And he thought it was great. He'd go, "Oh, you sounded great." And I'm like, "Oh my God...*you're a fucking idiot*."

ALAIN JOHANNES: Mark, as he grew older, his voice just had this *richness*. He loved using a Neumann KMS 105 handheld mic, but it didn't really matter. The vibration was apparent even when he spoke. But I think there's something behind his voice – it was his soul, his being, his way of communicating. The vehicle was the voice, but also, the lyrics. The whole thing together was impactful and was an intense, emotional experience to listen to.

When you explain who your favorite singers are, they move you or touch you at some point. They don't necessarily have to be super-technical. But Gladys Knight, Aretha Franklin, Stevie Wonder, Johnny Cash, Chris Cornell, and Mark – there was an ability to move you. Besides the richness of the tone and how cool the personality of it was, there was just something about the way that he made the "connect" and how one feels listening to it. You can't just *casually* listen to his voice.

GREG WERCKMAN: Lanegan is one of those guys that if he sang the phonebook, it would be worth listening to.

CHARLES R. CROSS: The greatest loss is losing that unique voice. That is a once in a generation voice Mark had.

Chapter 4
LYRICIST

In addition to being an exceptional singer,
Mark was a truly gifted lyricist and poet.

NICK OLIVERI: You *felt* his words – you could tell they were real. That's what I liked about it the most – it was things he had gone through or done or was doing. And also, he could tell the story of somebody else pretty damn good, too.

MEGAN JASPER: You can't read Mark's lyrics and not immediately understand he was raised as an Irish-Catholic kid – because there's *so much* Catholicism and imagery in his lyrics. But he's a fantastic lyricist. One of the things I loved so much about that last book that was published [2021's *Devil in a Coma: A Memoir*] was that it had so much of his poetry in it. But all of Mark's songs were poetic and so many of them were dark – and also, incredibly beautiful and not dark at the same time.

JESSE HUGHES: *True lyrics*…excellent lyrics, lyrics that are quality – they have a melody in themselves. There's a "music" to the words already. That's why when you study Shakespeare – in my experience, anyway – when I was able to get into it was when I was able to hear the music of the words. And his ability not to turn a phrase, because a phrase is something that happens within a paragraph or something. The entirety of the lyrical content of a song – in and of itself – made a complete thing.

And that's a very difficult thing to accomplish – even for TS Eliot or Mark Twain. To hopefully exist within the structure or within the mechanics of something that you're attempting to say with words, so that once it's completed, the whole thing together is Voltron. And maybe that's what he did. He had the ability to turn a song into Voltron. *Truly.* Everything he's talking about in "Methamphetamine Blues," once you listen to the entirety of the song – each verse – it's a complete thing. Instead of just random interesting lyrics – which is what a lot of music is.

Bubblegum hit me so hard because it is a masterwork. I don't give a fuck what anyone says – that album is *a masterwork.* Because the songs are seemingly effortless, they're uncomplicated in certain respects – but "easy" and "simple" are not the same thing. And it was easy what he was doing for him. And inside these intricate and incredible musical compositions is another difficult thing to do – lyrics which enhance, match, drive, and conform to clearly what the mood or the attempt of the song. When someone can call their shots in pool, you know they're great. When someone just hits the ball and they all fall into holes, that's just luck. Simply, what Mark is doing with his songs, when you look at the title, he's calling the shot. And his genius or the demonstration of his mastery was that he accomplishes that at the end of the song.

SALLY BARRY: Mark was kind of a master of showing and not telling. There's just nothing necessarily expected about his lyrics. Since he didn't consider himself a writer or a poet, it's the same as his voice – it's all very pure and very heartfelt. But he also paints really beautiful pictures. Right from the beginning on *Winding Sheet*, some of the lyrics on that are so beautiful. Like, the lyrics to "Mockingbirds" – they're so pretty, and really simple. Not trying to be clever at all. One of the things I really hate in any kind of writing is when somebody thinks they're really smart and they're trying to be really clever. And he never did that – he would paint these really cool pictures, or just sing really simple love songs.

CHRIS GOSS: To me, that was "the thing." "When Your Number Isn't Up," I mean, your friends are all dying and you're the only one alive in that song. He's "the night porter" – that's what's on his gravestone. "To janitor the emptiness" – that is one of the most profound lyrics of the last two decades. Like, losing Kurt Cobain and giant talents like that, and his friendship with Layne Staley, and losing those kind of comrades, and who else was there to replace them? I think that his poetry *was* Mark Lanegan.

JONATHAN HISCHKE: They're beautiful. They're so personal, and so expressive...it's cheesy to say they're "universally expressive" and they tell everyone's story or some shit like that. But, whatever it is about his delivery and the way he does it, I feel like anyone could tap into it and understand where he's coming from – even though they're about specific experiences of his. And again, that's not a common thing. When I think of great songwriters and lyricists, I'm thinking of all the obvious people everyone would think of – your Leonard Cohens, your Paul Simons, your John Lennons, your Bob Dylans.

But *his* version of it, I don't think he's taking years to write one line like Leonard Cohen did, and I don't think he's trying to be Bob Dylan and do what Bob Dylan did. I think it's coming more from a bluesy place and a personal place. Almost an aside about something – about whatever he's thinking about at the time. And it just seems casual, but deep in that way – the same as the singing. It's pure. It's not labored.

ALDO STRUYF: The language in Iran, they have like, 20 sentences to express "I love you." And it's always beautiful. In my language, Dutch, there are only two ways to say it. And Mark always found ways to talk about drugs, for example – there's nobody in Belgium that knows that *Bubblegum* refers to heroin. So, he always found this way to talk about stuff without really making it clear as possible – he could make it beautiful.

GARY LEE CONNER: On *Clairvoyance* we collaborated on stuff. A song called "Forever" – I remember writing that with him in the same room. I think "Lonely Girl," and he might have wrote a couple of things with Van. But after he died, I was listening to demos, and realized, "There were some good songs that we wrote together that was more him." There's a song I put on YouTube called "Baby Nicotine," that I wrote the music and he wrote the lyrics – a fucking great song. And I don't know why we never did it. There's probably about ten or fifteen songs like that, that maybe we'll release eventually. They're just demos – but it's him singing and his lyrics, that I think people would be interested to hear. But, we never did any of them.

And the strange thing is he never wrote for us. He wrote lyrics, and there are a few songs that Van and him wrote together – like on *Even If and Especially When*, the second song "Straight Out to Any Place." Or later on, on *Sweet Oblivion*, "Dollar Bill" and "Julie Paradise" were written by Van and him. And there was this one song that he wrote that's on one of his solo records called "Dead on You," and in the early '90s he had been learning to play guitar.

We were sitting around, and he was playing and singing it, and I was thinking, "Man, that's really good. We should do it." I thought maybe he'd have us do it, but he never once brought a song. And by the time we did *Dust*, he was on his second solo album – so, he was obviously a very good songwriter. I don't know if he was insecure about his songwriting or what – it was just really odd. That's one of my biggest regrets – that he never brought us songs and we could have had a whole other dimension to the band. But he never did.

ALAIN JOHANNES: He often had a lot of the lyrical stuff already sketched out. He didn't write music first. He wrote the melodies and the feeling of the chords – the harmonic atmosphere came out of the lyrics. And just his ability to dance around the darkness, but at the same time, *this strange feeling of hope.* I've never felt down from it. Like facing things that a lot of people don't dare face – and also accepting them and absorbing them to how to live life properly. He would send me a copy of the lyrics as we were doing the vocal.

MEGAN JASPER: I know he would sweat over the lyrics. He didn't just whip stuff out. I know he would sweat over words – to make sure it felt right and that it was *really* what he wanted to say.

MATT PINFIELD: I thought he was an incredible lyricist. That's why it was so great when they put out the book that just has lyrics [2017's *I Am the Wolf: Lyrics and Writings*]. He was one of those people who could just bring up this imagery – there was a dark and brooding quality and a beauty to it, all together.

JOSH KLINGHOFFER: I could speak mostly about some of these songs – especially off *Bubblegum* – that I've listened to a thousand times. Because when I was younger, I wasn't as intensely listening to the words – I just kind of took the sound in. But I think it comes with the experience. And then having a voice where you can say something so simply and maybe it doesn't mean anything to one person who is not familiar with you or your life, but if you are, saying something like, "To janitor the emptiness," and then say, "So let's get it on" [in reference to the song "When Your Number Isn't Up"], to be able to paint such an emotional picture – that's both specific and an abstraction at the same time – is such an amazing gift.

I can't say for sure what Screaming Trees records he wrote. I know he didn't write a lot of the early ones and some in the middle. But his solo lyrics, there was such an intelligence and such a self-awareness of the voice he had and what he could do with it. It's definitely something for me to learn from. I still feel like there are thousands of Mark Lanegan songs that I haven't heard or I don't really know well. He did so much, so I still have a lot to listen to.

ALDO STRUYF: His lyrics are amazing, and he's like a poet. I'm glad that he wrote a couple of books later in his life, and also the book with all the lyrics printed. I don't know if people in the States know this, but if you live in a non-English speaking country, the first thing that you listen to is the music, and the second thing is the lyrics. So, it's really different from an American English speaking person. So, if I listen to a song, the first thing that catches me is the music, then I start listening to the lyrics. The first album I played on was *Bubblegum*, and there's so much beautiful poetry on that album.

JOHN AGNELLO: *It's all Mark.* What he sings about is really interesting. I think that was part of the thing about him becoming a writer was because he didn't like Gary Lee's lyrics. And by the way, Mark was an amazingly read human being, OK? He turned me on to so many great writers. Cormac McCarthy – Mark read him *religiously*.

There's a bunch of other books that he made me buy to read, like, *The Fatal Shore* [by Robert Hughes] – which is the history of Australia. I think he got a lot of his lyrics from reading stuff like that. He was *really* well-read. And that's the thing – there were many levels of Mark. He was a smart motherfucker. He really was intelligent. But, he was also troubled. He could be violent and had a bad attitude sometimes. But he had a great sense of humor – you know what I mean? I've never met someone with so many layers.

CHARLES R. CROSS: The two greatest things about Mark were his voice and his lyricism. His spare, yet very moody lyricism.

MEGAN JASPER: Mark was a poet. But no one called him a poet – until I think he passed away.

Chapter 5
PERFORMER

What made Mark unique when he performed on stage?

GARY LEE CONNER: Later, he evolved into this…standing there, gripping the mic. But there's videos of him from the early days, when he was trying to do this headbanging stuff. He didn't like performing. I don't know if he ended up liking performing later with his solo stuff, but he never liked playing live shows. I don't even know why the fuck he did it. One time, I remember we were playing in New York at Roseland – we were opening for Alice in Chains, in '92. And before the show, he was so nervous he was throwing up in the bathroom. I can't remember what happened during the show – I think he was OK. But he didn't like playing live. Sometimes it seemed like he didn't even like singing – but he just kept doing it, because he cared so much about the music.

JOHN AGNELLO: Honestly, *the dude never moved.* He had his hands on the microphone stand, but he was so fucking compelling – you couldn't *not* stare at him. Even in the simplicity of just how he acted on stage, he was so compelling. Once again, once he opened his mouth, whatever came out was just genius. There was something magical about that prick. Even in Lausanne in 2017 [the last time John saw Mark perform], he had more of a husky voice, but he was *so* compelling. And not just for old dudes like me – young kids really liked him, too.

CHARLES PETERSON: Non-existent – to a degree. I know in his book he talks about how embarrassed he was at times with Gary's performance and histrionics on stage. But it's also kind of what made the band more exciting than they really were live, too. Obviously, if you're into the songs, it's exciting to hear them live, but you've seen Mark – he kind of just stands at the microphone and occasionally might push it away from him a little bit. "Morrison-type move." But beyond that, it always seemed like he was not comfortable on stage. Which I can relate to – and he talks about that in his book, as well.

SALLY BARRY: I saw Mark perform a bunch of times. I saw him perform with the Trees probably a half dozen times, and any time he was doing solo, I'd just show up and he always made sure I got back. But he was great. I'd seen him good *and* bad with the Trees. I'd seen him do performances with the Trees where he was in good shape, and I'd seen some pretty awful ones – because he was just too sick. But he was still a compelling presence and in his "static-ness" – just standing there, holding on to the mic. Pretty much every time I saw him do solo performances, he was really good. He was just one of those people – if he's on stage, you can't *not* look at him. If Mark's on stage, you shut up and listen.

ROBERT ROTH: In the Trees days, there was this brooding intensity. In fact, where you wouldn't want to fuck with him while he was on stage – you'd probably get hit by a mic stand. And the same goes for me in those days – you may get smacked by a guitar. It's just that intense state of being. When we played the Azkena Fesitval in Spain [in 2008], the Gutter Twins were on the bill, and he had really locked in more to this one stance – with his arm up on the mic. And meditative – focused on his singing, focused on his voice, and kind of living in that place where his voice resonates. Where he's not pushing it.

He changed as a performer and the focus was more on the sound of his voice. So, he didn't move around the stage. He wasn't trying to reach out to the audience. He was very much in himself, projecting from that inner-core – that spiritual core. That's the performance. It's not a matter of banter or interacting or swinging the mic stand around or anything like that. So, it went more from a shambolic thing in the Trees to a more "meditative, eyes closed, focus on being within his voice."

NICK OLIVERI: When we [Queens of the Stone Age] would do shows with him, I knew when he was going to come out we were going to be a badass band – and add something really great to it. He would walk out to the mic [mid-set] and he'd plant himself on the base of that mic stand. I saw some old footage of him with the Screaming Trees where he's jumping all around – I guess he stopped doing that at some point, and he would teeter on his mic stand.

A pretty fascinating stage presence – for somebody who's not running back and forth and side to side. Just being able to go out on stage with those guys was a fantastic thing. I look back on it now and I realize it was something great and special. I'd never been in a band like that before – it was a first for me…and maybe a last, who knows? It was an unreal thing – with Grohl on drums, Mark singing, Josh on guitar, and Troy Van Leeuwen on keys and lap steel [early on in the tour in support of *Songs for the Deaf*]. What a well thought-out band – everybody involved in it was for real and going for it pretty heavily, and playing and singing as hard as they could.

CHAD CHANNING: I saw him perform with the Screaming Trees and he opened for Johnny Cash at the Fifth Avenue Street Theater in Seattle, back in '95. That was really cool. I really enjoyed his performances. He was definitely one of those singers who it's sort of like "what you see is what you get." You never feel like, "Oh, *he's putting on a show*." Mark doesn't really put on a show – he just gets up there and he sings. Either he's your cup of tea and you like it…or he isn't. To me, I always liked that – he seemed just as genuine on stage as he was off. It was very cool that way – really a personal connection, I always thought.

JACK ENDINO: I saw him a few times here in Seattle performing. I think at least once performing with a small band, and another time I saw him perform with just Jeff Fielder on guitar – it was just vocals and guitar. You'd think that wouldn't be enough to sustain the interest for a whole set, but it worked fine. Jeff is a brilliant guitar player. He came and played the Moore Theatre here usually every year or two. I saw him at least twice – maybe more – as a solo performer. It was always great.

ALDO STRUYF: I think it's very unique what he does – just standing there, doing nothing else. And to get the lights down – it has to be as dark as possible. *No spotlights.* The way the stage looks for the audience, it fits his personality towards the outside world perfectly. When he was sober, he would sing it beautifully – it was hardly ever that he was out of tune. But of course, when he was not "clear in his head," then it was really hard – because he would forget stuff. But Mark was sober 90% of the time I was with him. But now and then, he would be wasted on drugs – and then, it would be really hard.

JESSE HUGHES: That motherfucker could stand in one spot and turn his head, and half the audience would be terrified *and* completely inspired at the same time. He has one of those performance capabilities where his very presence itself…I don't want to say it's a light, but it was more like a black hole. And not in a bad way. All the light was drawn into him, so that it gave an impression of darkness. That's an interesting concept that I'm going to get into – a black hole.

A black hole, what is it? It's considered the most powerful and impressive and mysterious phenomena that there is in the physical world. So mysterious, that life can't escape it. And all anyone sees is the reflection of something, no one sees the thing, they see the light that's passed off of it. Mark wouldn't allow any other light to be in the same room as him. It all came to him. When he was in Queens, he would only be on stage for what…20% of the set? And in that 20%, he commanded all the light. "Commanded" is a good word. Mark, in everything he did, *was a command*. Without meaning to be.

JONATHAN HISCHKE: Very compelling in that he was focused with his emanation of what he was presenting – but it was 100% through his voice. Because he wasn't drawing attention to himself or emoting in a physical way, obviously. And he wasn't moved by the music or the experience or the energy of the crowd. *It was all in his voice.* And I'm not saying he was trying to do anything – it was probably just how he felt comfortable. He just wasn't a big theatrical person. I never saw George Jones play, but a friend of mine I remember describing to me decades ago that he'd seen George Jones play, and George Jones had this thing where he was just sitting there playing, and it was so captivating, because there wasn't any extraneous bullshit going on. It was just watching him play, he was singing the songs, and every little movement meant everything.

I feel like that was Mark, too. I've never seen a performer quite like that. Especially the soulful versions.

Like, when I think of soulful people, I think more of an emotive way of performing – I'm thinking of Wilson Picket or Mavis Staples or Ray Charles. And not just somebody standing there still, hand on the mic – just looking up enough to get his mouth to the mic. It was really amazing. But at the same time, when you're behind him playing it – at least from my experience – it felt like the entire band was being funneled through him. He was like the mast of a ship cutting through the ocean. Just stoic and steadfast, and going straight into whatever was coming at him – without any hesitation. He was an unmovable object.

JOSH KLINGHOFFER: He's exactly the kind of performer I wish I was. He didn't have to do *anything*. He was a little more mobile back in the early days, but not much. He was so commanding, and he had the physical strength and an aggressive confidence in a way that he didn't have to do a goddamned thing. He stood up there in all black, and at the show I did with him [Stoned and Dusted, in 2019], I didn't think he wanted to do it. I think he was feeling nervous and exposed because he had never played with this band before. He was basically standing in the middle of the desert on a makeshift stage – which made the show for me all the more special, because it was so weird and it was not just your average show.

I think he was nervous – like he was playing a coffeehouse. But it didn't matter – he would be performing the same way if he was at the Glastonbury Festival. He would just stand there and sing, and he didn't have to do anything else. He smoked every couple of songs. It wasn't a performance – *he was being himself.* And he was feeling however he was feeling. I couldn't really see his face because I was behind him playing drums, but he seemed pretty commanding and forceful to me. Luckily, all that shit is on YouTube – I think you can watch that whole show.

JEAN-PHILIPPE DE GHEEST: There was this concert in Bilbao [the Bilbao BBK Live Festival, on July 12, 2013] – north of Spain. Five minutes after we started, there was a big storm coming up. So, someone behind the scenes just said, "We have to cut it" – because everything was going to be blown away by the storm. At that point, I saw Mark turn his back – to get off stage – and I never saw him as happy. Because he had this double feeling about playing – he would give the impression of not wanting to go on stage because he actually didn't like it. But also at the same time, he needed it – it was his life. He *needed* to tour.

There was this time we played at the Montreux Jazz Festival in Switzerland [on July 16, 2013]. Mark was always very "static" – he wouldn't move at all. And he put so much pressure on his mic stand at the time, that he broke it in two. So, he started shaking a bit – he was dancing. And the next day in the newspapers, they said, "It was an amazing concert – we've never seen Mark dancing so much!" Suddenly, he had to be this guy that he would not usually be.

CHAD CHANNING: If you've ever seen Johnny Cash, Johnny Cash is a very real person when he performs. I don't know if "real" is the right word – maybe "authentic." No need to throw on the bells and whistles. *Very genuine.*

JOHN AGNELLO: During those sessions [for *Sweet Oblivion*] when we were working, it was a Saturday I think, and there was a great show coming through town – it was My Bloody Valentine and Dinosaur Jr., I think it was at the Ritz on 54th Street. They had L7 opening for them, and somebody in L7 got sick, and they had to cancel. So, Dinosaur Jr. asked the Screaming Trees to open up for them.

So, we did a half day in the studio, and then we all went to the show. *It was one of the most amazing shows I've ever seen.* Watching the Screaming Trees open up, and then My Bloody Valentine – who I was a huge fan of – and then to see Dinosaur Jr...and this was before I started working with Dinosaur Jr. I was there with my girlfriend at the time, and it was the *loudest* show I've ever been to – but it was so much fun.

There was a thing – I don't recall how it went down – but the next day, Mark came into the session with a lump on his forehead. Apparently, he had thrown a bottle of beer at Mike Johnson while Mike was playing with Dinosaur Jr. It fell, and then Mike kicked it towards Mark, and actually kicked it so hard it hit Mark in the head. This is *while* they're playing...this is how nuts these guys were! That was one of my favorite nights. Even though seeing My Bloody Valentine, I had to hide in the bathroom – they played this one song last, that was just one chord that drones over and over again. It was super-loud and I started getting nauseous. So, I ran into the men's room for five minutes – until the song was over. And then, we started working again the next day – the Sunday after the show.

ROBERT ROTH: Sometime around '97, I'm on Capitol Hill and Mark yells out in the back of a cab that's going by, *"Hey Robert!"* Yells out his phone number, and says, "Get a hold of me. I'm making a new record – I want you to play Mellotron on it and some keyboards." He was working on a third solo record for Sub Pop – but this was when he was having some hardcore dependency issues, and was not at his best. I think he had fired Mike Johnson and three or four other guitar players during the making of this record. It was at a place called Ironwood – which is now Avast. So, I went down there and brought my Mellotron, my Wurlitzer electric piano, a Memorymoog synthesizer, and laid down a ton of tracks.

The tracks sounded great, but it was nothing like *The Winding Sheet* or *Whiskey for the Holy Ghost* – it was kind of like Lee demos and unreleased Trees songs. But he had top notch people playing on it. Brett Eliason was producing it and the tracks sounded great, but his voice just wasn't there. *Mark* wasn't there. At one point, he had fired the fourth or fifth guitarist. Now, I'm laying down acoustic guitar tracks, and he would sort of pop his head in, but he hung out in the bathroom. He called it "his office" – like the Fonz. He wasn't Mark – Mark was no longer in the building. It was sort of a ghost of himself. He would come in and say a few things to Brett and I about what he liked and didn't like, and was usually pretty favorable.

Then, Sub Pop asked us to go to New York for CMJ [for a performance on September 4, 1997, at the Westbeth Theatre]. Sub Pop put us up for a week in midtown Manhattan. The show though was on I think the second day. Truly had just gotten the green light to make this record for Thick Records – our follow-up to *Kid Coma*. But Mark had barely set up any rehearsals. I didn't really know who was going to be in the band. So, I used that time to record. I think I had been up all night in the studio, and then hopped on a plane the next morning. This was sort of his low point, but it was also a very memorable night.

The good thing is that he cleaned up after this – this was rock bottom for him. I show up and I'm supposed to be playing keyboards. We're supposed to be doing songs from his new record – I don't think we were going to do anything from the first two records. But the one rehearsal that they had scheduled was the first day that we had booked at Robert Lang's – to work on Truly's next album. So, I couldn't go to the rehearsal.

I get to the gig, and SIR Rentals had a full B3 organ, huge-ass Leslie speaker, I think they had a Fender Rhodes – big 72 keys. Just a shit-ton of these massive keyboards for me to play at this gig. I get there, and Mark says, "We're not going to do any of the new songs. We're just going to do stuff off the first two records. And Robert, *you're playing guitar.*" So I'm there at soundcheck, literally with a Walkman and a guitar I borrowed from Damian Jurado – who was a solo artist on Sub Pop – and was learning those songs on stage during soundcheck!

I latched onto it pretty quickly – all standard tuning, kind of open chord stuff. But Mark is disappearing every 45 minutes to an hour, and coming back, and borrowing money from somebody and taking off, coming back with…let me be clear – *he was copping drugs about every hour.* And he tried to convince me to steal the B3 organ, and "Just wheel it down the street" to a pawn shop he knew. Kind of amusing. I turned him down, of course – I thought it was fucking hilarious – and he just kept pushing the things like that, "Well…how about the Fender Rhodes? Let's sell *that.*"

I don't think I had slept much at this point – in fact, maybe this was the first day I got there. So, Mark and I took a cab back to the hotel, I took a quick shower, got the Walkman back over my ears, and had about a half hour to really dive in and learn the setlist. We get back to the Westbeth Theatre, and there's a line around the block – it's packed. And you can just feel the vibe – *they're there to see a trainwreck.* The rumors are flying about Mark's state. So, we get up on stage, and I think we played "Mockingbirds," and about three songs. It went pretty smooth but his voice wasn't the strongest. That was hard – because his voice wasn't there.

But we got through it and we got applause. And [guitarist] Paul Solger goes into the third or fourth song, and Paul starts playing the song we just played. Everything stops. I try it one more time…he does the exact same thing – starts playing the song we just played. So, I think we even may have done a third attempt, and Lanegan is looking pissed off – his reputation for just leaving the stage was pretty well-known to me through Mark Pickerel. And I could tell that was about to happen. So, I whisper in his ear, "Hey, let's play 'Where Did You Sleep Last Night?'" He goes, "Good idea." I sit down with the acoustic guitar, I start strumming the song…Paul goes into the song we had just played *a third time*. And Lanegan bolts.

It was pandemonium – people were freaking out. And towards the front of the stage, there were these really big, loud, obnoxious, drunk jocks – just *screaming* at him, calling him a "junkie." I had two full beers I didn't even get a chance to touch, and I poured both of these beers over these guys' heads. They started coming after me, and oddly, the brother of John Bigley – the singer of the U-Men – was there with a friend of mine, and they kind of stepped in and kept these guys from jumping up on stage and killing me. I ran off stage and got out of there. But that's how the show ended – three songs done pretty well, three false starts, and that was it. That was rock bottom. And I think from there, that record was rightfully canned and he got the help he needed. And thank God, because he went on to do some great music.

Chapter 6
SUBSTANCES

Did drugs help fuel or hinder Mark's creativity?

CLAY DECKER: I think his *life experience* enhanced his creativity all together. And I think drugs was part of his life experience. But he was just as creative and just as into music with or without them.

MATT PINFIELD: I think he had the creativity regardless. But I think there is a point – with anyone – where drugs can sometimes actually fuel creativity. And then other times, it can put things in a standstill.

MIKE JOHNSON: Oh, probably both. I don't know, because it hindered it probably from my perspective – at least heroin did. He sang way worse when he was on smack. That was part of the problem with our eventual split-up on *Whiskey*, because he was going in high and re-singing songs that he had sung ten times better – that were done. And he would go in and think that it sounded better – like it sounded like the last Billie Holiday records or something. It was like this slurring kind of...*really* not good. It was like, "What the hell? What are you doing?" That was awful. But later, I know that he once said that speed helped him write – I know other people have said that. It was never my thing, but some people can crank shit out of a high quality while on amphetamines.

SALLY BARRY: That's a double-edged sword, and I'm saying that as somebody who's been there/done that. There are times when getting fucked up just pushes you into moments of craziness, but it's hard to sustain. There's an ebb and flow to that. I don't think it necessarily did one or the other – because I don't think it does that. I think it's just part of who you are, and it is really difficult to sustain – especially as far into dope as Mark got. It's one of those things like, "How the fuck did you live through that?" It's by sheer luck really that you live through that level of addiction. But I think it helps *and* it hinders. Because it puts you in place that you normally wouldn't be – like, inside your head. And it gives you perspectives on what you're wandering through in the world that you wouldn't ordinarily have if you were completely straight all the time. It puts you in places that you never would be – and you have something to write about.

GARY LEE CONNER: The heroin definitely hindered it. The drinking…he couldn't have kept it up – he would have been dead. The thing about *Sweet Oblivion*, the problem with the collaboration is we'd have all these songs, but a lot of them were only half-finished lyrically. Because usually when I did a song, I'd finish the lyrics, and then Mark would just take them and change them up. But instead, he was singing stuff but without lyrics – dumb lines or joke lines. So, when we were in the studio, half or at least a third of the songs didn't have all the lyrics – or sometimes, even titles. We'd just have "Van's Song" and stuff like that. Mark would never tell me, "These are the lyrics I have." He'd just sing them and then we'd find out what they were. After about two weeks, we were ready to do the vocals, and they kicked us out of the studio.

But a couple of days or three days before, Lanegan had gone missing in New York on a drunken odyssey of God knows what happened. He was gone for three days, and when he came back, he was so fuckin' *massively* hung over. And if he doesn't sing all the stuff and have all the lyrics, the album's delayed. We were a little apprehensive, to say the least. I went to stay at my girlfriend's – now wife – because she lived in Upstate New York, and Van and Barrett probably stayed in a hotel. Three days later, Lanegan came back and gave us a tape, and we're just *floored*. We were like, "Oh my God. This is amazing." I think one of the ones I really remember the most was "Troubled Times," because we had this…I don't want to say what it was called because it was stupid! Well, I guess I can – it was called "Shit My Pants on Monday," because that was what he sang. He sang it repeated over and over again.

When you're writing songs, you just say whatever you can think of, and then you change it later. But then, our fuckin' A&R guy, we stupidly gave him a demo of that, and he thought that was really cool! He was going to release it on a goddamn 45 on vinyl – because he thought it was real "edgy" or something. He wasn't even going to tell us – our manager found out about it and told us. Luckily, it never happened. So, that was what we were dealing with, and all of a sudden, there were these really amazing lyrics. And that was the most edgy singing he ever did with the Trees. He really came through sometimes. That was the one that really made our career. I love the way he sang on that stuff, and really made the songs.

JACK ENDINO: I'm pretty sure he was using heroin during the *Whiskey for the Holy Ghost* sessions. I mean, I never saw evidence of it in the studio. People were not that stupid – I didn't find burnt spoons or any of that kind of tacky stuff laying around the studio. I'm sure whatever they did, it was off premises. So, I never saw any evidence of it – other than what I know now decades later, when everybody got clean and started talking about it. And I realize, "Oh…you mean when I was recording your record, blah blah blah was happening?" All I knew at the time was, "They're having some kind of 'sophomore jinx'." I was so naïve about this stuff.

CHRIS GOSS: Mark asked me to produce *Bubblegum*. I was really up for it – and he was sober at the time. He was very together and happy and sweet, and we were making plans for that record and getting along really well. And the week we started the album, he fell off the wagon. And I think there was a pressure on him when the record started. I don't know where it came from – I don't think it was from me – but just that he had this chance and he had an access to a lot of really good musicians at the time. But then immediately, a lot of drugs came into the picture.

Especially at that time, it was methamphetamine. I'm not a believer that meth is a good creative drug. But somehow, with Mark, lyrically it worked. Usually meth and lyrics are not a good combination. But his lyrics on that record are just *outstanding*. When he started getting kind of fucked up, his mood changed drastically. And it became kind of a sour affair at that point. I'm just pretty much a pothead in the studio. A pothead is kind of loose and almost groovy/silly. Someone who's on meth, who's just going a thousand miles an hour and no brakes applied at all…it turned weird.

CHARLES R. CROSS: Yes, that is true. [In response to the observation, "Unlike Kurt and Layne, Mark was not as well-off financially, so he had to continue to regularly record and tour despite his drug addiction"] But he also made life hell for everybody that tried to help him. There are numerous stories of people in Seattle music that were trying to help the Screaming Trees or Mark on his own – and he just burned through those.

That's either getting advances he burned through…he talks about some of that in his book, so it's not a secret. He burned a lot of people, and yet, he expected everyone to forgive him – because of his charm. *And not everyone gets forgiven.* There is again where there's a bit of the egotism I mentioned – a narcissism. All drug addiction – in a way – is a narcissism. And it's forgetting everyone else's situation. Certainly, in Mark's instance, forgetting everyone in the band that had tried and struggled so hard and created much of this work. Drug addiction eats everything up.

MATT PINFIELD: There were times people couldn't understand where I'd be out of it [due to substance abuse], and all of a sudden, I had to be somewhere or do some work, and they'd be like, "Holy shit! You snapped right out of it!" I can guess that may have been part of the process with Mark. Plus also, if he knew there were certain things expected of him, he could deliver.

CHARLES PETERSON: Reading between the lines, I would say "hindered." I think he even admits to a degree that it hindered his ability to – at least for that second album, especially – get it off the ground and think clearly. The one thing that you get out of that book of him writing about being a junkie is just how much freaking hard work it is, y'know? So, he was obviously spending most of his time scoring and whatnot – instead of making music. At the same time though, the Trees ended up doing some of their better albums – it's not like he didn't do *anything*. He did a lot with other people, as well – Mad Season and stuff like that.

Another story from that period that I recall – this must have been one of the sessions for his records – Mike Johnson said, "Why don't you pop down to Bad Animals? We're doing a session and Lanegan's going to be in it." So, I did pop down, and the band was all there – Mike Johnson, Dan Peters, Barrett Martin, and a few other people. Mark comes in, and he just looked like fuckin' death warmed over. I could tell he was kind of immediately embarrassed seeing me there. Like, "Shit. Charles knows me from a better state than this…and I don't want my picture taken looking like this." And he had some young stripper on his lap pretty much the whole time in the green room.

I took a few pictures through the glass of him singing, and then I felt like I was just distracting him and it wasn't really working out. So, I can't say it ever helped anyone. Of course, in the end, it maybe did help the songwriting, and that it made for a lot of great situations and stories – that were dark and bleak. It could be that the actual making of the music was hindered, but maybe he just needed to go through that for the experience.

ALDO STRUYF: In some cases it helps people to be creative. But in Mark's case, it would be more the opposite. When he was sober, he would do way better stuff. Also, work quicker. Certainly live he would sing way better than when he wasn't.

MEGAN JASPER: It probably hindered, because the material that he produced when he was clean – he produced more of it, and of equal quality to anything he did when he was fucked up. It slowed him down.

JOSH KLINGHOFFER: That's a hard thing to answer, specifically because I don't have the experience with drugs like he did. I wouldn't say this for everybody – if Justin Bieber was doing a bunch of drugs, I don't think they're helping him. But with Lanegan, it's hard to say that they hindered, because I think at the end of the day, drugs or no drugs, he *was* Mark Lanegan from Ellensburg, Washington, who had a difficult upbringing, had a lot of shit going on, and lived the life he lived, and all this stuff we know.

But him taking drugs, clearly him making sense of that life – he was someone who sang, wrote, and performed honestly how he was – so all the drug taking and all the abuse and the pain he was trying to run from or medicate, I think it was all part of him just honestly being him. I think it did probably help create, put him in a place, or get him as fucked up or close to dying, and then realizing that he didn't want to.

To write some of that stuff and to give some of those vocal performances…I'm not going to say the drugs helped. But, at the same time, him taking methamphetamine for weeks on end is not going to make your body last for a long time. Like, I don't think he was taking drugs to be creative. I think he was taking drugs because he was miserable and he didn't know how to deal with life. And I think sometimes it probably helped him make sense of things, and it allowed him to be creative and do work. And sometimes, it probably made his life such that the last thing on earth he wanted to do was be creative – or *could* do, because it's kind of hard to do when you're trying to cop all the time. In a way, to sum that up, he just was an honest person. And I think he was an addictive person and struggled with being addicted his whole life – and it just so happened that he was able to write and sing and create this great stuff. I think it helped *and* hurt.

JESSE HUGHES: I don't think drugs were an escape for him. I don't think he was trying to numb some painful memory. I don't think that was the cause. I think that he was enhancing…or I think he came to our world – which is showbiz – and that's the devil's world. But he didn't come pretending like he was showing up at a bible study. He knew *exactly* where he was coming. And when the devil offered him a deal, he was like, "OK. This is my job then." I almost feel like in a way he looked at it as, "This ain't no bible study. *This is what I do.*" And he had his dark delights – and these things were the addendum to him.

But every situation is situational, and something has a beginning, and then it will change. And there was a point...because sometimes the worst drug that you can be under the influence of is a human being. This is just my view of it, but as he began to hang out less with the people who truly loved him – like Alain Johannes, Joshua Homme – as he was further from them, he was most likely and possibly under the influence of people who were just along for the ride. And when you combine that with a drug – like especially, speed – that's a deadly, deadly combination.

And there is a *Spin* interview [an article entitled *Mark Lanegan Rails Against Technology: 'I Had My Own Private Snowden in the Room With Me'* by Tom Lanham, posted on May 7, 2020] – one of the last interviews he did that I read – that I was like, "My God. What is this? A TV *behind* the TV?" That was shocking to me. I was not happy with that. Not that I was mad at him – I was concerned. And I was concerned that he felt he needed to leave the country and be as far from everyone that he knew and loved. That to me was a demonstration or an indication of trouble.

JACK ENDINO: I'm sure it hindered it. But I don't know – there are people with drug problems who made amazing music. The problem is actually *finishing* any of that music. And the other problem is actually surviving the drugs. Because people can be extremely creative at certain times of their lives – whether they have a drug problem or not. And maybe the drug thing fuels the creativity to a certain point until it doesn't. I am not an authority on addiction, because I'm kind of the "straightedge guy" – I never did anything, really...other than psychedelics. I know that it was much difficult for Mark to finish the second record – I could see the torture he was putting himself through.

And the fact that he was a lot more moody and I had to talk him out of throwing the tapes in Bear Creek, because he was so critical of the record. By the time I worked with Mark at Bear Creek Studio, I think it was my second or third time working on that project over the course of an extended period of time. He was so sick and tired of revisiting these songs and singing them over and over again – trying to find the magic he was looking for – that he seriously wanted to scrap the whole thing and start over from scratch. After putting like, a couple of year's work into it.

And that was when I stepped in front of him and stopped him from taking the tapes out and throwing them in Bear Creek. Which is an actual creek that runs through the woods right behind the studio – it's literally right outside the control room back door. It's a lovely babbling brook. I had to talk him down from trashing the entire record. I said, "No. You are NOT going to throw the tapes in the creek…after all the work I put into it, as well as you and everybody else!" I just had to convince him that it was worth finishing. He just needed somebody to tell him that, I guess.

JOHN AGNELLO: You've got to say that drugs hindered his ability. Because I was in the room when he opened his mouth and sounded like shit – during the scrapped record for Screaming Trees [between *Sweet Oblivion* and *Dust*]. And I do have rough mixes of those songs with his vocals. I have a CD somewhere – I have to go find it. I didn't think *Dust* was as vibrant as *Sweet Oblivion* – it was a little more commercial. I wasn't super-fond of it. But you still can't take away the fact that he's a great singer and they were a great band. I think the drugs did hinder him at a certain point. I don't necessarily think the alcohol did – I think it was the heroin. Once he started doing the heroin, that was bad for him.

ROBERT ROTH: I would say hindered when it got to the point where we were in New York in '97. I've only found out recently the extent – through his books. I didn't realize how bad it had gotten after Kurt died. At that point, it was real detrimental to what he was doing. And prior to that, I don't think he was fucked up on drugs when he was doing *The Winding Sheet*. I think that started with the Seattle scene blowing up. And I think Gary Lee Conner wrote a lot of those songs.

His creativity blossomed when he got clean, honestly – if you look at his post-2000 career. That's his most prolific period. I would say no, I don't think it helped him. I wouldn't say that about everybody – I think there are some people where it opens up channels of creativity and its inspiring. And I'm not talking about heroin, crack, or meth – and I think those are the things Mark was dabbling in somewhere in the mid '90s to the late '90s. Those are not very creative chemicals. *At all.*

CHAD CHANNING: Honestly, if drugs hindered his creativity, then nobody would know who he was, maybe. What I'm trying to say is, if you ask that question about Jimi Hendrix for example, I would say it wouldn't have been a hinderance, because look at how great the guy was. Would he have been any better without the drugs? I don't know. I couldn't say. But I could certainly say it didn't have any hinderance – because I thought he wrote great songs.

NICK OLIVERI: Maybe on records it could help him, but live – when he was traveling – it was hindering. My take on it is it helped *and* it hindered. He wrote great stuff when he was sober and when he was off. He could make it work for him both ways.

CHRIS GOSS: I think at times both – as they do with everyone who mixes drugs and music. There are times when it works and times when it doesn't. I used to have this discussion with Ginger Baker quite a bit – the effects of drugs and music, and the psychology of those mixtures. Ginger was absolutely brilliant in his knowledge of that world and what the outcomes are – different drugs and music, and the ability to play or not play on particular drugs.

One day, Ginger and I had smoked some Thai stick. Back in the '90s, if you were able to get weed from Thailand, it was *super-extraordinary* weed. Now, that weed is everywhere. The power of weed is different. Anyway, we both had gotten really, really super-high off this Thai stick. It was a very heavy high – it wasn't a fun high. And I remember Ginger laying on the couch in my living room, and we had the *Band of Gypsys* record playing. "Machine Gun" started freaking me out.

And I had heard that album since I was a little boy – hundreds or maybe a thousand times. And in the middle of it, I said, "Ginger, I have to go out and take a walk around the block because I'm getting freaked out by this." And without even opening his eyes from the couch, he said, "*It was the cocaine.*" Legend has it that someone had brought Jimi and the band a wooden box of pharmaceutical coke the night of the Band of Gypsys shows [at the Fillmore East]. And that's why one of the sides of the playing was so fucking intense. And he knew that psychology so well, that knowing that *that* effect would have on not the player, but the listener 30 years after the playing.

It's pretty deep to realize that you're feeling that mixed emotion that was all those years ago. And it's still alive in that music. And he knew it right off the bat. When he said "It was the cocaine," it was like telling me "Don't worry about it. It isn't the end of the world." That song, it's one of the heaviest pieces that Hendrix ever did.

CHARLES PETERSON: After *The Winding Sheet* period, I kind of lost track of Mark – to a degree. I'd see him here and there on occasion through those years, and he always looked increasingly worse for wear. And I'd heard tales that he was a hardcore junkie. In fact, one time, my girlfriend and I – who at the time, she was dabbling in it, as well – we had to go over to an apartment that Dave Duet and Lanegan had been renting. I think they had both gone to rehab and given up the apartment, and we wanted to go over to help clean it out, so they could get their damage deposit back.

 And in the kitchen, I went to open a drawer – and the whole drawer was full of orange needle caps. So, I'd been kind of through the first "Seattle junkie wave" – seeing my girlfriend struggle with withdrawal, saving somebody's life at a party from OD'ing, and all that. So, at that point, I just didn't really want to have much to do with junkies anymore. And it's kind of a shame, because I should have been at *every* Nirvana show there was, every Lanegan show, etcetera, etcetera. But part of me was just like, "I can't really deal – beyond a professional capacity."

GARY LEE CONNER: He was completely sober – as far as I know – from right after that accident [at Twin City Foods] and *Other Worlds*, which was '85, until early 1990. He might have fallen off the wagon, I don't know. But if he did, I never knew about it or saw any evidence of it. As far as I know, he was completely on the straight and narrow. And I think the band really helped him to do that. In the early days, he was massively hypochondriac – he thought his eyes were sinking in or he had AIDS or something. One of the things that scared him was right after he had that accident was the doctor told him if he didn't stop drinking and doing drugs, he would die. But he was totally sober until early 1990.

In early 1990, we went to Europe, and there were all sorts of people giving us lots of pot. I don't know why they'd give it to us, like, "*Here's a huge bag of pot.*" [Laughs] People in Europe seemed to do that back then. So, he started smoking pot. And the whole year – including the time we were working on the first Epic record, *Uncle Anesthesia,* he was smoking *a lot* of pot. And I think you can kind of hear it in his voice on *Uncle Anesthesia* – his voice is a little mellower than it had been before. It lost its edge a little bit.

It came back after he started drinking again, because what happened was we had a van wreck. *Uncle Anesthesia* was coming out – early '91. We just got a brand new van, and we were using the van for equipment and we had a minivan. And Mark was riding in the equipment van with two crew guys, and we were in Wyoming – the first or second show of the tour. And it flipped on black ice – all the way over, on the other side of the freeway, upside down. And nobody was hurt badly – just minor injuries. Mark, I don't think he had anything happen – bruises or whatever. But a week later, we had gone to Chicago to regroup – to figure out what we were going to do – and he started drinking. And he didn't stop drinking – until he started getting into heroin.

So, I guess pot was the gateway drug for him – he started smoking pot, a year later he started drinking, and then a year or two later he started doing heroin more. But it's weird, because that tour that ended up being total drunk debauchery – except for me, because I just never drank very much. I drank a beer or something, or got really drunk once or twice. Because it was Van, and Dan Peters was our drummer, who was in Mudhoney – he was a big drinker, and with Lanegan, it was just crazy. But we couldn't even finish the tour, because he had gotten physically unable to keep going. We got about two-thirds of the way and then we ended up flying home and had to regroup. And that's the time we ended up doing *Sweet Oblivion.*

But what's really weird was the drinking is probably what enabled us to do *Sweet Oblivion* – it's horrible, but it's true – because he was so social when he was drinking. He'd come over and hang out and want to work on songs. He'd want to rehearse. He wouldn't stop. We would do stuff like "Nearly Lost You." We knew that song was kind of different, and we worked on it a lot – more than anything else. We'd just jam on it for ten or twenty minutes. It was like he was a different person, almost...a different really drunk person. [Laughs]

Like "Winter Song," we had just got the schedule and we were flying out to New York in a couple of days to do the record. And he shows up at my door at 6:00 in the morning. I'm asleep. And he goes, "You've got to drink beer." So, I tried to not drink it – I probably drank half a beer, and tried to dump it out. Then he called Van and he called Barrett, and we all got together and drove all over Seattle for some reason. And by early afternoon, we'd dropped him off downtown at this strip club, the Lusty Lady, because Nina Hartley – who was his favorite porn star – was performing or something. That was the end of that day.

But the weird thing is that night, I went back home and wrote "Winter Song." And that's always been one of my favorite songs of the Screaming Trees. My wife – she was actually my girlfriend at the time – was in New York, and suggested that I write a song like Cheap Trick's "Downed." The day of the craziness and that song were kind of inspiration for "Winter Song" – it has a similar descending thing. So, I wrote that and the next day I showed Mark, and he liked it a lot. That one didn't get changed much. But on the other hand, it starts out "Jesus knocking on my door." Originally, that was not "Jesus" – it was "Lanegan." [Laughs] So, that song was kind of inspired by that day.

JOHN AGNELLO: When we started *Sweet Oblivion*, Mark drank. There's a funny story of him going out one night, and not showing up the next day – because he ended up in Philadelphia. We don't really know how the fuck he got to Philadelphia. I'm not even sure *he* knows how he got to Philadelphia. He didn't tell the rest of the band or Don, but he confided in me. But during *Sweet Oblivion*, he kept his shit together. I don't think he was doing heroin – I think he was just drinking. And we would go out and drink.

But I did notice over the stretch of time of trying to finish *Whiskey for the Holy Ghost*, that took us over the course of six months or something to finish it. But in the beginning, he was fine. It was only at the end. By the way, we didn't work six months straight, we worked in stretches. It took six months on and off to finish the record. But by the end, it was back in the old days, so we recorded to tape and we mixed to tape. So, back in those days, when you sequenced your record, you literally had to put tape against tape in a row of the songs.

But I remember as we were sequencing the songs…he was nodding off. And I was like, "This is not like Mark. Is something going on?" And *that's* when I realized he was doing heroin. And that was bad. So, when we did the unreleased Screaming Trees record – the record after *Sweet Oblivion* – we did it in Seattle. And I have to be very honest and say as an ambassador for Mark Lanegan, I had a lot of stress going on, because he was kind of fucked up – *the whole time*. And the reason that record got shelved is because he was *so* fucking high, and he sang like shit. I could barely wake him up to get him to sing. He was really, really bad. And we had fights. I'd walk into the lounge and he'd be asleep, and I'd be like, "Mark! It's time for you to sing!" And he'd be like, "Hey man, *I'm sleeping.*" And I'd be like, "No! Fuck you! We're paying $2,000 a day for studio time. You're not sleeping, *you're singing.*"

We had these fights daily. I remember I said to him at one point, "You're not fucking sleeping. At home in your apartment, you fluff your pillows, you put on your pajamas, you go to bed and sleep. In the studio, you've got to sing – we're behind schedule." And I'll be honest, we loved each other so much as humans that even when I yelled at him like that, he rarely did anything to me. We really got along great. I'll be very clear – he kicked me in the nuts once. He threw a boombox at me and missed me by inches. But overall, we loved each other.

GREG WERCKMAN: There's an unreleased Screaming Trees album – and I remember Lanegan played me some of those songs. I was like, "Oh my God...*let me put this out!*" And he was like, "Hell no." I was like, "Please! These are great Screaming Trees songs." He would have none of it. There's an *amazing* record there.

GARY LEE CONNER: There were so many times in the old days where we thought, "*This is it.*" I know in the book, he talks about the time his arm got all infected. We were stuck somewhere in Canada in hotels while he was in the hospital. We were playing in New York, and my wife and I weren't married yet but we were engaged, and I had stayed with her, and the whole band came over for Thanksgiving – including Layne. They had some crazy odyssey in Philadelphia – he wrote something about it in the book. But a couple of days after that, they came out and I made them Thanksgiving dinner.

They didn't stay very long, and Mark and Layne spent most of the time in the bedroom or bathroom – doing something. And then I flew up to Montreal the next day for the next show, but Mark was in the hospital when I got there. And Layne came and sang "Nearly Lost You" – there's a video of it online. I think that was the only song he did. But then Mark showed up after the show and was out of the hospital, but then I think went back in the hospital when we got to Toronto. It spanned several days – with him in the hospital, and if his arm would get cut off. He *always* had to go to the hospital. Even in the old days, we'd always be like, "Watch for the hospital sign," because he may go to the hospital. But that time he *really* needed to go to the hospital.

KIM THAYIL: As with any elements of a person's life, drugs are a component of it, drinking, sex, relationships, money, the ability to be published, leisure time – does the person work all the time or do they have enough time to sit there, play their instrument and write songs? There are a lot talented and creative people who are unfortunately bound to perhaps their employment and maybe their responsibility, duty, and debt. These kind of things require time and money. But it's leisure time that affords you to sit next to your telescope for hours and hours every night, until you discover that one weird comet. Or to sit down with your piano or guitar and write a song.

Then when you produce stuff, it's a function of publishing and getting people to hear it. There are a lot of people who write songs out there, and a lot of them aren't heard – they're heard by friends of theirs. And maybe it doesn't move forward from their peers to other peers. Sometimes, it does – sometimes someone like Daniel

Johnston comes out, cassettes are spread around, and people have a reverence and curiosity for the work of Daniel Johnston. To the point that he starts making records, and a label picks him up. But it doesn't always happen that way. Maybe someone's music is not recognized by their contemporaries. Maybe it gets recognized later. We always hear about painters and visual artists who weren't recognized and don't become prominent until 50 years after their death.

Sometimes, you make those things happen for yourself – as did people like Hiro and Chris, who all the money that they got from work would go into buying themselves instruments or amps or recording equipment, so they could do what they really wanted to do. But sometimes, not everybody can do what they really want to do. And drugs are part of it. Is that a component of your personality that feeds into the songs you write? Or does it hinder your ability to perform well and write a song? Well, if you're spending all your time procuring for and addressing your addiction, that's time that isn't going towards you being creative.

But then again, are there other insights or pleasures you receive from attending to your addiction that are documented and prescribed in the work you do produce? I think if it's part of you and it's part of your personality, if you have a personality that engages in other activities that can hinder the time, the resources available, and spent to produce your creative work, or, they can be a source of inspiration. Or, they themselves can perhaps facilitate your creative work.

I've heard people say, "No great song was ever written when drunk." And I'm thinking, "That's bullshit. There's *so many* alcoholics out there – jazz guys and blues guys – that perform and produce great work, that had serious addictions or were alcoholics. I mean, how sober do you have to be to write "Louie Louie"? I think they're all part of the human experience and all part of the human condition, and all these aspects contribute to the work that someone might do. So, I think alcohol has impeded people and other substances like heroin have probably impeded people…and have probably facilitated and inspired people. It's not necessarily going to make things better – it's likely going to make things worse. If it's part of being a person, then it's part of your topography and biography. And then, it's a component of your creativity.

GREG WERCKMAN: That's the million dollar question for so many artists. I think it hindered. It maybe added to the darkness of his creativity, but he was *so* talented – he could have done so much. He could have been our generation's Tony Bennett. He could have kept going and performing with orchestras, making beautiful records. I don't think until towards the end did it really effect his voice. But his stamina…it was a negative, for sure. He would have been *extremely* successful without drugs.

CLAY DECKER: It wasn't too long after I tattooed Mark that I got a call from Shelley while I was in the middle of a tattoo, and Shelley said, "Mark's in the hospital." It was the day before he was supposed to go on tour with Queens of the Stone Age. So, I stopped in the middle of the tattoo I was doing, and I had a friend – who was a tattoo artist who was visiting – finish the tattoo. I raced straight to the hospital and pretended to be his brother, so I could go in there and see him. I met Shelley there, and I'd never seen him in a hospital before. I was rattled, really. I knew he was supposed to go on tour the next day, and I knew he wasn't going to be leaving on tour the next day. So, I called Josh, and Josh came down to the hospital. He looked at me, and said, "Man, *I've lost count how many hospitals I've seen him in*." Mark got sober for ten years after that. That's the moment that Mark got sober.

JOHN AGNELLO: I worked with him before and after he got clean, and it was amazing to see the difference. It was amazing watching him hang around Duff McKagan – his sponsor – and they both were doing great. I was so happy to see him get clean.

MATT PINFIELD: It's no secret that Mark and I both struggled with addiction and alcoholism in our time. And there were times over the years I would reach out to Mark when I was struggling, and he was there. I would call him and we would talk about it. I happened to actually be there the day he got out of rehab – when he got clean and sober.

I was in Seattle with Peter Buck, who was in an instrumental band called Tuatara, who I remember had released an album called *Trading with the Enemy* – which was named after the idea of the US government saying if you bought Cuban cigars, that you were trading with the enemy. [Laughs]

I happened to go to Seattle to hang with those guys to tape stuff. I remember being there and hanging with Mark right after he got out of rehab and he looked great. And I remember one other time I was up in Seattle, *and I was struggling, boy.* And I called Mark, and Mark was there for me.

MEGAN JASPER: He was able to turn it around…and he was able to turn it around *many* times.

Chapter 7
CLASSICS

Which songs or albums showcased Mark's talents most?

GARY LEE CONNER: I've listened to his stuff [other than the Screaming Trees] on and off, but he has *so much* stuff. I don't think I qualify to say about his solo stuff – because I don't know it well enough. The Trees stuff, some of the stuff on *Sweet Oblivion* definitely. Maybe "Troubled Times," and "Julie Paradise" has always been one of my favorite songs. It's kind of cool to step back and hear it, because I didn't write it. [Laughs] I always loved playing it live, too.

The earlier stuff, sometimes it's funny, because "Black Sun Morning" from *Buzz Factory*, I don't even know how I sang it on the demo, but it was kind of high. And it was weird, because sometimes our voice registers didn't match, and I never really understood, because sometimes I would sing stuff that would seem really high, but it wouldn't seem high for him, and vice versa. And that was one of the ones that was just too high for him, and he was kind of pissed off about singing it. A lot of people love that song – but it's not as good as his performance on say, when he does a similar type of thing on "Ivy."

"Ivy" was really great – really raspy. And another thing on "Ivy," I had that song for a year, but for some reason I was embarrassed to play it [for the others], because I took acid for the one and only time in late '86, and I got a lot of songs out of it! [Laughs] A lot of songs I wrote later, like "Transfiguration," "Other Days and Different Planets," a lot of the stuff on *Invisible Lantern*. But that song I wrote right after I took acid, and I was embarrassed to play it for everyone…and I don't know why. Maybe I thought it was too…mainstream? It's not mainstream at all.

But anyway, he was kind of mad – "What?! You had this song and you didn't tell me? *It's really fucking cool!*" Lanegan came up with this really cool descending thing [vocally], which is kind of derivative of a lot of garage rock. But the way he did it, it's not quite. He really made the song. Those are the kind of things he'd do that would take a song over the top.

And I think his vocal performance on "Strange Out Here" was probably one of his best. It was kind mellow, and he did this talking thing in the middle, where it's a "Doors parody," almost. But it was about getting out of Ellensburg. "Blood of a million dead sheep running down Third Street" – that's where the studio was, on Third Street. He wrote all those lyrics, so it was real heartfelt – as opposed to me singing about purple unicorns or something. [Laughs]

MEGAN JASPER: I love *Whiskey for the Holy Ghost* – but this isn't just his vocal performance, with that, I'm thinking of crafted songs. But I have to say *Sweet Oblivion* is maybe my favorite record to have come out of the northwest. And Mark's vocals are *so* good on it. And there might not be a better song than "Dollar Bill." And he *kills* it on that whole record. "Kimiko's Dream House" – there's something about Mark's voice in that song, it always comes to mind for me. There's something so tender and beautiful…and strong at the same time. It's a really beautifully-sung song.

CHARLES R. CROSS: I'm going to be one of the few people to say "Nearly Lost You" was great. That's definitely the best song on *Singles*. Mark and I specifically talked about that – he was shocked that it scored him a gold record. I like "One Way Street" off of *Field Songs* a ton. And "Resurrection Song" off that. *Field Songs* really was phenomenal – that, and *The Winding Sheet*. But I think *Whiskey for the Holy Ghost* is his best record. There are a bunch of songs on that, that are just *deep* – "The River Rise," which kicks that record off. And the Mad Season song he's on, that's just phenomenal – "Long Gone Day."

KIM THAYIL: His solo stuff was much more intimate and warm. I am a fan of the Screaming Trees because of course, I like Gary's guitar work and I like the type of songs they would come up with. I think the first Screaming Trees album I heard was *Clairvoyance* – I immediately loved the songs "I See Stars" and "Little Orange Airplane." I think of Lanegan singing that, and their taste in music that seemed to coincide with the parallel taste of Hiro and I, and that Ben had prior to and during Soundgarden. So, I think of those, but ultimately, I think of Mark's solo stuff as being a lot more warmer, intimate, and showing both melancholy and strength, and...I don't want to say "crooner," just short of that. *Contemplative.* And that's very different from the trippy and rocking stuff that the Trees do.

ROBERT ROTH: Pickerel quit when they did *Uncle Anesthesia* – he was already planning on quitting when we had got together [as Truly], but he said, "I have to go record this record." I heard "Bed of Roses," and I was like, "OK. I'm not going to say anything to Pickerel, but, *are you sure?* It's a great song!" [Laughs] I've always loved that song and his vocals are great on it. I think at that point he had kind of found his style. They had sped up tracks or something back in the earlier Trees days, and his vocals are great on *Buzz Factory* and those records, but I think it just got better.

As far as the more recent solo stuff, just hearing the stuff he did in the last few years with Soulsavers, Gutter Twins, some of his solo stuff...I mean, his voice got even deeper, even lower, even growlier. It just *lived there* – and it was impressive, to me. My voice is somewhere in the middle there – but he was digging deep into that texture with his voice. And then I heard things that weren't like that, that were recent, too – that were a little more high, a little lighter. That didn't even sound that much like Mark to me. I wish I could tell you what titles I'm thinking of.

I have seen some of it [a performance on YouTube from 2012, entitled *4AD Sessions*] and it's fantastic. I feel like somewhere in that time frame, he was really at this peak as a singer – really sounding like no one else and just having his own thing, his own niche. Which is a great thing. I finally found that for myself later in life – so it's interesting how some of these male singers like Mark and some of my heroes got better with age. I'm much more comfortable with my voice now than I was in the '90s.

GREG WERCKMAN: I loved the song "Bed of Roses" by the Screaming Trees. That is one of the quintessential Lanegan songs and Lanegan vocals. He wasn't too crazy about doing Screaming Trees songs – but that had very little to do with the music. On *I'll Take Care of You*, he did an amazing Buck Owens cover, "Together Again." It's on almost all of my playlists for drives. It's just sad and beautiful. He could have made a country music record that would have *killed* people. I remember when those Johnny Cash records came out that Rick Rubin did, I'd be like, "Mark, you need to make a record like *this*." And he agreed. He was like, "That would be cool to make a real sparce record." And a lot of what he did with Rich in Soulsavers led to that area.

SALLY BARRY: I think *Sweet Oblivion* was the peak of his vocal performances with the Trees. If I listen to *Dust*, I can hear how tired he was – and that kind of makes me sad. Because the band was cooking their brains out on *Dust*, but Mark was really tried. His vocals on *Sweet Oblivion* are great. A couple of songs that stand out for me from his solo work – I think "Resurrection Song" is just absolutely flawless. And his vocal on "Beggar's Blues" off of *Whiskey* I think is flawless. But for sheer vocal power, *Sweet Oblivion* – all the vocals are fantastic on that. And those two songs stand out to me as really perfect songs.

JACK ENDINO: I like the way he sang on *The Winding Sheet* tunes, because there's some vulnerability there. I just don't remember the song titles. I gave him an SM58 [microphone by Shure], and he just banged out the vocals in like…one take, two takes. And he never went back and hated on it. It was pretty painless. His voice worked the way he wanted it to work. He was very in control of the material. The band members were very simpatico. Mike Johnson was a crucial part of those first two records – I wish he got a little more credit, because he co-wrote a lot of those songs. Mike did a lot of "supportive work" – taking Mark's guitar ideas, and fleshing them out into something. Mark never claims to be a guitar player, but he's able to play enough to show people how his songs go. But very rarely did his own guitar end up on the recordings – it's usually Mike doing the guitar parts.

But Mark was very much in control – directing things. He knew how the songs were supposed to go. And I could tell that him and Mike Johnson had woodshedded on this stuff quite a bit – they knew exactly what they were going to do in the studio. "Mockingbirds" has Mark Pickerel on drums, and I'm playing bass. That's a lovely little tune. It's not intended to be a "rock record," but it's interesting that Mark chose to open with a rock song. "Museum" is a magical tune and his vocal's amazing. "Ugly Sunday," it's funny, because that's almost like a throwaway tune. I played bass on it, and I think I had to do drop-D on it – it's tuned way down. It's got a nice guitar part from Mike Johnson on it.

Mike Johnson plays a lot of very interesting guitar on that record. And being a Portland guy, he's very influenced by Greg Sage from the Wipers – as am I, and I'm not a Portland guy but I've absorbed a lot from listening to Wipers records as a guitar player. It comes up over and over again – I find myself going, "I wonder what Greg would have done here?" Mike Johnson definitely has a very strong style of his own, but there is a definite Wipers influence on what he was doing. Which was very cool, in my opinion.

MIKE JOHNSON: On record, there is a better version that didn't come out, but I would say "Riding the Nightingale." That's the one for me. But there's Trees songs that are maybe better...I don't know. But that was the one that I'm still like, "Somebody I knew could do *that*?" Even the first version was incredible. He re-sang that a few times, and it didn't get better. The best version was left probably on the cutting room floor.

MATT PINFIELD: I had always felt that Epic Records made a mistake by not releasing this one Screaming Trees song as a single – "Dying Days." It was a song I *absolutely* loved and was convinced could be a rock hit in that period of time. I felt like it was one of the strongest songs on *Dust*. And the label pushed back on it. But I remember spending time with Mark and Barrett, and them saying to me, "You were right about that song." I just felt it was this incredibly strong song all the way around – lyrically, the feel of it, and the changes in that track.

CHAD CHANNING: My favorite album of his is *Field Songs*. It has a Midwest meets Southwest sort of feel to it, that I really like. I grew up all over the place, and moved everywhere tons as a kid. So, half my life and my memories are in the backseat of a car, traveling through cornfields – or somewhere in the Midwest. So, there's a kind of style of song that hits me a certain way. Very few records can pull that sense out of me, but *Field Songs* is one of those, because it has that "flavor" to it. It's more a personal thing between me and what I'm listening to. "Resurrection Song" and "No Easy Action" are probably my favorites off the record.

CHARLES PETERSON: *Winding Sheet* is a pretty freakin' amazing record. And then the follow-up too, *Whiskey for the Holy Ghost*, and *Scraps at Midnight*. Those three records are pretty damn great. I like a lot of his later stuff – he put out *so many* records, I just get a little lost with it all. My go-to when I want to listen to Mark is the Light in the Attic compilation [2014's *Has God Seen My Shadow? An Anthology 1989-2011*]. I think Mark himself sequenced it, and I think it's a really good encapsulation of his career up to that point.

KIM THAYIL: Another one of the things that stands out for me was when he did the Captain Beefheart song, "Clear Spot" [included on 2003's *Here Comes That Weird Chill*]. I remember that Beefheart album was probably my favorite Beefheart album [1972's *Clear Spot*] – when I first heard it, in the late '70s. I took to Beefheart even more than I took to Zappa. But *Clear Spot* was *the one* – that was produced by Ted Templeman, who did the first few Van Halen albums.

And when I saw the title "Clear Spot" on the Alain Johannes-produced Lanegan album, I thought, "They wouldn't be doing a Beefheart song…would they?" And they did! It surprised the hell out of me. It's like when I heard Nirvana do "Plateau" by the Meat Puppets. I love the Meat Puppets, and my favorite Meat Puppets album is the second one [1984's *Meat Puppets II*] and my favorite song on the album is "Plateau."

And here's another one of my favorite bands doing my favorite song off my favorite album from one of my favorite bands! And then hearing Lanegan doing "Clear Spot," it's like, "He's doing 'Clear Spot'! I love that song!"

NICK OLIVERI: I think *Bubblegum* has got some great stuff on it. But I really am a fan of *Whiskey for the Holy Ghost* – "River Rise," "Carnival," and stuff like that. But *Field Songs* has some of my favorite stuff he's done – "Kimiko's Dream House" is an *amazing* song. And on *The Winding Sheet,* "I Love You Little Girl" – he had some great highs in his voice back then. I think "A Song for the Dead" [by Queens of the Stone Age] is an amazing performance – because it's more on the heavy rock tip, but still has his "Dark Mark" vibe. And I have to say a song he did on his Christmas record, *Dark Mark Sings Christmas*, of the Roky Erickson song, "Burn the Flames," is one of the most amazing performances I've heard him do – the vibrato in his voice is unmatched. *Amazing* vibrato.

JESSE HUGHES: I respect, admire, and love the Screaming Trees a lot. But me personally, I find that that's where he was discovering himself. So, it's not the things I focus on. But I don't think there's any denying that *Songs for the Deaf* is a crest. It's a highpoint. And "Hanging Tree" for me is "the one." The growl in the vocals…and this is another thing about him – when you're an engineer or a producer, if you have any sense at all, when Mark Lanegan is in your studio, you want to be able to be worthy of it. And if you're open to it, you'll be inspired. And you hear some incredibly inspired moments of engineering, incredibly inspired production moments that demonstrates the genius of Joshua Homme. But it demonstrates his genius too for being able to recognize genius, and simply attempting to capture it. And that was the hardest thing about Mark – to capture him. Like a giant, dreadful, terrifying leprechaun.

CHRIS GOSS: I'd say "One Hundred Days" [which Goss also sings on]. When we were younger, we both had girlfriends who were prostitutes. For me personally, when he says, "I stop and talk to the girls who work the street, but I've got business further down" – that puts me back to being 20 years old and high as fuck. And the sun setting in the city and running into the girls who were working on the sidewalk. That song, every time I hear it, it sends me back in a time machine. We both had similar youths around the time we were 20 years old. I was mainly in New York doing drugs, and Mark was in Seattle doing drugs – both of us being huge music fans at the same time, and the street life. So, that song does it for me – as far as capturing that vibe.

JEFF FIELDER: We never didn't do "One Way Street." That was kind of – for me – his "go-to song." He could sing it on cue, and it was just gorgeous every time. I loved playing with Mark – I loved hearing the sound in the room. It would change – what my favorites were. If I even had one. But we started doing "Strange Religion" towards the end of our tenure together – *because of Anthony Bourdain.* We did the Anthony Bourdain TV show [*Parts Unknown*], and we did "Strange Religion" at his request. The whole reason that came up was that Anthony did the foreword to Mark's book of poetry. So it was like, "You owe me one." And I was put in charge of all of it. Mark was like, "I don't know anything about restaurants in Seattle and shit." So, I brokered the entire thing. It was like my friend's place that we went to, the stage we performed on was another friend of mine. I sort of put the little band together. That was a cool experience.

And then after Anthony died [on June 8, 2018], we started doing "Strange Religion" all the time for him. Even though Mark comes across so bigger than life and bulletproof, he was really vulnerable to a lot of his songs. And he didn't want to play them because of that. And "Strange Religion" was definitely one of those – where he didn't like playing it. He didn't like singing it. I never asked him why, exactly. It's very heartfelt and you can kind of tell what it's about just by listening to it. I never asked him specifically why, but he didn't like doing it. It conjured up too much emotion for him. But we did it for Anthony, so we ended up putting it in the set. That was definitely a highlight of the set for me – in those times.

And this is just us playing together, but "Phantasmagoria Blues" I quite liked. And with the band, I *loved* doing "Bleeding Muddy Water." *What a tune, man.* That whole *Blues Funeral* record is quite astonishing, actually. I think a lot of people would say that – between *Field Songs*, *Bubblegum*, and *Blues Funeral*, it's just bulletproof material.

TRAVIS KELLER: I love the whole *Bubblegum* record. I love his cover of the Gun Club's "Carry Home." I love the Queens songs that he sings on, too – he was definitely the best part of that band, I think. Especially the songs he sings on *Rated R* – those are cool. I love *Field Songs* – that whole record is really cool. Honestly, I've been discovering a lot of the records I didn't know since, and it's wild. He was just *so* prolific.

JESSE HUGHES: *Bubblegum* – in my opinion – is one of the best albums ever made. I mean that sincerely – it's one of the most underrated and best records ever made. Every song off that album is a crusher. There's a melody in it, and he manages to use his voice in such a way that the nuance of the melody is almost disguised – without attempting to. Almost like an optical illusion or you think you're looking at an old lady…but it's a young lady looking in a mirror. He was more like the skull head with a bunch of naked bodies.

The song "Methamphetamine Blues," for me personally, is a dead-on, ringer of accuracy there. That sums it up. "Hit the City"…dude, I can go on for hours about that album, because I love it so much. And his band, he's got some of the finest musicians in the world. Which is another thing about him that I've constantly noted – even in his disconcerted or unbalanced, he was able to command some of the greatest talents in our business that the world knows, to be anonymous on his records. To perform without the normal fanfare or credit. That's really a statement.

And what a name for a record – *Bubblegum*. *Bubblegum* is the type of pop that is considered easy and light. And *Bubblegum* is a name for things that don't have much substance – that you just chew back and forth, and is anonymous. And that's hardly what that record is. It's almost like a study in intentional or designed contradictions. Which, I guess in that respect, they would become enigmas.

I related to *Bubblegum* – he was going through a break-up, and I was in the midst of a break-up. And that album seemed to me – personally – as if it was written for *me*. That's how it felt. Because in fact, the day I met him was the day I hit the city. And there's a song on there called "Hit the City." "Wedding Dress." All of these things I related to, and it seemed like…in the corniest of ways, but, strumming my pain with his fingers – that's what he did on that whole record.

NICK OLIVERI: I think they recorded that [a cover of ZZ Top's "Precious and Grace," with Mark and Billy Gibbons trading vocals] for *Lullabies to Paralyze* – as a b-side. That was a great song. Fantastic. I loved it. Just nailed it. What a heavy song too, and what a groove it has. It's just a perfect song for him to sing.

JOSH KLINGHOFFER: After I sort of distanced myself a bit from that kind of alternative music of the early '90s as I got a little older, I was going back and listening to older stuff – it was Lanegan's solo records that jumped out. And he was doing records unlike anyone else from that era. And his first solo record on Sub Pop I loved, and all those solo records I loved. But, when *Bubblegum* came out, that was when my obsession with his solo career began. I'd say some of my favorite vocal performances of his are "When Your Number Isn't Up" and "Strange Religion," songs off *Buzz Factory* and some of those early songs that in his book he would complain about being out of his range. I kind of understand what he was saying, but I think he always sang incredibly. And the first record he did with Isobel Campbell, *Ballad of the Broken Seas*.

There's a song recently that I became obsessed with, off that record he did with Joe Cardamone [*Dark Mark vs. Skeleton Joe*], they played it at his memorial service – "Hiraeth." Which is actually an amazing word. A friend of mine sent me a definition for it – it's a Welsh word, and whoever is the scholar who wrote it, likens it to "A homesickness tinged with grief and sadness." Wherever Lanegan came by that word, I would imagine that was perhaps what he was feeling. It's one of the greatest vocal performances I've ever heard.

Isobel Campbell being part of Belle and Sebastian – who was another band I was into around that time, and couldn't be more sonically dissimilar than some of the stuff Lanegan was doing, and the kind of light, very Scottish Belle and Sebastian. I wouldn't necessarily put them in the same breath, but I think there are a lot of similarities. And when those two voices met, I thought there was really a special thing. I think that was maybe the first time you really saw he was capable of moving in and out of all these different situations and environments. There was such a sensitivity to some of those songs on that record.

I think everyone and their mother probably compared it to *Nancy & Lee* [the 1968 album by Nancy Sinatra and Lee Hazlewood]. But it felt to me like something – at least in my myopic scope – we needed more of. I loved the idea of these collaborative records – one person from over here and one person from over here, that you wouldn't necessarily put together, but my gosh, they sound incredible together and they're doing emotional songs. I don't know if this is true, but it seemed to me that they made the record kind of fast. It was just very honest.

JONATHAN HISCHKE: I love the record with Duke Garwood that he did [*Blues Funeral*]. I love *Bubblegum*, of course. I love a lot of his guest appearances here and there. One of my favorite things that I can't stop watching is his performance of Queens of the Stone Age with him on "Song for the Dead" – they're doing it at Glastonbury [in 2002]. One of the great line-ups of that band – with Dave Grohl, Nick, Troy, Josh, and Lanegan singing it.

Again, he's just the mast of the ship on that one – just standing there while this crazy shit's going on behind him. Just the heaviest, biggest rock stuff, and he's just in it fully, and singing it but without anything going on. All the energy is circling around him and coming through him, but he's not doing it himself. It's just *so* cool. There's so much swagger in that. That's one that I always come back to. I also love the song he did with Masters of Reality ["High Noon Amsterdam"].

ALAIN JOHANNES: "One Hundred Days," "The Gravedigger's Song," "Morning Glory Wine," "Deep Black Vanishing Train"…but with Mark, it would be hard to just name a few. They hit me so directly every time he opens his mouth. I do prefer [Mark's voice] a little more "gravelly" on the later records – because it's even more resonant, which happens when people get a little older. And he did a great song with Ten Commandos [a band featuring Alain, Dimitri Coats, Ben Shepherd, and Matt Cameron] – "Staring Down the Dust."

JEAN-PHILIPPE DE GHEEST: I really love "I Am the Wolf." It's one of these songs where there's a *real* connection. Of course on every song he sings there's a connection, but on this song when I listen to it, it seems very clear. The song is just perfect.

CLAY DECKER: We had become really good friends when Greg Dulli and him started doing the Gutter Twins – that stuff was great. My favorite stuff by him was the stuff he would do with just an acoustic guitar player and him singing. Funny enough, I saw him perform like that at the cemetery he's buried at now [Hollywood Forever].

JOSH KLINGHOFFER: One of the saddest things about Mark not being around anymore is that he seemed to be able to do great work with everyone. I like nothing more than that it's being made out of love – love of what they're doing and love for each other. I feel like Lanegan was kind of generous in the sense that he would let other people dictate the way the music was going to sound, and then he was always confident in what he was going to bring to it. Even within his own solo records they would change from time to time. Or even with *Bubblegum*, within the same album, there was a different approach. "When Your Number Isn't Up," "Strange Religion," and "One Hundred Days" – those three songs are some of the best songs I have ever heard.

MATT PINFIELD: I thought the thing that was very interesting about Mark was just how diverse he was. He certainly lyrically and poetically had a thing that was uniquely Mark's, but I felt that after Screaming Trees, he went and experimented in many different directions. "Experiment" might not even be the right word, because I think he just saw all his different musical influences and he could branch out and go in so many different directions musically. If you were a Mark Lanegan fan, wherever he was going, *you went with him.*

MEGAN JASPER: I don't know that there's anything Mark did that I didn't like.

Chapter 8
COLLABORATION

What was it like to work – in various capacities and on various projects – with Mark?

KIM THAYIL: We played shows with the Trees, and Mark Pickerel used to joke about how the Trees were compared to the Doors – because on the early Trees records, people would describe Lanegan as having a voice that was reminiscent of Jim Morrison. And in our early days, in the context of playing for punk audiences, we were Zeppelin-like – for good or bad. So, the joke that Mark Pickerel would make – and I think Lanegan made it, too – was, "We should tour together. It would be like the Zeppelin/Doors tour that never happened!"

GARY LEE CONNER: We decided to do solo records in 1989. It was going to be like the Kiss records [from 1978]. I don't know if Pickerel was going to do one or not. But Lanegan ended up doing the Sub Pop record, and Van and I did records that were on New Alliance – which was a subsidiary of SST. So, he had been writing songs at that point. He had moved to Seattle. That was a thing that happened – we worked in Ellensburg on *Even If and Especially When* and *Invisible Lantern*. Then sometime in 1988, he moved to Seattle – so the vibe got a little different then, because we weren't all in the same town all the time. And he ended up working on his solo album, too.

But later in '88, I had written a ton of stuff – and that was when Van had quit the band for a while and Donna Dresch played bass with us. And we recorded the record in Los Angeles that was going to be *Buzz Factory* – but we didn't have a title yet. We spent two weeks before a tour with Donna recording it, and it didn't turn out the way we wanted it to…at least the way Mark wanted it to. He was always 100% the guy who made the decisions on everything. If it was up to me, I probably would have put it out – but I listen to it now and it's a lot of the same songs that were on *Buzz Factory*, and some of the songs were on my Purple Outside solo album [1990's *Mystery Lane*]. But then Van got back in the band, and right at the end of the year, we went into the studio with Jack Endino to record *Buzz Factory* – in Seattle. That was the first time where we recorded outside of Ellensburg. Van had just had a kid, and had three jobs, and couldn't go on tour, because we didn't make much money.

JACK ENDINO: *Change Has Come* was the last thing they did at Reciprocal. Screaming Trees were hip enough at that point that Sub Pop didn't want to be left out, so they said, "We know you're going to sign with a major label, you gave your notice to SST." SST by the way, they always did single album contracts. People forget this about SST – SST never did multi-album deals with bands, which was kind of the standard for other labels. Nobody ever owed SST another album – it was always one record at a time.

So, the Screaming Trees decided to go off and talk with a major, and Sub Pop was able to insert themselves into there at some point, and say, "Just give us a single!" So, they sent them into the studio and I was able to record two songs – I think they were "Change Has Come" and "Days," and the other three were the ones that Steve Fisk recorded. I don't remember much about it because it was just two songs, and we probably did it in a day. I will say – oddly enough – Mark Lanegan continued playing that song, "Change Has Come," in some of his solo sets for quite a long time. I saw him do that at a solo show.

MIKE JOHNSON: He had been working on stuff with

Kurt – he was going to do that Lead Belly record that I'm sure you heard about [a project reportedly called the Jury, featuring Mark, Kurt, Krist Novoselic on bass, and Mark Pickerel on drums]. I think he changed his mind or he wanted to do something else – he had this idea of doing an actual solo record [*The Winding Sheet*], and that's when I got a phone call. And he and I talked to each other semi-regularly and wrote letters to each other, sent tapes. He was like, "Hey man, would you be interested in making this record with me? I've got a solo album." I was like, "Where do I sign up?!" He sent me a tape of these demos that he had, that were all pretty simple three-chord songs – with really cool melodies and words.

So, I drove up from Eugene to Seattle. First, we four-tracked the songs – the whole part of writing intros and any middle break type stuff. Then, we went into the studio like, a month later – with Jack and Pickerel. We must have practiced with Pickerel, but I don't remember. But anyway, it was really quick. It was like, three days – just in the studio, laid down the stuff. First, I think we did the tracks that Pickerel played on, band tracks, the basics, the acoustics with Mark doing guide vocals. So, it was really fast and simple.

The story I would always tell is, "The first album was three days…and the second album was *three years*." *The Winding Sheet* was all very new to me – it was the first professional album I had anything to do with. I'd only recorded singles and tapes with my band. And song-wise, I remember putting the most effort into "Mockingbirds" and "Ugly Sunday." I remember Steve Fisk telling me about the piano part I wanted to play on "Mockingbirds" – "Dude…that's going to sound like *Bob Seger*." And I'm like, "No, it's not!" Which it didn't. I don't think I was there when he did the vocals. I think he and Jack did the vocals.

JACK ENDINO: There were two songs [recorded by the Jury] – there's "Down in the Dark" which Kurt sings a harmony on. It was on the same session. Kurt came by the studio to do a backing vocal on "Down in the Dark" and I ended up doing a kind of guitar solo on the song – it's the only time I play guitar on the record at all. But the other song, "Where Did You Sleep Last Night," was recorded at a completely different time – as part of a project called the Jury. And that was going to be a collaboration between Mark and Kurt – with some friends helping out, because supposedly, they had written some songs together. But by the time they got in the studio, Kurt explained to me, "Well, we forgot all those songs we were writing together. So, we've decided we're just going to do some Lead Belly covers."

So, they did "Ain't It a Shame," which ended up on the Nirvana box set [2004's *With the Lights Out*], and they did "Grey Goose," which Mark was supposed to sing…but he didn't. So, there's nothing but a one-riff piece of music that just plays one riff over and over again, with no vocals – and that ended up on the box set, for some reason. And there was "Where Did You Sleep Last Night," which we sort of "repurposed" for Mark Lanegan's record. Because that was the one that Mark song on, and he thought, "Well, this other thing never went anywhere. Why don't I just put it on my first solo record?" I think we may have recut the vocal, and I remixed it – because the Jury thing we never did real mixes on. So, that ended up on Mark's record, too – even though that was from a completely different recording session at another time. That would be the only track that has Krist playing bass on it.

CHARLES PETERSON: Unfortunately, I wish I read all of that while Mark was still alive and was able to talk it out with him – I guess I didn't realize just how fully upset he was at the time by that photo [that was used as the front cover image of *The Winding Sheet*, which according to Mark in *Sing Backwards and Weep*, resulted in him confronting and almost assaulting Sub Pop's Bruce Pavitt in his office]. Along with Bruce, I helped in choosing it – guiding everyone towards that image. There were other ones like it – that were also candids.

I did not know that Bruce put the record out with that cover without Mark's permission. Bruce came to me and said, "Give me your thoughts." I thought it was great. I thought in the same sense of a Nick Drake record, or Tim Buckley – that it just had this picture of the singer-songwriter on it. And I thought – especially at the time – where Sub Pop was at, the Screaming Trees weren't that widely known, you need a picture of this person on the cover, for people to really identify with the album. So, we went through all that, and then I just stepped away. I was like, "*Whatever*. It's not my final say."

And they were slides – I didn't have to make prints or do any of that stuff in the end. Mark will be resting in peace knowing that all of those originals have been lost. I wouldn't be surprised if the Poison Idea drummer [Steve "Thee Slayer Hippy" Hanford] took them – in that madness that he writes about there. Unfortunately, they're all missing, and that's kind of a problem with the reissue – that's why the reissue cover actually looked worse than the original cover. But I would love to go back and see all of those. It's because Bruce and I, we took Lanegan down to the ruins of the Western State Hospital down there in Steilacoom, and did a bunch of shots – one of which ended up on the back cover of the album.

But Bruce just didn't think they were striking enough for an album's front cover. He really wanted that classic portrait of the musician to sell a record. So, Mark and I went back and did that session. I kind of had the idea, "Let's at least cloud it in red light or something." Mark was OK with that. The ironic thing is that album cover probably got him way more pussy than any other album cover he ever put out. [Laughs] To be crass about it. It's like, "Dude...*come on!*" I'd have to talk to Bruce about the truth behind that whole office incident – whether Bruce actually cowered on the floor or not.

MEGAN JASPER: I got *a lot* of those phone calls from Mark, where was just fuckin' *livid* that Bruce had chosen this photo that Mark was just appalled by. So, although I got a lot of the sweet moments...I also got a lot of the just, *"What the fuck happened?"* moments – which were scary. But that said, I always felt like he was kind to me. It's funny, because I'm certain I was there [in the Sub Pop office, at the time the supposed confrontation between Mark and Bruce occurred] – and I do remember him coming in to talk to Bruce. I remember them getting into it, but I don't remember anything becoming physical. But I remember him *hating* Bruce for it.

JACK ENDINO: For *Sweet Oblivion*, there was the need for some b-sides to go with the CD singles they were putting out. And they needed three b-sides – most people have not heard all of these b-sides. One of them was "(There'll Be) Peace in the Valley," which I think is a traditional tune, and one of them was a Black Sabbath cover, "Tomorrow's Dream." I had to show Gary Lee Conner how to play the guitar part – because he was trying to do it in standard tuning, but you have to be in drop-D. And he didn't do a lot of drop-D. I said, "No, no, no. Drop that E string down to D, and that riff is super-easy to do." Which of course, is true. So, that was amusing – hearing Mark Lanegan singing Ozzy. It's very interesting because in the bridge of the song, Ozzy goes up an octave – he sings a very high part – and Mark goes down an octave, instead. It's very "Lanegan," actually. I think it's a lovely version.

And then the other one was a song called "Winter Song." There is a band version of it on *Sweet Oblivion,* and what we did was an acoustic version. I ended up playing slide guitar on it and they couldn't credit me, because they're on a major label, and they're all musician union members…and I was not. Therefore, I could not be credited on the record. And I said, "Whatever, I don't care. I'm credited as the producer in any case." We probably spent a day in total doing all three songs – it was very quick. It reminds me that I played bass on a Hole tune once, "Beautiful Son," and they couldn't credit me for that, either – I think it was the same story. But that acoustic "Winter Song" is pretty cool. Again, it has a *great* Mark Lanegan vocal in it.

MIKE JOHNSON: That record [*Whiskey for the Holy Ghost*] was a completely different story. Then, I moved up to Seattle, and then it was going to be serious. We talked about this idea that he had – he wanted to make an all-acoustic album, and I was very excited about it. Like, all *Astral Weeks* [Van Morrison's 1968 album]. So, he and I went down to Bud's Jazz Records – which is a well-known jazz record store in Pioneer Square, in Seattle. We talked to Bud – the guy who ran the joint – "Do you know any jazz bass players who you think would be up for playing on an acoustic album…by some derelict rock guys, *like us*?" [Laughs]

And he gave us the number of Phil Sparks – the guy who played stand-up bass on the album. We went and met him, and he was totally cool and down to do it. I think the three of us jammed once or twice at his house, and we went into the studio. It was just the three of us – we laid down basics. So, it was stand-up bass, me playing guitar, and Mark sometimes plinking along on guitar, and sometimes singing guide vocals. That was going great. He didn't completely have all the songs for it, but he had a lot of it already.

And Sub Pop called us in the middle of recording, and actually pulled us out of the studio. They said, "It's over. We're not going to fund this. You're not doing this." We were totally pissed, and, "*What the fuck?!*" And that was the end of that. Which was really a tragedy, to me. That always really bummed me out, because it never happened. One of the songs ended up on *Scraps at Midnight*, "Wheels," and everything changed. Sub Pop had lost funding – they ran out of money. So, that put the kibosh on the record for a while, and then in the interim is when I joined Dinosaur Jr., and had to go out to Massachusetts and learn how to play bass for that band. And then, the Trees went on tour.

But Mark and I were always talking, and then he didn't want to do the acoustic thing anymore. We got back together and he had some new songs. We started practicing those – they were going to be electric songs. We did a couple of songs with Mark Pickerel and we did a couple of songs with Dan Peters playing drums. The two Dan Peters songs were "House a Home" and "Borracho," and there's also another song that got left off. And by then, Mark had started drinking. When I met him, he didn't drink at all. And then, I was drinking with him and we were getting kind of crazy. It was off and on like this making the record. And then things just kept – personally – spiraling more and more out of control. Like I said, it ended up being three years and I don't know, six engineers or something.

And then he started doing heroin and stuff, and I

didn't think he was ever going to finish the record. Because it seemed then he was just trying to get money out of Sub Pop for drugs. He called me to do a session in New York, and I was like, "I'm not going, dude. I'm done. I have done all the guitars and the bass. I've done everything. *You've got to finish the record.*" Which, he did. I felt like that was the only way I could get him to do it. The end product is not as good as it could have been. It could have been two different records – it could have been a double album. But it's still probably my favorite of his albums.

JACK ENDINO: Mark started *Whiskey for the Holy Ghost* with Terry Date – if I remember right – and got some songs recorded, got partway into it, didn't finish anything. And then someone may have worked on it in there – I think Ed Brooks. At some point, he brought the two-inch tapes to me, we did more work on it, and we tried to finish the record. I think I worked on it several times. But I found myself working with him at Bear Creek Studio at one point and I only tracked a few songs on that record, myself – most of them were overdubs I was working on. Which, mostly would have been vocals. There may have been some guest musicians, too.

But we tracked "The River Rise" at Reciprocal and we tracked a few other songs. And then, the rest of it was redoing the vocals on these other songs and adding overdubs to these other songs that he had already recorded with Terry Date or Ed Brooks. And there were many songs on quite a few reels. There was a lot more material that we worked on than what ended up on the album.

And the problem that I had was that Mark was having a "sophomore jinx." Which meant that he was his own worst critic of everything he was doing – which meant that no vocal track would satisfy him, no performance of himself would satisfy him. He was very self-critical. By comparison, *The Winding Sheet* took I think just a matter of days to record and mix. I keep thinking six or seven days – it may have been less, it may have been more. But it went very painlessly and very quick. It was kind of magic, actually. I even ended up playing bass on about half the record. But *Whiskey* took a couple of years, and as I said, I think four different producers. Finally, John Agnello is the one who ended up bringing it over the finish line and mixing it.

    At one point, Mark and I mixed the entire record. And it was literally the last couple of days before Reciprocal Recording was slated to close for good. And even as I was mixing this record with him, he was deciding to redo vocals all over the place. So, the last studio day of Reciprocal Recording, it must have been about an 18-hour work day, because we literally stayed there all day and all night, and we were there at 9:00 the next morning, when Chris Hanzsek pulled up with a truck to start pulling the gear out of the control room – because that was the last day of the studio. So, Mark – even though I was mixing the album – was still insisting on re-recording all the vocals, as we were mixing it. And this was *many* months into the project.

    We were completely insane by the time we finished it in the morning. And I thought, "Well…maybe we mixed it. Maybe the record's done?" I didn't really believe it. Of course, he ended up going off and screwing around with it some more and redoing vocals and changing out some more songs. I don't remember if my work at Bear Creek Studio took place later or before. There's a good chance it was later. I wish I knew what happened to all my mixes of the record – I don't know where they are. Maybe Sub Pop has them in a vault somewhere. Because there were a few songs I remember that didn't make it on there.

    It was crazy – I think Mark was having "junkie

issues," and that was the reason for his tremendous self-criticism he was going through at the time. He was depressed – he wasn't satisfied with anything. And I've worked with people having heroin problems since then, and I recognize it now – as something that some people become so critical of themselves that absolutely nothing is good enough. And I think Mark was probably clean and sober when we did *The Winding Sheet* – which is how we managed to do the record in under a week. As opposed to a couple of years and four different producers to finish the second record. Of course, the proof's in the pudding – it's an amazing record.

JOHN AGNELLO: "The River Rise," I had Mascis from Dinosaur Jr. play those cymbal swells – Mark loved that idea. We recorded in this interesting studio called Messina Music, that had millions of cookie jars. And the intro that was the whistling and the jingling is a cookie jar. Mark thought it was amazing, so I put a mic on it, and that's how we started the record – which I thought was hilarious, and really thinking out of the box. I came in and finished it. He started it in Seattle and was miserable about it – even though it was fantastic. They played me the rough mixes, and I said, "Get your ass to New York City…we're going to finish this record. *This record is a masterpiece.*" And honestly, we did it on and off – he was touring a bunch. He hated the record until we finished it, and then he realized it was great.

SALLY BARRY: I was like, "What do you want me to do?" [Barry sings on the track "Sunrise" from *Whiskey for the Holy Ghost*] And he was like, "Do whatever the hell you want to do." He just threw me into a booth and we were working with John Agnello – who was a princely person, and also an amazing producer and engineer. It was just very casual, no direction, no stress, no nothing. And that's why I ended up hanging out for a lot of those sessions, because it was just really fun. It was just a great place to be. And to watch Mark working was really nice. He was insecure a lot of the time – about his vocals. He would come out and be like, "Is that OK?" It was like, "Dude…stop. This is *great.*"

He was one of those "sour candy people" – he was kind of gruff on the outside, but on the inside he was a very soft person. I remember one time when we were hanging out during the *Field Songs* sessions, we were sitting in his car smoking or something, and I had made a little book of some art and poetry I'd done, and I was like, "Hey, I made you a copy of this book I made." And he was looking through it, and was like, "Wow…this is amazing! I wish I could write poetry." I was looking at him like. "You are. You're an *amazing* poet." And he was like, "Nah." He was just so critical of himself. And really generous with himself, too. If he liked you…I always say Mark treated me like gold, all the time. He always made sure that I knew that he thought I was awesome. He would do that for his friends.

MIKE JOHNSON: I was the star [in the "House a Home" video]! That was weird, because the guy who directed the video didn't know I actually played guitar and co-produced the record. Because of the way I looked, he knew me from around town or something, and was like, "Hey man, do you want to be in this video? They want you to do this stuff in this video, that has this narrative to it." I was like, "Oh yeah! Cool. It will be fun." And at the end of the shoot – because the last thing we did was the playing guitar with Mark singing part – he goes, "Oh. I didn't know you actually played guitar with him!" I'm supposed to be some sleazebag door to door salesman, who's seducing the women that he goes and tries to sell stuff to. It was pretty vague – where it seems like there's a story…but maybe not.

JOHN AGNELLO: I worked on about three or four of his solo records in different locations. All of them were just wonderful…but *Whiskey*, there is just something special about that record. "House a Home," I'm surprised that's not covered more by people like Johnny Cash or someone like that. That song is a *legendary* song. You should be hearing that on the radio all the time. Like, Chris Stapleton should cover that song!

MIKE JOHNSON: That was much different [comparing working with Mark to J Mascis]. With Mark and I, we were genuinely collaborating. On the solo records I worked with him, I was like…his right hand on that stuff. So, it was very much collaborative – where it was the whole conceptualizing of what it would be like, what it was going to sound like, what we were going for. Whereas with J, I was hired into the band and the band already existed as "his thing" – and he already had his sound. So, that was more like, "I'll just come up with a bassline," and, "Do you want to play guitar on this or sing on this?" It was less collaborative. Whereas with Mark, I was in on the whole vision part of it.

KIM THAYIL: In 1996, we did the Lollapalooza tour – with Metallica headlining. Metallica was approached to do Lollapalooza, and they were asked who else they would like on the bill, and they said, "Soundgarden." Which makes sense, because at that time, Metallica had more of a commercial/mainstream audience – as well as a metal audience. And Lollapalooza was more alternative, and we had some success in both the alternative *and* metal genres. They asked us to tour with them, and then we were asked by the promotors of Lollapalooza, "Who would you like to have on the bill?" And we said, "Screaming Trees! The Ramones!" So, they got the Ramones on the bill, and we really pushed for the Screaming Trees. That whole tour that summer was the Trees and us together. And Josh Homme was touring with the Trees. And some of our roadies that were working with us were friends of the Trees and their roadies – so there was a little inter-family "picnicking" there on the Lollapalooza tour.

JOHN AGNELLO: I think we did *Scraps at Midnight* at Robert Lang Studios, in Seattle. I don't remember much about that record because it was probably just me in there twiddling knobs alone with him. I remember *Field Songs*, because we had Ben Shepherd playing on it and Mike Johnson – and everybody was jamming in the room. That was really epic. It's just different when you're alone in the room, mixing and twiddling knobs. It's not that epic – it's really kind of boring. I mean, boring in the sense that it's just a guy and a big console turning a knob. I don't have much fond memories of that record. I like the record very much – don't get me wrong – but I can't place myself in that room right now. I can't remember what that was like.

MIKE JOHNSON: It was kind of like getting back to the first album type of thing [for *Scraps at Midnight*]. He called me from Pasadena, and he's like, "I'm in a halfway house. I'm out of rehab and I want to make a record. Are you up for doing it?" And I was like, "*Totally.*" And he was like, "Do you want to come down to Pasadena?" And that's what I did – I went down there and we started writing on that one. That was more collaborating – trying to bang stuff out. I think he was so fragile at that point…but he was of this really good frame of mind though. We were back to joking. That's the thing – throughout everything, there was always massive amounts of humor with him. It was great. He looked great. It was like he was learning how to write songs again – trying to hit it fresh. It was really a rebirth at the time.

At that point [*I'll Take Care of You*], he was back in Seattle. He was just kind of winging it again – he didn't have a firm place to live. He was living here and there – hotels. He would come over to my house every day – we'd shoot the shit, smoke cigarettes, drink coffee, and listen to a record. He'd hear something and be like, "Let's do *that*." We booked a few days with Martin Feveyear, and we'd go over to his studio that was out in Magnolia in Seattle. That was the year that it rained for three months straight. It never ever stopped raining. It was so dark, wet, and cold. *All the time.* Because we were both smoking, and we couldn't smoke in the studio, we were outside trying to stay dry.

But it was good. It wasn't done in one shot. It was like, piecemeal – record a few songs. And we did some original stuff at the time, too – which ended up on *Field Songs*, eventually. It was put together on the fly. He had started that without me. The first thing was the song "I'll Take Care of You," and that was with Van and Pickerel. So, he had done that one song, and he was like, "Let's do a covers album." Then, we just started piling on stuff, and seeing what worked and what didn't work.

GREG WERCKMAN: He was working on *I'll Take Care of You*, and Sub Pop wanted a picture for the front cover. And there were a couple of things that Lanegan hates – and one, was getting his picture taken. He *hated* seeing himself, and he absolutely, positively went to war with Sub Pop. He let them put his picture on a previous record [*The Winding Sheet*], and he was like, "I'm digging my boots in. There is *no way* I'm letting you do this." So they were like, "Well Mark…give us *something*. Tell us what you want on the cover. You have 24 hours – if we don't get anything from you, we're running with this picture." And it was basically, a picture of his face.

Without me knowing, he faxed them, "To Sub Pop, from Mark...here's my album cover." And it was a blank piece of paper. They got it, and they're like, "Yeah, this is funny." And he goes, "No, no. *This is it.*" And Sub Pop I think tried to teach Mark a lesson – they did it! That album is just a white cover. I was like, "Mark, I understand you not wanting your picture on the cover. I get it – there's a lot of artists like that. But when people walk into a record store, this is the cover they're going to see! You're kind of shooting yourself in the foot." And he just laughed. He was like, "Nah. *Fuck 'em.*"

MEGAN JASPER: I remember him being as particular with his own album art as he was with the music. The memory that always comes to mind – because it always makes me laugh – was when he was recording *Field Songs*, when he saw the image of that record, he didn't mind the photo. He liked it. But it was *the color*. There was almost a salmon-y hue to it – but more in my memory, brown than anything else. But he called me up, and was like, "That record is looking really pink. Is it *too* pink?"

CHRIS GOSS: *Rated R* [by Queens of the Stone Age, which Goss co-produced with Josh Homme] was a lot of fun to record. It was the album that kicked off their mega-success. So, the bad side of things – the money, the pressure...it's funny, the more money you get, the more pressure there is. Which is so odd. But it was a very good time for all of us. A pleasure to produce. I remember Mark when he did come in to do some work on that, was in a great mood. The same with Nick Oliveri – his first recording with the Queens, really. Mark was on the money. Mark was in good spirits and not so fucked up – and that goes for everybody in the band, as well. It was "innocent days," I guess you'd call it.

NICK OLIVERI: We had another version [of the Queens of the Stone Age song, "In the Fade," which Mark sang on] called "Universal Subconscious." It sounds more Nirvana-esque, real heavy. It kind of follows that thing with the bass and the guitar. But we got to a point where that song wasn't going to make it, so we did a "bass day" and I came up with a bassline for it. We kept the drum take that we had from the heavy version, I threw the bass thing down, and Josh did some great swells and stuff. He said, "Well, maybe we can have Mark come in." And I was like, "Wow. That would be unreal." Because Mark was working on *Field Songs* [his 2001 solo album] at the time. I had met him, but only in passing. He came in, and was super cool. I was stoked to meet him and it was great having him because he really made the song something else.

They went to go eat – Josh and Mark – and I sat there working on some lyrics, and they picked them apart. I had something like, "Cracks in the ceiling and spurts of light that never come," and they changed it up a little bit. They came up with "Live 'til you die," which I thought was great. The song is one of the best ones on the record. It's the only song that Mark is singing lead on. He sang background on "Auto Pilot," but we could have done it like we did live and had him sing – it was a much better song when he sang it.

I would have loved to have him sing on that, as well, but Josh didn't know what he wanted Mark's role to be in the band – if he was going to be in the band or just come in and sing the song. But I can think of some other songs on that record that would have been great if he sang on. It would really would have opened up a lot of the tunes, because he has that power in his voice, for sure. But that writing day was a special day for me, because that was the first day I met him and was spending time with him.

Right away, we were working in the studio, and to watch him work was great. He would sing a line, and at the end of the line, he'd go, "DAMN IT!" – because he thought he sang it wrong. And we'd go, "Dude...that was perfect. What are you talking about?" I think he was recording some of the first stuff sober at the time – so he was uncomfortable, maybe. It ended up being the versions that we used were the ones that he thought weren't good at first. I'd never worked with someone up to that point that could sing like that.

He started with the tour for *Rated R* – we had him do some stuff with us live. We had him sing "Auto Pilot" and "Walkin' on the Sidewalks" – so he had more numbers to come up for. It was kind of a mutual thing, I think – Josh and him were talking about doing some shows together, being in the band, touring with us, and coming in for the tunes so it would be a "three-singer band." That was the *Rated R* era. It seemed like once he was in, he was in, and we were giving him more to do and he was writing more stuff to be on. It was a mutual thing – we wanted him as much as he wanted to be in the band.

MIKE JOHNSON: *Field Songs* was like the "sober version" of doing *Whiskey* again – because it took a long time, and there were some aborted studio sessions. Some stuff worked, some didn't. Because it started in Seattle, and then it ended in Los Angeles. We ended up recording it at Duff's house. So, that went on and on. At that point, I was not in the best of shape, and I didn't contribute as much to that record...I'm on everything and I definitely was in there, so I shouldn't say that. I guess I did. But it was more difficult for me. Probably less difficult for him.

JOHN AGNELLO: *Field Songs* was the one that I started with them, and having Ben Shepherd from Soundgarden play bass, Mike Johnson play guitar, and Dan Peters from Mudhoney played drums. It was so much fun. But again, controversial – Ben Shepherd got really mad at one point, because he couldn't get a part right, and he threw his bass and he was spitting. I had to kind of calm him down. I think he referred to me as either "coach" or "sergeant." Like, "Hey coach, what do you want to do now?" He was super-nice – in fact, in the middle of all this shit, he basically got me a hotel, because he felt bad that I was staying at the studio and he felt that I needed to get out of there. So he just booked me a hotel for two days. It was so nice of him to pay for it.

And I love working with Mike Johnson, because we've done Dinosaur Jr. records together, and I did a solo record for him [1996's *Year of Mondays*]. We're very good friends. Back in the mid-90's, I think we both broke up with our girlfriends the same month, and we consoled each other in New York – we hung out a lot. I was really close to Mike, really close to Mark, and was really fond of the other guys. It was just magical having them all play. Mark's live vocals I've got to say, I could have kept all of them and that would have been it. But he wouldn't have it – he wanted to re-sing them. But he was such a great singer. One live vocal take is all you needed from him. What was great about Mark is it was pre-Autotune, so nobody gave a fuck if he was a little out of tune – it didn't matter. If he was alive today and we were doing vocals and my engineer wanted to Autotune Mark's vocals, I'd punch him in the face!

SALLY BARRY: I worked with him also on *Field Songs* – but that song never made it on. Mark was intensely critical of himself as an artist. He would not ever let something go that he didn't feel was *really* good. So, we had done the entire song…and then he scrapped it, because he didn't like his lyrics. Which is a shame – because I thought they were great lyrics. But it's something that will never see the light of day. The song's working title was "Joy Division." It was more about the actual Joy Division [not the band] – which were the Nazi brothels. It was more like a song from a man to a woman. But he hated his lyrics, so, we'll never know what it's really about. But I did a whole bunch of vocals on that. They sounded really cool – because John Agnello was running the board again, and he's such a great engineer. He makes your voice sound amazing.

ALAIN JOHANNES: For *Desert Sessions 7 & 8*, we were supposed to meet for breakfast at 8:00 in the morning – everyone was staying in hotels nearby. I got there are 7:45, and everyone had gone [for breakfast elsewhere] – except for Fred Drake, who was living at Rancho at the time before he passed away. And he said, "Dude, they didn't wait for you. I'm sorry. I'm going to make you some eggs." So, he made me eggs.

I sat there on the couch, was inspired by the environment, and I wrote "Hanging Tree." And the way that I wrote it, the original version is slightly different – it has the major-minor touch and release than the bluesy way that they did it [Queens later re-recorded it on *Songs for the Deaf*], because they didn't quite remember how it went, because I had played all the parts. It's a darker kind of vibe. So, I wrote the song, and then everyone came back from breakfast and we started to record it – and that's when Mark asked me to help him [with the timing/when to start singing].

It's got such few words. It's got the image of people hanging in a hanging tree. The visual in my mind started to play out – just being in the desert. And I pictured this song about being betrayed – I guess it plays into Christian theology. And also, being completely left alone, left for dead – doesn't actually mean the person is done. All the images of Joshua Tree – desolate, open space, "Swaying in the breeze" all that stuff. And then "As we two are one" is the relationship between light and dark – kind of transcendence through a portal. All these things were just coming to my mind. Really, there are only six lines in the whole song.

CHRIS GOSS: Rancho de la Luna – where I had originally wanted to record [the 2001 Masters of Reality album, *Deep in the Hole*] – was booked, so I kind of threw together a studio in a rented house in Joshua Tree. And Josh was doing some Desert Sessions work at Rancho – that's why I couldn't get in there. So, a lot of people were available who were doing Desert Sessions to drive literally a mile to come to where I was making the *Deep in the Hole* album – with Mark singing on "High Noon Amsterdam." I have photos of Mark singing on that record. It was also a good time for Mark – he was gracious and friendly, and relaxed at that time.

To indicate how astute he was musically, I'll never forget this, Mark did a European headlining tour – this was the Masters of Reality tour with Nick and Josh, actually – and three shows we did with Mark, opening for Mark. I know London was one of them, Glasgow, and one other place. And I remember I changed one of the lyrics in "High Noon Amsterdam" after we released the album. And I mentioned it to Mark, saying, "I've got a better lyric for that line, but don't worry about it." And he goes, "Well…what is it?"

The original lyric was "Stuck my nose in the rose in the hole and it smelled like a dream," and then I changed it afterwards to "it started to bleed" instead of "smelled like a dream." He got that immediately. The rose is like a junkie reference – there's a million references to roses when you're dealing with bloody syringes. I just remember the professionalism of that – of not having to remind him, just all I had to do was mention it once, tell him the new lyric, and then he comes through and did it perfectly. On stage he never missed a fucking beat. As a live performer, he was on it. *Really* on it. He was always there, coming in when he was supposed to.

GREG WERCKMAN: [The material that was eventually released as *Houston Publishing Demos 2002*, in 2015] was one of those moments where Mark was down on his luck and he really needed money. I had a friend [Randall Jamail] that was in the music business in Houston, and he paid Mark and bought some of Mark's publishing. And one of the caveats of this publishing deal was that Mark write some original songs for the deal. And it was *mind-blowing* – Mark when he wanted to, could sit down and make these songs.

For years, Mark and I would talk to each other, and say, "Is anything ever going to happen to these songs?" Because they were *so* good. They were not, "Give me my $20,000, here's your crappy songs." They were such great songs. It took a long time, but finally, we convinced him to put them out. At this point, I think I had given up and Randall had given up, and out of the blue, Mark maybe called one day and said, "Some of those songs on those Houston demos are pretty good. Let's put them out."

CHRIS GOSS: I was present for some of Mark's work on it [Queens of the Stone Age's *Songs for the Deaf*]. Because I didn't produce it, it wasn't so ingrained in me. Josh and Nick had committed to do a Masters of Reality tour that year – while they were recording *Songs for the Deaf* with Eric Valentine. And the plan was that we were going to rehearse in a room in Eric Valentine's studio – do tour rehearsals there while they were recording the record. But the recording with Eric wasn't going very well – vibe-wise. I think Eric and Josh were locking horns on a lot of things. Even some of the work I did on the record, Eric was at the control board and I was playing, I felt like I was being put through the ringer a bit, y'know? Like, "This isn't your band anymore, Goss – *I'm* producing this now" kind of vibe. I think it was "The Mosquito Song" – I did some nylon string guitar playing.

In the middle of that – about two weeks before the tour is about to start – Josh said, "I hate to tell you…I can't do this tour." I was like, "Well, I hate to tell you…*you have to.* The promos have been put out, your name is on the posters, this is quite a big deal." Having Josh and Nick as half of the band on that tour was crucial at that moment. I just said, "You can't back out of it. It will crush me. I'd have to find two players in two weeks." So anyway, it turned out in my opinion, that's *exactly* what they needed to do – get the fuck out of that studio. We rehearsed about four or five hours – literally – for the whole tour. And that kind of reminded them what it was all about. Like, "Fuck it. Let's just go out without much rehearsal and make this up." It was fantastic.

This veers away from the Lanegan subject, but the state of mind of everybody at that time, it turned out that when Josh and Nick got back from the tour, that's when they decided to not work with Eric anymore – and Josh finished the record by himself, basically. So, I think doing that tour with me kind of reminded them, "*This can be fun.*" That's what it's about for me, anyway. And that brings you back into "Lanegan world" – the difference in when he's sober and when he's not sober, and what is fun and lovely and friendly, turns into harsh and ugly at times.

NICK OLIVERI: Josh is really smart, but he was

incredibly smart back then when he produced the record. He put the right people in place to be on it and to be in the band, and to share the front spotlight with another frontman was a key to that band's success. Being able to put your ego down and share the stage with these guys, Dave and Mark. It's really a reason why this record is special – because there are different frontmen on it. And Dave on the drums is "a frontman." He hadn't played drums on a record in a while, so Josh was a smart guy to put these people in place that really made the band special.

There was so much going on at that time, because we had been writing the stuff, and showing Dave songs that were already ready to go, and then him writing this amazing drum part for it and then we'd go and record it. I remember a lot of it was working on the music stuff, and then the vocals came after that. On "Song for the Dead," Mark sings it so raw, so rough, and so good. It really is a great performance on that one – he's really laying into it. The deep voice thing is not always easy to sing at high volume – as far as I know. But he was a really powerful singer, with that low growl. And he had some highs in his voice, too – which he didn't use as much as he did working with some of the earlier recordings. There's some stuff on *Whiskey for the Holy Ghost* where he's singing some higher pitch stuff. So, he had great range.

I really love "Hanging Tree." Alain Johannes wrote this crazy time signature music for it. I think the verses are very interesting, because it's one line for the whole verse – Mark sings one line at a time. It's word by word. I don't know of any songs that do that. And with his voice you could do that – sing a word and hold it out, and one sentence is the whole verse. "God Is in the Radio" was a Desert Sessions song. I don't know if it ever came out on that, but I know that they recorded it for Desert Sessions. It was a good song for Mark, and with Josh and him singing it together, I think their voices worked really good together. There was some weird, eerie thing about it that was really cool. Very melodic…but still very dark and eerie when their two voices are singing together – I think on "Song for the Deaf" they do that as well.

I had the bassline [for the song "Song for the Deaf"] and it inspired from there, it started moving from there. There wasn't any, "Hey, I've got this song." We were jamming in the room and I started playing this bass part and Josh liked it and started jamming on it. Then other parts came to me. The jam part in the middle, I wanted the song to be a longer tune because it was the title track. Mark and Josh singing together on it really makes it special. I think their two voices together with the falsetto [Josh] and the low [Mark] is a real treat for the ear. It's a nice, eerie kind of sound while being melodic at the same time. I think the song holds up to be the title of the record. Lyrically, Mark wanted to go for a deaf, dumb, and blind kind of thing. That was the inspiration behind the lyrics that Mark was trying to come up with there.

The video was directed by Dean Karr [for the song "No One Knows"]. He had us doing some crazy stuff – like strapped to hoods of cars. My girlfriend at the time went to the taxidermy store and got a deer, and they put mechanical pieces in it and made it into this little robot that could move and smack us in the head! It was quite fun. I recall being stuck in the wall with our heads through the wall and Mark being sick. [Laughs] And Dean Karr putting grocery bag handles on his ears and Mark going, "You son of a bitch…I'm going to kill you!" It was the funniest thing ever because we were strapped in the wall. It was a long one, but it was a fun day. [Note: When asked what were Mark's songwriting contributions to the song – as Mark and Josh are listed as its writers – Nick replied, "I think I remember him writing 'We get these pills to swallow, How they stick in your throat, Taste like gold'"]

I think [the *Songs for the Deaf* album] holds up as strong as anything out there, if not better. To my ears. But my head's growing as I'm saying that! I'm quite proud to be on that record because I think it can hold up with anything that's out there. I think it's a well-made record. The songs are well-crafted. I know I, Josh, and everybody who played on it gave everything they had. Everything technically they could do and everything in their mind they could come up with that was "next level" than what they'd done before – myself included. I've watched Josh over the years try different things and push himself to the end of his ropes. And myself, as well. It really made me a better player at the time – *big time*. Because you're playing with these great players and great singers, and it's like, "I have to step up my game. I don't want to be the weak link." It really had me playing better as a player – Josh too, and everybody involved. Everybody was bringing what they were bringing, and all for the greater good of the band.

And Mark was always a champion. He was this bad-ass, and one of the best voices I've ever heard sing. And Dave pushed himself – "Hey guys, you have to leave the room. I have to get this right" – working out parts that he wanted to push himself to do. And I know with every song we did that. So, I think that record really shines through like that, down to the mix. Everything about it is very well thought out. Every single instrument on it, where it's placed in the mix, if you put on headphones you can hear it come from one side to the other side or in the middle. Everything was very strategically done and I think that shines through for the listener. It's definitely the best record I played on.

I was at Brad Cook's, recording [Mondo Generator's

2003 album, *A Drug Problem That Never Existed*]. And I was trying to sing this song, "Four Corners." I did I don't know how many takes, and I came back another week to do it again, and it just wasn't what I was hearing to be right. And I was like, "*I wonder if Mark would sing it?*" So I called him up, and he said, "Yeah. I'll come down and do it." He changed a couple lines in there that he didn't feel comfortable singing at the time, and he came in and nailed that thing. That song *makes* the album, because his performance on it is so good. I'm proud to have him on that, and that I'm on there with him. That tune really turned out special. I wrote the lyrics because I blacked out, and when I came to, I tried to remember what the hell happened. I was trying to figure it out – and those are the lyrics that came into my head.

CHRIS GOSS: Around the time we got done making *Songs for the Deaf* is when we began talking about doing *Bubblegum.* We got through most of *Bubblegum* and basically finished it. We mastered the record – this is after Polly Harvey cut a couple of tracks ["Hit the City" and "Come to Me"]. As the producer, I felt, "OK, it's a great record." And then – without being notified at all – he took eight or nine songs from *Bubblegum* and released *Here Comes That Weird Chill.* And I didn't even know about *Here Comes That Weird Chill* being made or being constructed from a lot of the tracks from *Bubblegum.* And here I am under the assumption that we're done, and at the same time, he started cutting more tracks for *Bubblegum* with Alain Johannes. This was without my knowledge.

Eventually, word got to me that he was recording more tracks for it. And I thought, "Wow. We have a great finished product as it was." It was brilliant. And he added probably seven or eight more tracks to what he hadn't used on *Here Comes That Weird Chill* – maybe even more than that – and extended the length of *Bubblegum* quite a bit. *Bubblegum* is a great record, but I think what he did with *Here Comes That Weird Chill* and *Bubblegum* I think both records suffered a bit. Instead of having one really incredible record, *Here Comes That Weird Chill* was good, *Bubblegum* was great…but could have been perfect, if he hadn't made that move.

Even contractually it was kind of fucked, because basically I produced *Here Comes That Weird Chill* and I'm not even sure if I got a fuckin' production credit on it [according to Wikipedia, Mark is solely listed as producer]. I was turned off at the time, and I have a tendency when things like that happen, I'm not the kind of guy that calls my lawyer and says, "Let's get to the bottom of this." *I walk away*. I'm kind of like, "If that's the way you want to do it, fuck you. Go ahead." So, that went down that way. And then when I finally heard *Bubblegum* in its finished form, it was really the first time I had heard seven or eight of the tracks. And there's a big difference between the tracks I cut and tracks that Alain cut. I just think it was too long.

I thought we had a good package, but he made *two* packages out of it. If he wanted to do that, I could have helped him do that. But that's what I mean with meth – you can't negotiate with meth. I kind of fell out of me giving a shit after this stuff started to happen. I worked a year on *Bubblegum*, and in this life, there's not too many years. And when you put a year of your life into someone else's project or someone else's music, you become emotionally involved in it – very much so. And emotionally involved with the people who are making it and the artists themselves. So, you're not *only* their friend – you're their friend, producer, and psychiatrist. You fall into a lot of roles.

ALAIN JOHANNES: With Goss they were making the record, and I think they were pretty close to done, and then Mark just wanted to try a few songs in a different context – and that's when he came to me. We just did it and it ended up going on the record, and I'm not sure if things were left out or if he needed more songs or they were supposed to record those with Chris. I never found out – we never spoke about it. But it was never an issue because Chris and I have been friends the entire time – and he came down and played stuff on *Blues Funeral*.

CHRIS GOSS: And I recall at the Rancho de la Luna segments of *Bubblegum,* Mark insisted on working on Christmas Day. And I wouldn't work on Christmas Day. To this day, that's an issue that I have with musicians on particular holidays. It's like, "No. I'm going to be with my family." I mean, Mark was still gracious after all that stuff went down, and we were still gracious to each other. Like I said, I didn't go to war in any sense. I was like, "Hey man, it's your career – you do what you want."

I know that contractually I was probably fucked by him doing that – I was supposed to be *the* producer of *Bubblegum*, and then it got split by a number of people. I know he liked working with Alain a lot – in that sense I'm glad he found a producer that he was happy to be with for that long. But I can't take that heavy emotion. It's rock n' roll and it's an artform, and in Mark's case, it's a very serious poetic artform. *It's heavy.* Sometimes you can do it and sometimes you can't. And I know the more advanced in years I become, the less I'm going to emotionally invest in someone or that period of time anymore. It's just too much.

ALDO STRUYF: *Bubblegum* was the first time I worked with him. I went to the studio in Joshua Tree, Rancho de la

Luna. I was on the plane on Christmas Eve [Aldo is from Belgium], so there was nobody on the plane – except for ten people. So, it started really weird for me. I arrived and his manager drove me to Joshua Tree, and they were waiting for me there – with a bottle of tequila and some weed! A couple of songs were already recorded – or at least parts of it – but I was there with Mark, Chris Goss, Josh Homme, Dave Catching, and also a girl that played bass on some songs and sang a little bit [Molly McGuire]. And then more and more people came over, and I noticed I didn't produce that much stuff – because I was a bit intimidated by everybody that was there.

And then that second day in the evening, he said, "OK. Everybody can go home now and stay home for three days – because now, we're going to record with Aldo." He sent everybody home, and then we worked for a couple of days on nine or ten songs. That was surprising that he sent Josh Homme home – to work with me. I worked on a song that PJ Harvey had sung on, and other people I admired – Dean Ween from Ween. And I'm a big Ween fan – I have a Ween tattoo on my back. The songs were *so* good – and there were some beautiful songs that didn't get on the album, because he said, "Too much 'Nirvana' songs. Let's drop it." But it *wasn't* a Nirvana song and it was great. There was a lot of beautiful stuff being recorded by beautiful people and great musicians.

NICK OLIVERI: I remember going over to see Mark when he was working on lyrics for *Bubblegum* – he was staying at the Beverly Garland Holiday Inn. He used to stay there when he was off tour – he'd live in this hotel. You'd go visit him, and everything is everywhere – CD's, records – and he's writing lyrics. I remember him being in this zone while writing these lyrics. No matter what hour, he'd be working on lyrics. He came up with some great stuff. I remember when we were doing the oddities one [*Here Comes That Weird Chill*], him going, "Yeah, *I was hanging out with Winona Ryder.*"

ALAIN JOHANNES: The first time we worked – just the two of us – was a cover of a Kinks song, "Nothin' in the World Can Stop Me From Worryin' 'Bout That Girl," and I ended up arranging it in a weird, slow, Carnatic meets hillbilly music. I put it up on YouTube. It's just harmonium and cigar box guitars and percussion, and I had just gotten this microphone which was taken from a military helicopter from the '60s – it had a very frequency-compressed sound, and his voice sounds amazing on it. We did that in two and a half hours – just flowing.

And then we were in Queens of the Stone Age together, and in that time period was when he kind of fell off and had to leave the band – so he could focus on his health. He was in a hospital and then got clean in 2005. And then we stayed friends, and the next time we got to work together was *Bubblegum.* I played lead guitar on "Methamphetamine Blues" and other stuff. He actually came over for a couple of days to 11AD – which was the house studio that Natasha and I had – and we did "Morning Glory Wine," "Driving Death Valley Blues," "Head," and one other song. Just him and I.

[Alain's studio, 11AD] was on Kilkea and Oakwood. If you're familiar with Los Angeles, it's about three blocks from Canter's. It's a house on a corner. I did soundtracks for the videogame *Tom Clancy's Ghost Recon* and there's a video of the house there, and there's a Cornell EPK [for *Euphoria Morning*] with the house in it. It had really tall ceilings and there were two rooms with drum sets in them. One room was glass and tile – with the Eagles of Death Metal, kind of trashier/aggressive sound. And the more majestic sound was the big living room. We could do stuff and the neighbors never complained – we'd go until 10:00 or so. It was amazing. It looked very much like a French salon – where we did Eleven, *Euphoria Morning*, the first two records of Eagles of Death Metal [2004's *Peace, Love, Death Metal* and 2006's *Death by Sexy*]. It was just a house with gear everywhere. The entire place was mic'd up and ready to go at all times. It would make it really fun.

Natasha was joining us for lunch or just chilling in between. She ended up singing on "Sympathy." That was the first real, "OK. *We can do this.*" I recall him coming over and just him and I created this entire sound of a band. We also did a cover of "Clear Spot" [which appeared on *Here Comes That Weird Chill*]. I'm playing drums, bass, organ, electronic drums, and clavinet on "Head." It was just a couple of days, just like *Dark Mark Does Christmas* – we did that in a day. He'd come over and I'd go into kind of a trance, where I was being "guided." And then as I was hunting for the sound and for the part, he'd be right there – and I'd feel him getting excited or approving. Or, if I started going down the wrong path in terms of the sound and the part, I could sense his silence – he'd start getting a little grumpy. [Laughs]

JESSE HUGHES: He performs on [Eagles of Death Metal's] *Death by Sexy* – which is an interesting moment, when he came into the studio. Because there are some video clips of it, where it's "Move in the Night," and the lyric is "Oh yes we move, yes we move, yes we like our dancin'." And he's like, "Oh yes we move, yes we move, yes we like Ted Danson." He was kidding – he was trying to be funny. And everybody was like, "Oh yeah, *joke*. Got it, got it, got it."

JEFF FIELDER: Once we started working [on *Hawk*, the third album credited to Mark and Isobel Campbell], it was really something. It was just the three of us. And I was curious to see how it was going to turn out. But I wish I had tapes of those original things, because all my parts got edited to fit a "whole band mix." But all the acoustic guitar on that record is *me* – and there's a couple of electric things. But mostly, all of the acoustic rhythm stuff, we did just then and there. And the band was put on later in Scotland. And we did a bunch of tunes – we did that and two more over the course of the week. I think we ended up with about seven tracks by the end of the week. And then she did the rest of it with her guys back in Scotland. And then that was done, and we didn't talk much – me and Mark. We just did the thing and then he split. And then getting into 2010, I just basically wrote it off as, "That was a cool experience."

And I get a random email from the management – this woman Lisa, who was this British lady that lived in LA – *and all of these tour dates.* They go, "We'd like you to be in the band if you're available." And I had never seen anything like that in my life. Like, *everywhere.* I had never been much of anywhere – except for the places I lived, which was Texas, Alaska, Washington State...I've been to California, Canada couple of times. But never anywhere, really. And I was just blown away. So I said, "Yeah!" And then, joined the band. Everything was so new to me, and seeing all these places. It was a little intimidating – seeing all these crowds. I hadn't been exposed to all that stuff yet. And everybody else was really seasoned.

Giant Sand were the touring band, more or less. The rhythm section. And then it was me, Mark, and Isobel...and Isobel's guitarist, who's on everything. But once I got more comfortable with it and Mark started talking to me, and he would have me do announcements after the show about the merch – because he was all about the merch and he was all about signing autographs. That carried on for years. Because he's like, "That's how I make my money, man. So, I gotta sell these CD's." He would sell his own kind of bootleg live stuff that he was already doing.

And then I found out during this time, that he was playing with Dave Rosser as a two-piece. And I'm not sure what was going on with that – Dave was also in Afghan Whigs, and they were starting to become a little bit busier coming up. I knew this project was short-lived, and we were doing all the festivals and all over Europe. I was like, "This can't stop" – for me. And I just admired Mark so much from a far. I started to really understand his music, I felt like. I was just like, "Man, I've got to work with this guy." But you can't just go up and talk to him. So, my mission in life was to get him to recognize me, somehow.

And we did this small tour of Scandinavia. We did all of these little runs, and I got more and more used to doing it – tour buses and all that stuff. It was pretty rad. It was a crazy time. This is all throughout 2010 – it was really concentrated, the touring was *a lot*. So, we did this short run of Scandinavia, which was acoustic – it was just me and an upright bass player. And that was the time where I caught his attention, somehow. We only did about six gigs, and at the end of that run, he comes up to me in the dressing room – and that was rare of him to just talk to me, one on one – and he said, "Hey man, make sure I get your number before we all go home, OK? I might have some work for you from time to time." And I was like, *"Fuck yeah."*

We got home, it was like four days and he called me, and said, "I'm doing this run up the west coast. Do you want to do it?" And I said, "Yes." I had all these questions, and he's like, "Dude, I don't care. Just play the songs." So, I had all of Rosser's stuff, and I learned all his arrangements and I took it really seriously. And I just learned everything I possibly could. And then once we started playing together, it was only like two days of rehearsal – maybe only one – and in that time, I discovered what I needed to do. Of how to support his voice and how to be the thing that needed to happen to make the music work. And that was quite an experience. He gave me a lot of leeway.

He was difficult to be around – especially at that point, I was a little green and he is really intimidating. He makes his presence very known. Getting to know him, it was sort of this "dance," of "Don't talk to him *too* much. Just enough to figure it out. Don't piss him off, for Christ sake. Just pull the gig off." And I got *really* scared. Our very first show together was at Hollywood Forever Cemetery, oddly, in this masonic hall. It was some sort of ritual, man – some sort of "bloodletting ritual." It was only candlelit – there were no lights on. Sold out. It was probably 250, maybe 400 people. It was rather small. And we had to walk down the middle of the audience to get to the stage – in complete silence. Nobody said a word. And I was first, so as soon as my foot hit the stage, the place erupted in applause. And then we played to candlelight, and these *huge* shadows were cast behind us. And the hall is so ambient – the sound of it.

And I got it. That was the night I understood what we were doing and what my role was in it and everything. And then we did the rest of the tour in sort of regular venues – mostly theater type things. But I always reference that first gig, because that's the way it was supposed to be – *dark.* The mood of it, the candlelight, the almost church-type vibe. Later, we would do multiple tours of churches. I wasn't in the Mark Lanegan Band for another three years, so, it was three years of me just being his "side guy" – when he would do these either special events or solo tours, without a band.

ALAIN JOHANNES: *Blues Funeral* was the same kind of idea [as *Bubblegum*] – "The Gravedigger's Song" is just me and him playing all the instruments. And we invited Jack Irons, who was in Eleven with me and was the first Chili Peppers drummer. So, Jack played, Goss came down, Duke Garwood would send stuff from overseas, Dave Catching came in, Dulli…it became this revolving door of friends. That was the template – that, *Phantom Radio*, and *Gargoyle*, we did at the house [11AD]. And then I moved out, and we did *Somebody's Knocking* and *Straight Songs of Sorrow* at his place. I basically took a mini version of my studio and set it up in his garage.

ALDO STRUYF: *Blues Funeral* was the next one he invited me to play on – and that was at Alain Johannes' place. It's a beautiful house and very inspiring – lots of instruments. Alain is a sweet guy. And the songs were really good. I think that album is also one of my favorites. Here we were just the three of us most of the time, so it was different from Rancho/*Bubblegum* – except for the two days he sent everyone home, there was always way more people around. And here, we could *really* work on the album – in this little studio room with Mark. I was in the living room and I was on my own, making keyboard sounds and recording some horns. For *Bubblegum*, I was in the States for five or six days. For *Blues Funeral*, I was there for two weeks – at least. I had way more time to find great melodies and keyboard lines to put on the album. I think that album is unbelievably good.

That performance [*4AD Sessions*, uploaded to YouTube on May 8, 2012], I think that band was four Belgium guys. I won't say it's better than his other bands, but we played the music like it was on the records. And later on, when Jeff joined the band, he had his own style, and Jeff played it beautifully. He's a great guitar player. But he put his own influence in the music live. Back then, for the *4AD Sessions*, we just said, "We're going to play it like the record – as good as possible. The same sound, same vibe, same guitar lines, same keyboard lines. *Everything*." That was maybe the fourth time we played together. The first show was in Paris – that's also on YouTube and is also four or five tracks in a studio, with an audience. But that *4AD* performance is a killer set, and he's singing so good – and the way he looks, also, is amazing.

GREG WERCKMAN: So much of what Mark did too was wanting to help others. He was like, "I've got this friend, and he just doesn't get any attention." Because he sent me a Duke Garwood record, and I thought it was good, but I just didn't know if Ipecac could sell it. And finally, he was like, "I'm going to do a record with Duke. Will you do *that*?" I would never say no to Mark – literally, any record that he was involved with that he brought to me, I'd be like, "Yeah. I'm going to do it." Then he sent me the actual record [2013's *Black Pudding*] – that I agreed we would do without hearing any music – and I was like, *"This is great."*

MIKE JOHNSON: Mark emailed me out of the blue. We hadn't probably talked in maybe six/seven years at that point. I had moved over here [Paris], and he had been doing the Queens – we just kind of drifted apart. He asked me if I wanted to come do that [2013's *Imitations*], and I was like, "I don't know." I wasn't really connected with doing that anymore. But I did. He was like, "Dude, I just want you to be here. Let's just do it." And I was like, "OK." And it was a good time. We got along really well and we had a lot of laughs. I didn't end up playing on everything, and I mostly just was there – hence, the "vibes coach," I guess. [Laughs] I played some, but Jeff Fielder plays most of the guitar on there – he's a much better guitar player than I am.

JEFF FIELDER: And I did a record with him called *Imitations*, which was that second covers record. We did that in Seattle. He wanted to do *Imitations* with Martin Feveyear. I could be wrong about the details on this, but he's English and he was a young soundperson – kind of front of house guy/engineer – that got hired on a middle-later time Screaming Trees tour. And those days were insane. I didn't know *that* Mark. The Mark that I knew was different than that, but once I got to know him, I got to hear all these stories – especially later.

I knew Martin already – just because he lives in Seattle. But I didn't know the *whole* story. Apparently, he was touring with the Screaming Trees, Mark got pissed at Martin, and they just left him in Seattle! The tour bus left. And he stayed, got married to a Seattle woman, and got his visa. Never went back to the UK. He owned a recording studio here [Jupiter Studios], and everybody knew Martin. So later, they became friends again, and Martin made *Field Songs* – which is a lot of people's favorite record.

So, when it was time to make that next record, he wanted to make a covers records. He wanted to use strings, do almost a Sinatra-type vibe on some of the stuff. He wanted Martin to produce it. So, Martin's in Seattle, and I became more or less the "arrangement guy." And then, we just brought in *everybody*. It was a really cool experience actually, making that record. Duff was there, Barrett Martin which was neat, Mark Pickerel which was great. Making that record was great.

It was a little bit difficult – there was one point where we were listening back to everything…and he just wanted to scrap the whole bit. "I hate it," y'know? And Martin was like, "Hold on love, just give me a minute." We put the strings on it – Andrew Joslyn made these beautiful string arrangements – and then once it was more in place, came back and listened to it, and he goes, "This is the most beautiful thing I've ever heard. It's like a dream come true."

And after that record was done, that was the beginning of the touring that I got used to with Mark – which was this kind of "family vibe." I met Fred Lyenn who played bass in the band, there was a string section – just a two-piece string section – and enter Duke Garwood. So, at that point, I met the whole organization. Aldo would come to the gigs when we were in Belgium, and I got to know Aldo. And it was really like a family.

ALDO STRUYF: For [2014's] *Phantom Radio* album, I didn't do that much. In a way, Mark was really OK with working with Alain. I remember for that album I was feeling a bit down. One day, we talked on the phone, and I told Mark that, and he said, "Wait man, I'm going to book you a flight." It wasn't the intention I think – to play on the album. Because I was also living in Belgium and a flight to the States is expensive. And he said, "Come over and we're going to record a new album. Set your mind to something else and have a good time." And again, I played on a few songs. Mark was changing the vibe of the album a little bit – he was listening more to new wave music, like Joy Division and all those bands. For me, it was the first change into going more electronic, more danceable music. He really wanted more electronic stuff to be on the album – and of course, that was fun to do. But Alain did most of the stuff.

For [2017's] *Gargoyle*, he also invited me over, but that was a bit of a different situation, because I went to his place – I always stayed at his house – and he was doing lots of pills. When I arrived, I think the next day, he had to go off and kick the pills he was taking. So, I didn't really see him in the period that I was there. Me and Alain recorded some stuff, but we didn't have the feedback of Mark. Because I always record ten different things, and then he chooses one or two that he likes. So, *Gargoyle* was a bit more difficult because Mark wasn't there while I was there – because he had to go to a rehab.

JEAN-PHILIPPE DE GHEEST: Basically, I'd communicate with Alain Johannes [on the three releases JP played on: *Phantom Radio* and *Gargoyle*, plus the *No Bells on Sunday* EP]. He'd send me tracks, and sometimes Mark would say, "Try to do Pink Floyd-ish, 'In the Beechwoods' drums." Then, I did one track, and at the time I had just broke up with my girlfriend, so I was sleeping a bit everywhere. I would just play some drums on my laptop with the built-in mic, send it to Alain, and he'd say, "Yeah, that's nice." Then, I'd play the real part, I would send it, and then I would get no news. *Nothing.* And then…the album would come out, and I would discover my parts on the album. There was not much of an exchange, like, "Maybe we can do it like that or like this." It was just me in a room, recording drums – with no feedback. I'd just send it, and that would be it.

I never really worked "for" someone – having to play exactly what the leader wants me to play. So, since his music was recorded in the studio with Alain Johannes, there was a lot of layers. We were not enough in the band to reproduce the record, so we had to play with computers and tracks going on – with a click track on a couple of songs. For some songs, he'd give us some space – we could adapt to ourselves and play a bit as we would like to play. But most of the time it was really "play what's on the record." He loved the live shows to be very close to the record. It was really like a job in a way.

It wasn't really my style in a way – I'm not a "square

drummer," I'm more like a jazz drummer. I improvise a lot – most of my bands, we improvise and there's a lot of freedom. So, it was really the opposite of my way of working. But Mark has this huge, dark voice – it's really alive. So actually, when you play behind this kind of artist, it makes you forget about the instrument you play. I wasn't playing drums…I was just sitting on the tip of his tongue in a way. I was following the voice.

ALAIN JOHANNES: *Gargoyle* is where we opened up a little bit more to Rob Marshall – he contributed a lot of the music on that. And then we just layered on top of the stuff he sent us. It has a little more aggressive sound. That one is probably the least amount of stuff I'm playing on it. It was more like playing stuff here and there, and helping him to arrange some of the things he'd been sent – as musical beds to write to.

I was on tour with PJ Harvey around that time, so we did it in between some of the times I was home. *Blues Funeral* is probably my favorite of all the ones we did. And there's something about *Straight Songs of Sorrow* that is very direct and powerful. But *Gargoyle* was a really cool move in a different direction – it has a little more aggressive and intense vibe than the previous two we worked on.

JONATHAN HISCHKE: So, that happened [Jonathan's first performance with Mark, as part of a benefit for Brian O'Conner], and I didn't see him until a few years later – when I was hanging out at Rancho again, working on something with Dave Catching, and he mentioned that he was going to play a show with Mark for another event out here. A festival [Stoned and Dusted]. And he was kind of not that excited about it, because it was a low-paying thing. And Mark wasn't able to afford to have a full band. He was just going to do it with a couple of guitar players – including Dave. Like, an acoustic kind of thing. And Dave was kind of lamenting, like, "I don't know how it will be. We're playing in between these loud, psychedelic bands. I think it will be weird." Right then and there, I said, "*I'll do it for free.* If I put together the rhythm section, do you think he'll be into it? For free – people he doesn't have to pay." Dave called him, and Mark said he would.

So, the first person I thought of – who I knew would want to do it and wouldn't be offended by the lack of payment – was my friend, Josh Klinghoffer. I play in bands with him, and he was the guitar player in the Red Hot Chili Peppers after John Frusciante left – he was in there for ten years, between John Frusciante's stints. He was just let go right before Covid. And before that, he played wih PJ Harvey. Now, he's in Pearl Jam…and Jane's Addiction apparently, too! He's all over the place. But we're close friends, and I know that he is a Mark *worshipper*. It was like a golden goose for him.

He never played with Mark, he never talked to Mark – he was just in awe of this guy. And he plays really cool drums. He's not known for being a drummer, but that's his original instrument. He has a really cool feel – not what you'd call a technically proficient drummer, but he's just *full* of feel. It's like Levon Helm, Mo Tucker and people like that all mixed in there. Just very loose and feeling the music in this cool way. And I knew that he'd be great for this. And I knew that he loved that record, *Bubblegum* – that's what a lot of this material was going to be. I guess when Mark comes out to the desert, that's his catalog.

So, I called Josh and he jumped at it. He was freaking out – he was really excited about it. He showed up and he already knew all this stuff. I bet he knew it all by just listening to it so much. And he made some requests. I remember he *begged* to do "Strange Religion." Mark OK'd that, so we added that to the setlist. And I remember there were some country covers in there and some other stuff. He had the same experience I did – Mark showed up, we'd rehearsed a little bit with the band, who I think that one was Dave Catching and Mathias Schneeberger on guitar, me on bass, Josh on drums, and Shelley and Mark. And that was it. Josh, I remember – after he talked about the experience of Mark showing up and opening his mouth and singing – said, "It's like being in the room with Johnny Cash." Somebody of that stature or importance. That much soul and that much history in their voice. We were just losing our minds that we got to play with *Mark Lanegan.*

I remember we went out to the show [on May 26, 2019], and it was way out in the hills. It was outside at this makeshift amphitheater out amongst the boulders out in the desert. It wasn't at a formal venue. And I remember that Mark at that point – I don't know how much reality there was to this – was very paranoid about somebody stalking him. It was dangerous – at least in Mark's mind. So, he actually cancelled the show, formally. And then…we showed up anyway. It was like "a secret appearance." All the people were thrilled – the energy was real exciting. We just showed up and played. I remember it being a real magical night, because it was cold – even though it was in the late spring/early summer. It was *really* cold.

And we were playing just as the sun was going down. So, we had dusk, and over the course of our set, it got dark, and they started projecting these crazy psychedelic lights on the rocks behind us – the boulders. You can watch this stuff on YouTube. It was really special, and one of those things where you could hear a pin drop. It was really gentle and sensitive – the performance was very sensitive and just letting Mark lead it. We were all very in tune with one another, and it was really special – musically speaking.

After that, he booked me right on the spot for some gig that was coming up – that I wasn't able to do. It didn't work out schedule-wise. Then we were talking about doing some other stuff and emailing back and forth. And even though he didn't have the money to pay anybody else to do that show and I told him I didn't want money, I remember he sent money anyway. Which is a really nice gesture – even though he didn't need to, at all. I even said, "I'll send this back. I don't want it." And he insisted on me taking it. He was very cool like that, I found. He probably dipped into his own pocket for that, which I thought was really upstanding.

JOSH KLINGHOFFER: I think I was on tour with the Chili Peppers and I was in an airport, and I got a text from Jonathan Hischke, and he said, "Hey, do you want to do a show with Lanegan, where you play drums?" I hadn't played drums in a long time. But at a show with Lanegan…of course! I half-jokingly said to Jonathan, "I would totally do that. But we have to play the song 'Strange Religion'." Kind of thinking that the gig wasn't going to happen. But it did. And we played that song. As it got closer and closer, I heard what the gig was going to be like – out in the desert in the middle of nowhere, these people try and do something like what those desert people used to do with generator parties.

And apparently, Lanegan was so pissed that he said yes to this – it was just like a couple hundred bucks and it really wasn't worth it. And it was a band that was put together. But he showed up and sang, and it was fun at rehearsal. And I think he had something going on at the time where someone was harassing him, and he had a stalker. Because that was the first thing that he said when walked into rehearsal – "Is there anyone outside who looks weird?"

We did the show, and met up at Dave Catching's

house before the show. We hadn't spoken much, but he knows that I'm in the Chili Peppers as the guitarist. I still looked kind of young, and it probably doesn't compute that I'm "that guy." He comes up, and he wanted to pay me. And I said, "With all due respect, *there's no way*. I cannot. This is such a thrill and an honor for me. Just to play with you, hang, and meet you." And he kind of gave me this faux "Are you really going to emasculate me like that and not take my money?" And at this point of his life, I think he was reflectively almost performing like he did his whole life, like, "This is what I'm supposed to do. This is who I am." But I think he was touched. He just said, "Thank you," and walked away.

We did the show and the show was great…and I drove out to the desert. He was in the front seat, and Shelley and Jonathan were in the back seat, and he was talking about his mother being a Trump person. We were kind of bonding over that silliness. So, we got a little bit of a "hang" in. And at the end of the night, I gave him a hug and said, "Thank you so much for having me. I'd do that any time." He said something very sort of "him" and poetic – "You've really brought a smile to this old grizzled soul." I had a text with him the next day, and I thanked him again for having me. And he wrote back the sweetest thing – "You were such a kind person. I really need more people like you in my life. Let's be friends. Let's stay in touch." I said, "I would love that." And we never did after that – Covid happened, I heard he moved, I think I heard from someone else that maybe he was back on some sort of uppers. I never reached out because it was a weird time. It wasn't like you could say, "Hey, *let's hang out.*"

TRAVIS KELLER: I was a cameraman [on the 2019 music video for "Stitch It Up"]. Joe Cardamone directed that one. Mark asked us to do that, so it was our first time working with him as peers. But I was a cameraman, and so was Jacob Mendel – and Jacob ending up editing it with us. It was just a crew of three of us. And then Donal Logue acted in it. Just being asked by Mark to make a video for him was like a teenage dream. And also Donal – I was obsessed as a teenager in the '90s with his MTV character [of a cab driver] that he played in the video. So that was kind of a "going full circle moment" for all of us.

Mark is a fun guy – before you get to know him, he's kind of intimidating, kind of stoic. But he had a great sense of humor and he really got into dressing up into all those characters that he played. As he changed the characters…I think at one point he shaved his beard. We shot all of that in one day. We were just pretty much laughing at Donal the whole day – because he was in character from the get-go, and we just sort of drove in circles for hours, while he went over topics that we'd bullet point for him.

I took a couple of different batches of promo photos for him – for [2019's] *Somebody's Knocking* and [2020's] *Straight Songs of Sorrow*. I went over to his house, and it was kind of an honor – because I knew he despised taking photos. So, the fact that he asked me to do it and asked me again just felt cool. I knew that he dug what we did, and I always tried to get it done as quick as possible. He would just get nervous and he couldn't stop talking – which when you're taking a photo of someone, you're like, "You've got to stop moving your lips, dude."

It was kind of a battle between telling him to shut up for a bit, but then he would get nervous and tell amazing stories. He would just rant off Kurt Cobain stories. The first time, he was coming along with his book, so he was verbally telling me a lot of those stories – which I later read in the book. And he would just tell me stories about Layne or different people. And he always liked to bring up the fact that we have the "Eastern Washington connection" – because we were both born up there and grew up in the Pacific Northwest.

JONATHAN HISCHKE: He sent me some very funny emails. We had an email back-and-forth about some stuff – the way he wrote emails was so dry and so self-deprecating and so funny. There are some things that I still quote from and say all the time – because they're so funny. There was some thoughts about some gigs that never materialized. The second gig happened in 2018, and at the beginning of 2020, I'd asked him some questions about some stuff. Just small talk – "Hey, I was thinking about you. What's going on? I haven't talked to you in a while." And he wrote me back this *tome*. Really going deep and inside about business stuff, about some money problems he was having, problems he was having with his label, his management, his this, his that, some gigs getting cancelled and screwing him up in this way and that way. It was really intense and really down a deep hole. And went on forever.

It was kind of like one of those things where I was like, "OK. I need to respond to this, and I will. But I need to process it a little and take my time." I was trepidatious. I didn't know quite how to deal with it, because I didn't know him that well. And it wasn't that funny. There was *some* humor in there, but it was pretty serious and pretty…I don't know if "bitter" is the right word, but it was pretty stark – how bummed out he was, about his situation at that moment. His book had just come out, and I think that was going well for him.

Then Covid hit, and things got weird. My life kind of fell apart in the meantime, too – this relationship and this desert situation I was in. It kind of slipped by me to find the energy to respond. I regret that now, because that was the last thing I heard from him – was that email of him upset about things. Because I think that he obviously trusted me and wanted to be at least "pen pals," if not friends – and bounce stuff off me. I didn't know where that was coming from. And then I talked to some people that were closer with him later, and it sounded like he was going through all kinds of crazy stuff – obviously health-wise, and it sounds like mentally a little bit, too. He was down a dark hole. And I didn't even know that he'd moved to Ireland until after he was gone.

ALDO STRUYF: Mark is the kind of guy who wants to move on quickly. He stayed at my place in Belgium very often – he preferred staying at my house rather than going to a hotel. And when he was here, I had a little set-up where I can record stuff. He would ask me to record his voice for some projects like Not Waving [the 2019 release *Downwelling*, credited to Not Waving & Dark Mark]. And he's a guy who wants to do it one time…at most, two times. So, it has to sound perfect for him, too. But he was always enthusiastic afterwards.

ALAIN JOHANNES: The original version of *Dark Mark Does Christmas*, he just made vinyl that he sold on tour. The first version came out in 2012 – we did six songs – and then he added to it in 2020. So, in 2012, I would say it was after *Blues Funeral* that we did it – because I think he took it out on the road for that Christmas of 2012. He just made limited vinyl.

It's super-raw – it's just his voice and an instrument or two. And then the 2020 version, he asked me to remix it and remaster it, and he added three songs to it. I got stuck and I couldn't get home – I went to Chile after I got Covid to play Lollapalooza, and they locked us down and my flights got cancelled. *I was there for six months.*

JEFF FIELDER: [A video performance of Alice in Chains' "Nutshell"] is the last time I actually worked with Mark. That was a really intense time right there. If you kind of fast-forward through that first *Imitations* tour with Duke Garwood, all the way up through me joining the proper band – the Mark Lanegan Band – in 2015, and then me being his guitarist for that entire time, up to the last tour, in 2019. I did everything that he did. Well…not quite *everything*, but live, I was "the guy."

The last tour in 2019, it started at the end of October, and went all the way up through right before Christmas. It was intense, man. All the tours were really intense, but this one in particular was just like…I don't know what kind of hex somebody put on us, but everything that could go wrong did go wrong. Shelley got sick, and we had to leave her in Spain. First of all, it was too long…it was hard living right there. The band was hot as shit though – we had a new drummer and the band was really well-rehearsed and really great. But man, it was *grueling.*

So, by the time I got home from this, Christmas and New Year's 2020, and then me really wanting to make a new path – not knowing what was going to happen. So, I had this long talk with Mark around the middle of January, and I'm like, "I don't think I can do this shit anymore. I want to still work with you…but I can't do this anymore, this grueling pace." And we had a great talk. We talked through all this stuff. Because whether he wanted to admit it or not, we had become friends – just because we were together so much. And a lot of times, it was just the two of us – in these dressing rooms, for hours. We kind of worked it out. It was time for a change for everybody on some level. So, we agreed that it would kind of go back to where it was before I was in the band – I would do the special gigs, just the two of us. And in fact, there were a bunch of gigs booked for 2020 – we were going to play Red Rocks [with the Avett Brothers], which is amazing. We were going to open for X at a series of gigs. And then, *the shit went down.*

Once the shit went down, we had talked a little bit...and you probably read that *Spin* interview with him right around that time. He was talking all this stuff. I know my fair share of conspiracy-type guys, so it wasn't anything new to me. But I was like, "*Oh, man.*" And especially early on, when everyone was still kind of like, "What's going on?" Because we had all these gigs booked like I said, and I was like, "Are we doing this?" And he goes, "Oh no, man. You've got to get the fuck out of here. The world is over!" So, all that was cancelled. And then I didn't hear from him for a while – he was living in LA.

And then I was slated to be the musical director on this Alice in Chains thing. Every year, the Paul Allen Museum, which is now called MoPOP – it was once called the Experience Music Project – I had been working with them for years and was really tied in with them. Every year, they would do some kind of private show – honoring a certain luminary musician. Robbie Robertson one year, Jackson Browne one year – that kind of thing. And often I was in the band, and often I was the band leader. So, I got the call in 2019 to be the musical director for the Alice in Chains year. I was stoked about that. And of course, when everything went down, I was like, "Well...that's not happening, either." And then as the year progressed, I was making videos and doing livestreams and had this whole room set up like a TV studio. I got really on top of it – and made sure that everything I put out was really well-done and edited.

And by the middle of the year, they were like, "We're going to do it and we still want you to be the guy. It's just going to be a virtual gig." So, there was going to be a live component – which was the stuff that was with Krist Novoselic and Liv Warfield. All that stuff was going to be live. And that was the first time that anybody had played in months. And then it was my idea, "Can I make a couple of videos? Because I think I can get some cool things together." Because at that point, I was already working with Nancy Wilson and making videos for her, because I know her whole organization. And then I said, "I think I can get Lanegan to do it." Because everybody was like, "There's no way he's going to do it" – because he just didn't do shit like this. But if I asked him to do this for Jerry [Cantrell], I thought I could get him.

I called him and he said, "I'm in Ireland." I'm like, "How the fuck did you get to Ireland?!" I didn't know you could leave the country. I mean, *this is full 2020 lockdown*. And I didn't know you could leave the country. And he said, "You could fly into Scotland." That's the only port of entry. And this is right before Brexit went down. So, from Scotland, you could get into Europe. And he's like, "I sold the house. I'm out, man. America's over, dude." His idea was to move to Portugal, but he ended up in Ireland – at his buddy's, he had a lot of land. And they really liked it there. He used the word "holding" – "We're holding in Ireland." He seemed in good spirits.

And I go, "Well, I got one for you, man. If you can do this thing for me, it would be amazing." And it was my idea to do the song. I was like, "If we can do 'Nutshell,' it would be amazing." And he goes, "Dude, I would do anything for you brother, and I would do anything for Jerry. So, whatever you want." So, the way that happened is I recorded the song first. The way I would do things back then was I recorded the entire song myself – so everybody who played on it could have something to play to, that was kind of finished. And then I would slowly replace myself – the drummer replaced the drums…it was all the guys that are in the current Heart.

And then, I had this great track and I sent it to Mark. I said, "Just get a decent video, *please*." And he knocked it out of the park. I was so happy to get that video recorded really well – he had some guy there in Ireland who he was already starting to work with. And I was really expecting this "cell phone video," and he gave me this great, beautiful, hi-res video. I sat there and watching it over and over again – I was kind of enamored by it all. I spent a lot of time editing that together.

There was a director of the overall show that thwarted all my stuff – he re-edited it, and that's the one that everybody has seen, is the one that he did [with intercut footage of Alice in Chains members]. And I thought that was OK, but I was like, "Man, you really shouldn't cut into Mark's performance. It's only two verses and it's extraordinary to watch him sing it." And they cut all over it. I was really bummed out. It took on so much weight after Mark passed that it was a little overwhelming for me for a while – to watch it. [Jeff would later post "The Jeff Fielder edit" of the performance on YouTube, which features Mark more prominently]

I was working with Nancy Wilson – I still am – and I just thought it would be great if they did something together [a cover of Alice in Chains' "Brother," also for the 2020 MoPOP Founders Award]. I was working with Nancy a lot during that "2020 remote thing" – I was helping her do videos. When I approached Lanegan about that thing, that was one of the sellers – "Do you want to do one with Nancy Wilson? I think that would be really cool." And he was like,

"Oh man…that would be awesome!" And again, Liv Warfield was the other singer, who is fantastic. I thought it sounded really great – all of us together. I made a video for that, too – like I did for "Nutshell" – but I never put it out. But the track is great. In fact after that all came out, Lanegan was like, "When we tour next, we'll do 'Brother' in the set." But of course, that never happened.

Original Trees in Seattle
L-R (both pix): Mark Pickerel,
Mark Lanegan, Van Conner, Gary Lee Conner

[Photos by Charles Peterson]

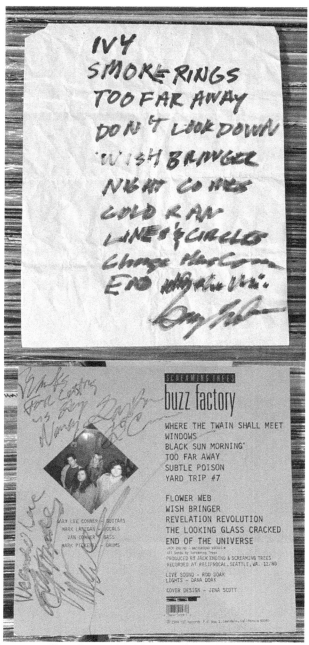

Trees setlist circa 1989/1990 (location unknown) +
autographed back cover of *Buzz Factory*
[Photos by Greg Prato, courtesy of Record Reserve]

Winding Sheet/Sub Pop single photo session: 1989
[Photo by Charles Peterson]

The ruins of Western State Hospital:
Steilacoom, Washington (*Winding Sheet* era)
[Photo by Charles Peterson]

Mark and the Trees at CBGB's
New York City: October 18, 1992
[Photos by Steven J. Messina]

Gary and a Les Paul (that once belonged to Chris Cornell)
CBGB's: October 18, 1992
[Photo by Steven J. Messina]

Van at CBGB's: October 18, 1992
[Photo by Steven J. Messina]

Gary Lee at CB's!

Mark, Barrett Martin & Van
CBGB's: October 18, 1992
[Photos by Steven J. Messina]

Charles Peterson's 1967 Buick Skylark
Georgetown, Washington: 1993
[Photo by Charles Peterson]

Charles Peterson's 1967 Buick Skylark
Georgetown, Washington: 1993
[Photo by Charles Peterson]

Mark enjoys a cigarette: 1993/1994
[Photo by Charles Peterson]

Mark takes a seat: 1993/1994
[Photo by Charles Peterson]

"He just looked like fuckin' death warmed over."
Mark at Bad Animals Recording Studio in Seattle:
mid-late '90s
[Photo by Charles Peterson]

Screaming Trees at Lollapalooza: 1996, New York
Barrett, Mark, Josh Homme
[Photo by Steven J. Messina]

"It looked so much like she would just beat his ass!"
Seattle's Little Saigon/Chinatown: 1998
[Photo by Charles Peterson]

Queens of the Stone Age's Nick Oliveri and Mark
Roseland, NYC: September 5, 2002
[Photo by Steven J. Messina]

Chapter 9
RELATIONSHIPS

Some of Mark's most notable relationships over the years.

SALLY BARRY: He would kind of break away from them [the other members of the Screaming Trees] as much as possible. There were times we were all hanging out in a hotel, and he would kind of get his own space going. They were like a weird mix of people.

JOHN AGNELLO: He beat the shit out of them [the Screaming Trees] – not physically, but verbally. He was mean and dismissive. He was *really* tough on them. I couldn't believe it – I would stand there watching them, and be like, *"Holy shit."* But he was kind of the boss, so he could get away with it. It was brutal. And with the unreleased record, once he started being all fucked up, they were not happy with it, either. And they were right – he was really in bad shape.

MEGAN JASPER: I would describe [Mark's relationship with Sub Pop's Bruce Pavitt and Jonathan Poneman] as being all over the place. I remember him disliking them *immensely*, and I remember him also having a lot of respect and gratitude. And I think much of that depended on what their working relationship was at the time, and also, what Mark's state was at the time. There were times when those guys just sort of severed ties – partially because it was just too much. Because Mark could be *a lot.* But, I would say when Mark came back to Sub Pop after having gotten clean and started making more solo material, I think he dealt really well with Jonathan.

GARY LEE CONNER: We saw Nirvana…we heard a

little bit about them. It was real early – in '88, they came to Ellensburg and played [on June 17th]. And there was almost nobody there. Maybe ten people, maybe twenty the most. Because nobody had heard of them, really. There weren't too many shows – we played at a place, the Hal Holmes Community Center, and there were a lot of people when we played, because we were like this oddity, like, "Who the hell are these people? The Screaming Trees...*from Ellensburg?!*" When we played there in early '86, we had a record out but we weren't on SST yet. And I think we played there again in '87.

We were kind of like "the music scene" – us and King Krab. Nirvana came over and played, and a few of those people came to see them, and I think Lanegan was totally blown away. And I was totally blown away. To me, it was like seeing the Who when they were unknown or something like that. They weren't always great live, but that time, something clicked – and I felt like I was seeing...they kind of reminded me of Blue Cheer or something. Because Kurt was this little guy who had a huge voice. The only thing I was disappointed in was that "Love Buzz" was a cover. [Laughs] But still, they made it their own. So, that's the first we heard of them – seeing them, and we got to know them.

And I think when Lanegan moved over to Seattle, he lived with Dylan Carlson in Green Lake, and I'm sure Kurt must have visited a lot. I think that's probably the first time he got to know him. And we played with them several times, too. I don't really know much about the relationship – other than they were really good friends. And when Kurt died [on April 5, 1994], Mark was pretty broke up about it. The relationship never really came into the band, though – it was a really personal relationship. It wasn't like they were hanging out when we were around, too much. I don't know how much he hung out with him after Nirvana got big.

But I know the one thing that happened later – after Kurt died – was that song, "You Know You're Right," when we were working on songwriting for *Dust*, during that time, Mark is like, "Courtney wants us to do a song." And it was that song – "You Know You're Right." So, I got a tape of it and we learned it. We never recorded it. But we learned it without Mark, and Mark came down to sing it...and he couldn't. He changed his mind. And that was the end of it. But who knows? We could have had a big hit with Kurt's song. [Laughs] I'd imagine it would have been a pretty big deal – in '95 or '96 to release a cover of an unknown Nirvana song. I don't know. That was the idea. But I don't know if it was the idea of capitalizing on Kurt...although we could have used the money.

That was another horrible thing about the '90s – we spent it chasing the money. And there was a lot of artistic stuff going on, but especially those two years when we were trying to come up with something for *Dust*, it was just kind of like...I like to call it the "STP sickness." Because Mark was telling us to write songs like Stone Temple Pilots, or shit like that. And we tried...and we couldn't do that. I know a lot of people really love Stone Temple Pilots, and I appreciate a lot of their songs. But their first record [1992's *Core*], you can't get around the fact that there was "the Nirvana song," there was "the Pearl Jam song," and there was "the Alice in Chains song." And they were the first three singles! [Laughs] Later, they got to be pretty interesting.

Apparently, Van tells me – I can't remember – that one time we hung out with Scott Weiland, in 1995 or something. We were doing an interview on a radio station, and he was around there, and we went out to dinner. I don't know if he asked if I liked them or something, but I was like, "Eh, I don't really like it too much." I do like that "Interstate Love Song." I said something about that. I would do that a lot – I'm slightly autistic, I don't understand how to get along with people. He wasn't mad or anything. But I remember Scott was making up songs that had cool melodies – at dinner. Singing them. I appreciated that – it was pretty cool. And I like some of their later stuff – the song "Vasoline."

But yeah, Lanegan was trying to get us to write a "grunge hit" or something like that. And he was so distant because of the heroin during that time – from mid-'93 to…he cleaned up some later on, when we did some demos, in like '98/'99. And when we actually did the record, *Dust*, we all got along pretty well during that time. He was like, "We don't have enough songs" – even though we wrote songs for two years. I had brought my four-track out to LA, and I've released two or three songs that we didn't put on *Dust*. One was called "1,000 Pound Hammer," another called "The Royal Star," and one of Van's – "Comes to Nothing (Venus in Red)." That's on YouTube.

MEGAN JASPER: I remember Mark being around Kurt way back in the day. I knew that they were close – and then they became even closer as time went on. Because it was all about Mark, Dylan, and Kurt. Those three were *super* tight. When I first moved to Seattle, Mark was living near Green Lake, and Dylan Carlson was his roommate. I feel like they were always around together. I don't remember him ever saying a shitty word about Courtney Love – when the rest of the world was psyched to share shitty words about her.

CHARLES R. CROSS: I think early on [Mark and Kurt] were friendly because of their music. Both of them were two men that kind of felt "not pretty," and outsiders. Their relationship was also based, however, on drugs. And in that world of "drug buddy-ness," the drugs are ahead of every friendship. So, no matter how close you are to somebody, drugs play a role in it. What I will say about Mark – for all the junkies I knew, he was pretty self-effacing about it. He didn't hide the fact that he was a junkie. He wasn't like Kurt. Kurt often did interviews and said, "I'm clean. I'm doing better than I ever have." Mark didn't have that duplicity to him. He wasn't good at marketing himself. But he'd pretty much given up the idea of being a pop idol, I think.

JACK ENDINO: I'd imagine [Mark and Kurt] were drug buddies on some level. But, they were also simpatico on a creative level, as well. Unfortunately, there were no results as far as songwriting that anybody knows about. I don't know what they might have done together – in terms of collaborating creatively, other than these Lead Belly covers. And Mark is only on "Where Did You Sleep Last Night" – he has no involvement in the other two tunes we recorded during the Jury session. Kurt sings one of them and Mark's not there, and nobody sings on the other one and Mark's not there, either.

It could have been something very interesting – if they had actually done something with it. It seemed like a great idea on paper. Sub Pop paid for that session, and ultimately since they ended up paying for *The Winding Sheet*, they got one song out of the Jury session that we could add to that record. It's funny that that song got a lot of mileage – that arrangement of the song has been copied by other people quite a few times.

ROBERT ROTH: Kurt was obviously a huge fan of *The Winding Sheet* and his records, and influenced him – especially the unplugged Nirvana stuff. They had a mutual appreciation. I think that maybe Kurt looked at Mark like a big brother in some ways. Amongst the Seattle bands, Soundgarden, Alice in Chains, and even Mother Love Bone, they came from more of a "hard rock" side of the fence, slightly. And I think the Trees, Nirvana, Truly, and even Love Battery, we were coming from more of a psychedelic side of things, but making it heavy and keeping it intense…but not with such a spandex/metal thing. So, there was common ground there – in terms of coming more from the punk rock side of the fence.

But then, punk is a limited term, because Lead Belly, I think that we all can probably consider him "punk rock" in a way…maybe it's not accurate, but in our minds, it was a type of folk music that was visceral and real and genuine. So, things like that we all related to – the Velvet Underground, more of that. We all loved Sabbath, Zeppelin, Stooges, Black Flag, and all that stuff, too. But I think there was this other side of the fence with the Trees, Truly, and Nirvana, where there were these more sophisticated musical influences coming into it, that I think the masses of grunge fans probably don't realize those sort of records were on our turntable as well – Roxy Music. Things off the beaten path – Os Mutantes. *Just weird shit*. I think we all shared what cool stuff we were into.

CHARLES PETERSON: I was not privy for that. From the sounds of it, they had a good relationship, but also from the sounds of it, Mark was even exasperated by…the second biggest junkie in Seattle was exasperated by the first biggest junkie's habit – having to score for him and do all that.

MIKE JOHNSON: I only met Kurt maybe once or twice. All I remember was Mark talking about Kurt here and there. I know that he admired him a lot and thought highly of him as a person and as a musician.

CHAD CHANNING: I never really knew Mark not to get

along with anyone. It always seemed like a good, friendly relationship between the two. I can say we were definitely Screaming Trees fans and went out and saw shows. And I know Kurt liked them – we were total fans of Mark and the band.

NICK OLIVERI: Mark said he wrote some lyrics on "Something in the Way" with Kurt on *Nevermind*. But Kurt had played on some of Mark's solo stuff, *The Winding Sheet*. So, instead of getting paid, they just did this thing where, "Hey man, I added a lyric on your song and you added a lyric on my song. Let's just call it even. Whatever happens, happens." Little did Mark know, if he would have had publishing on "Something in the Way" on *Nevermind*, he would have had *a lot* of money. I remember him kicking himself in the butt a little bit about that – "*If I had that 'Something in the Way' publishing…*"

CHARLES PETERSON: He talks more about Layne than he does about Kurt [in *Sing Backwards and Weep*].

MIKE JOHNSON: Layne I met a couple of times…actually, on Lollapalooza, I met him often [when Dinosaur Jr. and Alice in Chains were part of the 1993 line-up]. We didn't talk about Mark that much, because Layne was kind of kept in seclusion by his management at that time. He didn't really hang out much. I know Mark loved Layne, and he really worried about him before he died [on April 5, 2002] – he really wanted to help him. And he thought that he was in a *really* dark place. I know that he cared a lot about those guys.

ROBERT ROTH: Layne was roommates with a guy named Damon who was a DJ. I remember going over there, and Layne and him had been listening to the first Truly EP [1991's *Heart and Lungs*] a whole bunch. That was real early on. But once [Mark and Layne] hooked up, I think there was a lot of heroin going on, and I wasn't in that loop when it got to that level. I never ended up becoming a heroin junkie.

GARY LEE CONNER: I guess that's when he got *real* into heroin. It might have been a little before that. But we spent the summer of '92 doing a lot of European stuff – we did the Reading Festival – and then we came back and did a tour with Alice in Chains. I just remember there were a lot of drug problems – like, not having drugs mostly. Usually, the drug problems that other people see are the "not having drug problem." They can't get the drugs.

And Layne was always really cool – I thought he was a really nice guy. He was probably on heroin pretty bad by that point, I guess. They had a weird vibe though, because the other guys – probably Jerry and maybe the drummer [Sean Kinney] – they would do coke a lot. And "coke guys" and "heroin guys" don't seem to mix. They wouldn't spend a lot of time together. And Jerry on the other hand, he'd hang out a lot with Van – because Van would do coke. I never did heroin or coke, thank God – which was probably why I was able to keep writing songs and keep the band going. Otherwise, it wouldn't have gone anywhere.

TRAVIS KELLER: He just always talked about how Layne was his best bud, and that Kurt was almost like a little brother – but still like a best bud.

MIKE JOHNSON: Mark, he used to always say to me…because he knew I worried about him, and he knew he was in a spot that was different than the spot I was in. He'd be like, "I'm not self-destructive, man. *I don't want to die."* He used to always say that. And he was off and on with it, too – he managed to get clean at a point where he was really deep into a bad spot with heroin. And those guys didn't – Layne didn't. I don't know what his story was. I don't know why his sickness was so deep and destructive.

CHARLES PETERSON: Mark had that "inner-farm boy strength" – that I guess those two [Kurt and Layne] didn't have.

CHARLES R. CROSS: My relationship with him was, he knew that I knew those skeletons. I had been in that Harborview apartment he lived in, so there was no secrets. I interviewed him a lot. I'm not pretending that Mark and I were great friends, but we were definitely friendly though. So, I interviewed him at least a half dozen times. It depended on where his current sobriety state was – I don't think Mark sober or unsober was necessarily an easy interview. He didn't really like talking to the press. He didn't like talking about himself, and he certainly didn't like being asked about grunge. But it was a different standard in Seattle. But remember, Mark has got some convictions and other things in his background, so trying to talk to people about that kind of stuff – he didn't like being questioned by any authority figures.

But generally, at *The Rocket*, we had a different relationship with the Trees – we wrote about them more than any other publication, ever. So, we were "the friendly guys." Morally, I still wonder if the work that I did at *The Rocket*, we were primarily writing music stories, but where was our responsibility to cover the "off the stage stuff"? We generally held the rule that if they're arrested and it's in the press, then we might write something about it. But our job was not to talk about people's individual demons. I was looking through some old *Rockets* just the other night for something on Lanegan, and saw we did write a story on when he got arrested one time. But our job was mostly to write about the music and the story behind the band. Mark had a lot of troubles with the law – he put those in his book.

JEFF FIELDER: [Mark and Duff McKagan's relationship] was really special. He felt like he really owed Duff a lot. He felt like Duff saved his life at one point. And I'm sure he did. It was one of Mark's lowest points. And Duff took him in – like a little broken winged bird – and kind of nursed him back to health. I think that Duff had a house and he just let him stay there and got him together – and really started working after that, really proficiently.

They were great together – they were fun to hang out with. There was only a couple of times – we made the *Imitations* record and Duff was there, and we actually opened for Guns N' Roses. I'd assume that was all Duff doing that. We found out really quickly we were not a "stadium rock band." [Laughs] Those were *really* difficult gigs. I wouldn't trade it for the world, and what a thing to say you got to do – open for Guns N' Roses. *In Spain*. I think we did four or five shows. But they were all terrifying and they were all kind of terrible. But, it was great.

There were three bands on the bill – we were in the middle – and the first band [Tyler Bryant & the Shakedown] were these young guys. All I can remember is the guitarist, his dad is Brad Whitford from Aerosmith, and they were in their mid-twenties and had a '70s rock vibe, and all had long hair and Marshall stacks. The crowd just *loved* them. And then we came on – all dressed in black, standing still, with no nothing…we were set up really tight in the middle of the stage – and I don't think they knew what to make of us.

We didn't get booed or anything – but they weren't *that* excited. I think the audiences were just vastly different – at least in Europe. I just remember being *so* freaked out. The last gig was really good, luckily. Because every gig was kind of a nightmare – until the very last one, I think in Barcelona. We just had fun, and it went over pretty well.

GREG WERCKMAN: He had friends all around the world. I'll be honest – I don't know if all of his friends *should've* been his friends. Because in the music industry, there are people that just want to attach to you because of who you are. But Mark saw through most of that. There were a fair amount of people who just wanted to hang out with him and get high...or maybe ride his coattails.

It was stressful [being Mark's manager for a period], because he tended to want to fight people and he always got the feeling that he was getting screwed over. Look, Mark was not a "market person." Mark was not a rock star. Mark had this amazing voice – his talent. But everything that went with it, he wasn't comfortable with. He didn't like how he looked, he didn't think he was as good of a singer as he was.

So, getting on stage was not easy for him. Getting him to do interviews was not easy. Getting him to get pictures taken was impossible. But he was a real human being and he was a real artist – and had a soul. He just didn't quite fit in – in the music industry. But with his talent, he could have been a successful singer into his 70s – that's the type of voice he had, that he could have kept making beautiful, beautiful records.

I enjoyed the challenge of working with him, but it *was* a challenge. My career has been like that – I've only really worked with challenging people. I think it's kind of boring otherwise.

JOHN AGNELLO: He spent a lot of time with Sally Barry. Mike Johnson was really close to him. Mike got sober too, by the way – because he blew up his pancreas. I remember Mike in the sessions with a stomach ache while working with Lanegan – it might have been *Field Songs.* He was complaining about having stomach aches, and within six months his pancreas blew up because he drank so much whiskey. He got sober and he's doing great, living in France – he seems really happy.

SALLY BARRY: *Field Songs* I wasn't there as much. The *Whiskey* ones seemed a lot more organic. *Field Songs* just seemed like it was a very separate thing. I wasn't around when the rest of the musicians were there – I was only working with him on the vocals. During *Whiskey*, everybody was dropping in and out. That's when we were hanging out the most. And I think that was part of the reason he and I went out drinking a bunch. He and I were really comfortable around each other. When he and I went out together, people just kind of left us alone – because we were obnoxious. And also, Mark constantly had women hitting on him, and I think him having me with him kind of put that off a little bit, and made it a little less for him to deal with.

We got thrown out of a couple of bars together. [Laughs] That actually brought about one of the best things anybody ever said to me in my life – we were in this Irish bar, and we were just *obliterated*. We were yakking with the bartender, and one of us told a joke – I can't remember which one. But it was so funny that we both literally fell off our stools, were rolling around the floor – cry-laughing. The bartender came around the bar with a broom and pantomimed sweeping us out the door. [Laughs] We couldn't stop laughing. We were sitting on the curb outside, and I said, "Mark, why do we do this?" And he said, "Oh, you know why we do this. *We do this so we don't have to give a shit about the fact that we don't give a shit.*" Which I thought was beautiful. He was a really good friend. If Mark was your friend, he was a good friend – for all his foibles. Just funny as hell, and just a good person.

JEFF FIELDER: [Mark and Isobel Campbell] had a brilliant working relationship. They both appreciated that. They're very much their own people and their own "artist" – they had their own needs. I didn't envy the tour manager. [Laughs] To Mark's credit on that one…because that was Isobel's project, and Mark was almost like a studio musician on that stuff. And he gave it 100%. The shows were really great all the time – and he really just let her do her thing and take the lead.

It ended on not such great terms, because we did a show outside what we were supposed to be doing – he did a solo show with me. And she didn't like that very much. But I think in the end, everything was cool with them. I think Isobel might have wanted to work together again with Mark, but it never came to be. And three is kind of a magic number with those records, y'know?

I think Mark looked back on it fondly – and that's how we met, so it was cool. But it was interesting – where his head was at with his own music and what that music was, was *so* different. It gave him that outlet, but I think he was getting further and further away from any sort of acoustic-type music.

GARY LEE CONNER: I don't think they [Mark and Chris Cornell] were that close of friends. But we got to know those guys pretty early – Mark Pickerel had set up a show in Ellensburg, and they opened for Faith No More with their original singer [Chuck Mosley]. They were getting popular at the time and there were quite a few people there. And that was the first time we saw Soundgarden – in '87. We played a couple of shows and we got the same manager. That was our main connection – Susan Silver managed us and Soundgarden, and Chris co-produced the *Uncle Anesthesia* record. Van, Mark, and Chris would play basketball a lot.

KIM THAYIL: Chris was basically assisting Terry Date [co-producing *Uncle Anesthesia*]. Terry had produced *Louder Than Love*, and would produce *Badmotorfinger*. And for a brief period, Susan Silver was managing the Screaming Trees, and she connected Terry with producing *Uncle Anesthesia,* and Chris got on board, too. The Trees were interested in Chris helping out, because he had a lot of experience recording with his 8-track and 4-track. Chris was always eager to learn more stuff in the control room, Terry was eager to impart that information, and they all worked on that together. I don't think I dropped by the studio – Terry invited me to drop by, but that would be one of those things that would be kind of weird, where you sit in the corner and interrupt some other band. [Laughs]

Chris was a friendly guy – very outgoing. He could be kind of corny and goofy, but generally, he was quiet and somewhat introverted, and private. And Lanegan was similar – he could be very outgoing and friendly, and he could be kind of withdrawn. So, I think they got along just great, but both their personalities…they were both the type of singers who were a little bit more subdued or withdrawn. That would impede the initiative required to establish and maintain a close friendship. I think they had mutual respect and they liked each other, but I think their personalities were such that someone had to keep putting the foot forward to do the maintenance on the friendship. Look at both the nature of Chris and the nature of Mark – buddying around together didn't seem to be either of their styles.

CHARLES PETERSON: I guess in the sense that they were both wallflowers, in a way. I still am somewhat of a wallflower, too. Us tall, silent types, that move to action quickly when it's needed.

JACK ENDINO: There was a similarity in that Chris was also pretty hard on himself sometimes in the studio. But not nearly the scale that Mark Lanegan was. Occasionally, Chris would have a bad day. His voice just didn't work, and there would be certain days when he would come in and be flat. And we didn't have Protools – we had to get it right. And he would just have to hang it up and say, "I'm just having a bad day today."

One time, Chris got *so* upset that he actually kicked a small piece of furniture across the room – a little stool that I own. I still have the stool – he broke it and I fixed it. He felt really bad about it later, but I told him, "Don't worry about it." That was the only time that I saw Chris Cornell even remotely angry. *Ever.* It was the day we recorded their Beatles cover, which was a b-side – "Come Together" [included on the "Hands All Over" single]. "Turgid" is the best way to put it. It was a slow, heavy version – it didn't really work very well. It was the only recording they ever made with Jason Everman in the band. And that particular day, Chris was having a terrible time hitting the notes. It's not that the part was difficult – it's well within his range. It just wasn't working for him that day.

Other times, Soundgarden was painless, no problem. A lot of work, very meticulous, very serious, laser ears, very in control of what they were doing – knew exactly what they wanted. And I had a great time working with them. They were very, very particular, very perfectionist – but not neurotically so. There wasn't this feeling of a band shooting themselves in the foot – like I got with Lanegan.

The problem with Mark Lanegan is the tape would be full of tracks. You had 24 tracks to work with – the drums, the bass, there's a couple of acoustic guitar tracks, there might be a violin, there might be keyboards, there's overdubs, percussion…and you're left with maybe two vocal tracks to work with. And now, if you want to redo a vocal, you have to decide, "Well…which one of the old vocals am I going to erase?" And if you think it's easy to erase a Mark Lanegan vocal track, it's a *terrible* decision to make. I had to make those decisions in the studio, because I would get it so we'd go back and forth between two tracks at least. I always tried to have a few tracks, so we could comp something together.

But if the tape didn't have any more tracks, and Mark said, "We're going to record it again," and you had to erase it, then that's what you had to do. And there were some great vocals that got away. I would be sitting there, just wanting to kill myself, because I would know that Mark sang it great five takes back. But now, he's going to sing it for another half an hour, and he's going to hate it more each time – and it just drove me nuts.

But, this is the problem that we had in the days of analog recording – when people would get "perfectionist," the performance would go over sort of a bell curve. You'd go over this hump where the magic happens, the artist keeps going, and unless somebody stops them, it just gets worse and worse. And you couldn't tell Mark, "No." If he was going to do it, he was going to do it. It was hard, because I knew that he would come back another day and sing the whole thing again. And of course, that's what he would end up doing.

KIM THAYIL: I'd say "friendly acquaintance" [is how Thayil described his relationship with Lanegan], because although I feel like I saw, called him, or received calls from Lanegan more in the late '80s, he was definitely more of a reserved, solitary kind of person. Of course, it made perfect sense that he toured with Ben Shepherd after Soundgarden broke up – Ben played in Lanegan's band with Mike Johnson for quite a while.

CHARLES R. CROSS: The person I knew the best in the Seattle music scene – in a way – was Chris Cornell. Partially, because he was around for so long, and that meant that I had decades to know him. And we had more of a personal friendship outside of business. But with both Chris and Mark – both of whom died in the last few years [Cornell passed away on May 18, 2017] – it became more complicated to talk to them because every time you talked to them, someone else died. So, it felt really horrible. I know Mark was greatly affected by the death of John Baker Saunders [Mad Season's bassist, who passed away on January 15, 1999]. He doesn't get talked about nearly as much, but I know that *really* ran deep for Mark. But every time you talked to these guys, more people had died.

ALAIN JOHANNES: We [Alain, Mark, and Chris] never hung out at the same time all in a room – but they all spoke really highly of each other. I was trying to figure out a way to get them to do stuff together. Chris regarded Mark really highly – songwriting-wise and everything.

Polly [PJ Harvey] used to reach out quite often to give me and Mark kudos. They both had tremendous respect for each other. And she was a big fan of the last 15 years or so [of Mark's music]. For *Straight Songs of Sorrow*, she sent me a beautiful email about how much she loved it. I would definitely say he was on the short list of Polly's artists that she likes and listens to. And I would say the same thing for Mark.

[Mark and Natasha] were really awesome. There's a song called "Sympathy" – that was one of the b-sides for *Bubblegum* that we did – it's so great because I hear her voice and his voice, and I'm playing some weirdo trumpet, cello, and whatever. They had a tremendous respect for each other and Natasha really appreciated his voice and him as a person. She was kind of protective of me, and she was really happy that we were friends and close. And it was so much fun on those few shows we got to do during the first period of the Queens – to have Mark. Because we finished *Lullabies* after he went home and got clean. But it was quite something to have such huge personalities in the band.

Natasha, I had a dream I was going to meet her, and I met her in 1984, and we would be together 24/7 – like soulmates, almost like a musical connection like that. And the same thing happened with Chris Cornell – the three of us had this *amazing* connection. This ability to "flow" together and create music – which is unusual. There have been groups or duos that complete each other in a certain way, and Mark and I had that.

And one of the things I have to deal with is that Natasha, Mark, and Chris are now gone – so I'm just sitting on my own, trying to figure out how to keep the legacy going.

GREG WERCKMAN: Alain was one of those guys that would do anything for Mark. Al was always there for Mark. Mark would be in a bad way, and say, "I need to make music," and Al would be like, "Come by the house. Let's make music." They made *so much* music – that is probably never going to be heard.

[Mark and Mike Patton] were friends. Mark really looked up to Mike – which was a little awkward, because Mike would always be like, "Jesus. You've got the voice of God. *You're* the one we all need to look up to." But Mark really looked up to Mike. And Mike loved Mark. There is a secret project that was not quite off the ground yet that Mike was working on, that Mark was hopefully going to be part of. And every musician that knew Mark was a fan of Mark.

The same thing with Buzz from the Melvins. Buzz and Mark had known each other for a long time, but Mark was always awkward around Buzz. Buzz always laughed at it. Mark was never quite comfortable in his own skin. I'm friends with the Avett Brothers, and they had shows that were cancelled at Red Rocks because of the pandemic [in 2020], and Lanegan was going to open up one of those shows. They *loved* Mark.

CHARLES PETERSON: I don't think Mark ever came up [in conversation with Eddie Vedder]. I'm sure Eddie is [an admirer of Mark's music]. The Trees or Lanegan, I don't ever recall discussing them with Ed or those guys.

JOHN AGNELLO: I remember going to see them open for either Oasis or the Spin Doctors, I forget now. I got on the tour bus to talk to them, and you could tell they weren't vibing with the headliner. And they were *really* unhappy. And the headliners hated them. It might have been the Spin Doctors. But then when I read his book, I read about how they almost beat up the guy from Oasis [singer Liam Gallagher] – Van hit him with the head of his bass or something. Honestly, if I was in a band like that and these guys opened up and they were fucking around or doing fucked up stuff, I could see people not vibing with them, either. But on the other hand, J from Dinosaur Jr. was very patient with them – that's why he was cool with them opening up for them, because they all got along.

GARY LEE CONNER: I don't know why [Mark and Liam] rubbed each other the wrong way, exactly. I like Oasis – they were kind of '60s derivative, which is right up my alley. I didn't think they were the best thing ever, but I thought they were pretty cool. It wasn't that long of a tour – it was like, ten dates. And I thought it was their first time touring the US, so they weren't playing giant arenas – they were playing small arenas, like, 5,000-seat arenas. But the first show, Liam didn't come – he was having some argument about his model girlfriend with Noel [Oasis' guitarist and Liam's older brother], and it was Noel who played the show himself. The first time I saw Oasis, it was Noel singing all the songs.

And then Liam shows up, and apparently, there was some off-hand comment that Liam made about, "What are your guys' name? Screaming Bushes?" Or "Howling Bushes" or something like that. And that made Mark really mad, I guess. They spent three or four dates of this tour…every time we got to the show, it would be like, "Are they going to fight?" It was kind of entertaining in a way. [Laughs] And it was more entertaining a few years ago when they rehashed the whole thing and were going back and forth [via Twitter].

The best thing was…right after the book came out, a lot of people were like, "I can't believe Lanegan said all that horrible shit about you." But then all of a sudden, it turned into "Liam Gallagher" – so it kind of took the heat off of me having to worry about it. I was like, "Well, people aren't talking about what you said about me, now they're just talking about Liam Gallagher." They never fought, and the thing is Lanegan was pretty out of it drug-wise, so Liam probably would have got him. [Laughs] It was just a lot of stupidity, but when you're on tour, anything like that is entertaining – the ongoing drama. Especially when you're not directly involved in it. As opposed to, if he was saying bad things about *us*.

JESSE HUGHES: There were topics with Mark where you kind of got a sense that you're rolling the dice if you ask about them. But I've got to be honest with you, man…if you get an idea of what that was about, I would like to know. Because if ever there were two worlds that truly shouldn't give *a rat's ass* about what the other one thinks…I'm sure that Billy Graham didn't give a fuck about what Satanists thought about his preaching – because they're Satanists! Because what they were demonstrating to me was the appearance of a rivalry of some sort. But how? Different sports. There's no way to compare it. There's a reason why you don't see a lot of matches of karate champs versus boxers – because it's pointless.

Mark was also a clever, clever person. And a person who understood show business better than anyone. And he was definitely a child – if you will – of Ringling Bros., if you know what I mean. And I wouldn't be entirely surprised if they weren't friends, and that was an amazing…you know that Warner Bros. cartoon where that sheep dog and the coyote walk in and they're holding their lunch boxes? "Hey Ralph." "Hey Joe." They clock in, and then they beat the fuck out of each other for 40 minutes, then they clock out, and they're friends again.

Mark was one of the most savvy and perfectly political persons I've ever known. And I learned a lot from him about having to negotiate the personalities and the politics of rock n' roll. That was one of Mark's geniuses – he could seemingly demonstrate to you in his presence exactly what he was about, without telling you a fucking thing. I think anybody who has been in a room with him would agree with me that you would be certain of what he was about – without having any idea. That's a talent, man. And that's certainly not accidental.

SALLY BARRY: When he was in the Trees, he was friends with the whole crew. John Hicks was a really good friend. And I know he and Josh Homme were real tight. I know he and Kurt were super-tight. He and my ex-husband, Justin [Williams], were really good friends. He and Layne.

JACK ENDINO: And Josh did some time in the Screaming Trees – he's not on any of the records, but I think there are a couple of songs on *Last Words* that he does some extra guitar on. Because he was in the band for a couple of tours – he was "the other tall guy" in the band. They were the tallest band ever.

NICK OLIVERI: Josh was probably one of his best friends. Clay Decker, who is a tattoo artist – I know they spent a lot of time together. Greg Dulli was one of his good bros. Chris Goss was friends with Mark pretty good. Dean Karr was a good pal of his. I'd like to think of myself as a good pal of his. I know Josh was, for sure – from back in the Screaming Trees days. Josh was like the equalizer in the band, to keep the peace – because all the other guys would fight each other. Josh was like a breath of fresh air in the band.

CLAY DECKER: He always made me feel like I was one of his closest friends whenever I was with him. He told one time when I was at his house, "Y'know, I think I've spent more time just one on one with you than with anybody else

I know." I can count all the friends of mine that met my parents on one hand – and he's one of them. He came out to the Big Island of Hawaii – which was rare enough that anyone would come out there – and that's when I went snorkeling with him.

I'm one of the few people that ever saw him in swim trunks. He looked at me with the most serious look he'd ever given me – more serious than when I got him drugs in Japan – and he said, "Man, don't you fuckin' take a picture of me, motherfucker." I'm like, "I'm *not* taking a picture of you. I never want to see you like this again!" He got in the water and no matter where he went, I could see him – because he was like an albino dolphin down there. Me and Shelley's dad were up on the boat most of the time they were down there – just kind of laughing.

ALDO STRUYF: I think Greg Dulli was one of Mark's best friends. They really cared about each other. I don't know if they saw each other a lot, but they certainly called each other a lot. I'm sure they were planning on making some new stuff – Mark sang on the new album of the Afghan Whigs [2022's *How Do You Burn?*], and Greg did some stuff on the last Mark album [*Straight Songs of Sorrow*]. When Mark was in trouble or wasn't on the right track, Greg would call me and tell me, "Hey Aldo, call Mark and see how he's doing – because I think it's not OK at the moment."

CLAY DECKER: [Mark's relationship with Greg Dulli] was wonderful – they seemed so genuine and so close. There was no judgement passed by either one on each other at all. They both always spoke incredibly highly about each other. It wasn't that often that I saw them separate, really. [Mark and Dylan Carlson] knew each other a long time, and it seemed as genuine and real and authentic as two old friends that both endured the passing of another friend [Kurt Cobain] could be. The people that Mark called friends were *really* friends. And Mark accepted them for who they were and vice versa.

GREG WERCKMAN: Greg Dulli and Rich Machin – those were Mark's people. They had to deal with so much crap from Mark, and also, had so much joy and were responsible for helping him so much. Rich and Mark made two records together [2007's *It's Not How Far You Fall, It's the Way You Land* and 2009's *Broken*], but they should have made so many more records.

And Rich would have been the guy to have taken Mark to that place – like Tony Bennett. To this crooner-singer, singing the standards – Rich found the beauty of Mark's voice, and was able to use it like no other producer that Mark worked with. He gave it the space, but he also augmented it with the right instrumentation. Those Soulsavers records, man, those are things of beauty. And that could have gone on *forever*.

JEAN-PHILIPPE DE GHEEST: Aldo was really close to him. He was really his friend. Aldo is a very loving person – very kind. He would do anything for anyone. So, that's what he did for Mark – he tried to look after him.

JEFF FIELDER: Sitting there and talking to Anthony Bourdain, he was just a *master* interviewer. In the show, I think they had me say a little bit, but I was almost Mark's "buffer." So, Anthony would ask me a question – to get Mark to open up. He would have me talk, and then shoot it over to Mark. He was just a master of getting people to feel comfortable and feel at home – not only us, but the staff and everyone there. And then after the cameras stopped, he started talking to us about his life. It was so interesting – he was talking about his new girlfriend.

It felt very close to before he died [on June 8, 2018]. I just couldn't believe it – he was just talking about how amazing his life is. Lanegan and I had a funny thing, starting with David Bowie – we would text about somebody that would die. Like, I told Lanegan about David Bowie, and we had this text conversation. Bourdain, we had a long conversation about that, too. And when Chris Cornell died, we had a long conversation about that. It was kind of weird.

But as far as him and Bourdain go, they just seemed like such good friends. I think Bourdain had such respect for Mark – because they led similar lives in a lot of ways, and went through a lot of the same kind of "dark places." So, I felt like they were kind of kindred spirits in that – coming out the other side, and brilliant at that they do, respectively. Similar to Duff…except Duff and Mark go back so far that it's almost like they're brothers. Bourdain, it felt like they were spirits that matched. So, every time another one of these people would die, it was just another "notch." Lanegan never said anything like that, but it just felt like it notched him down a little bit more.

CLAY DECKER: Right after Anthony Bourdain passed away, I showed up at Mark's place in Glendale and stayed with him – and he spoke incredibly highly of him. He was really crushed about his passing. I asked him about some of the rumors on the internet and what he thought, and he concluded that he did kill himself.

CHRIS GOSS: Yes. [In response to being asked, "Did you see any similarities between Mark and Scott Weiland, both of whom Chris worked with] They're both redheads. Including Ginger Baker, Josh Homme…I worked with a lot of redheads, and a lot of them were notorious drug users. Yeah, there *are* similarities. There always are with people who are not too happy with the condition that they're in. Hence, what comes out of that towards someone like me – the person they're working with – sometimes it's strained and uncomfortable. And tense. But the first time hanging with him, when they were doing *Dust*, he was so shy and laidback – almost hiding, in a way. Then, I got to know him more down the line when Josh Homme joined the Screaming Trees for a while.

What had happened was I'm not sure the year it was, but Josh wanted to cut some tracks in Seattle. He was going to school in Seattle – this must have been around the same period, almost. Pre-Queens of the Stone Age. Just post-Kyuss. And Josh wanted me to come up to Seattle, and cut some tracks. I advised him to get Van Conner to play bass on the tracks – which puts that in a timeline that I would have known Van well enough to have him come into the sessions. Josh originally released it under the name "Gamma Ray." But there was a German band that already had the name, so he put out a split record – a "Kyuss/Queens of the Stone Age" record. It was a very busy, blurry time for everyone involved, really.

JESSE HUGHES: Joshua Homme, chief among them. And not just a friend – but a guardian. Because Mark also kind of needed that. That was why Queens for him was like a perfect thing, in a way. Because just like Nick Oliveri – who was dangerous – there was potential for collateral damage. So, Joshua protected everyone from each other. And clearly, as much as it seems that Mark didn't care what anyone thought, he most certainly had to, because the quality of his music improved. And it doesn't happen if you don't care. That's one thing that I would think about Mark – Mark was truly a man of his word and his actions. You got to know things about him by what he did, because he certainly wasn't going to tell you.

But Nick Oliveri was also definitely one of his dear friends. Alain Johannes...again, people loved him. They wanted him to succeed, they wanted him to not be the victim of his own...but he was on the one-way ship to hell. That's what he's kind of singing about – a dark road. Head on down the road, head on down the street. So, to him, it's like, *"This is what I'm doing."* But the people around him, they didn't want that. I can personally tell you as a witness that when Mark passed, that hit my best friend [Josh] harder than I've seen a lot of things hit him. It hit him hard and it hurt him badly. I can't say this for certain, but if I had to be a person observing a friend, I would say he felt this, "Why didn't I do more? Could I have helped him?" But nobody is going to tell Mark to do anything.

CHRIS GOSS: I think it was good [Mark's relationship with Homme and Oliveri], because he was offered such a sweet job – when he was touring with them. There's that short period when Grohl was doing the drums on tour, so the quality of touring upped quite a bit. All of a sudden, now there were some private jets and Mark had an easy gig to come out and sing four or five songs. And he stayed sober through most of that tour. And just would sit on the side of the stage – smoking cigarettes and drinking water. So, he was happy with that position. And having three singers – Nick was singing vocals as well, at the time – it was really nice, for a band to split vocals three ways in a show. And, also having Dave Grohl on the drums. It was quite something at the time. And just *the juice* with that record – to really put them over the top.

NICK OLIVERI: Dave Grohl is a monster on the drums and a cool guy. Everybody got along really well on the tour. Mark and Dave were friendly with each other. They weren't like, palling around late-night, walking the streets or anything – but they got along great. *I loved Mark.* Mark was my friend – I could tell him anything and he would listen to me. If I needed some words of advice or just a laugh, he was great. He had a way of calling me in the middle of the night, and saying, "Hey, do you want to take a walk?" He liked to walk really fast, like he had somewhere to go. But we weren't going anywhere – we were just outside, smoking cigarettes. We had some pretty funny talks on our late night walks.

I remember one time, there was an incident where I went out with some girl after a show, and I thought I'd sneak back into the hotel without anybody seeing me. As I'm getting out of the cab, I see two boots hiding behind a bush or something in the darkness. A cigarette hits the ground with sparks, and he says, "*On your anniversary, you son of a bitch?!*" And he walks away really fast. I'm like, "Wait! Wait! It's not my anniversary! What are you talking about?" [Laughs] Also, when Troy Van Leeuwen joined the band, he called Mark "Laney-poo." And Mark goes, "Tell that new guy if he ever calls me 'Laney-poo,' I'm going to kill him." And me or Josh heard him, and said, "OK, *Laney-poo*."

JESSE HUGHES: Even in light of that [when Mark criticized Jesse via Twitter in 2018, over comments Jesse had made concerning the March for Our Lives movement], in light of something that would normally inspire a blood feud, I respected the man. And I never really took it personal. And there's not many people in my life that are able to accomplish that. I take shit *very* personally. And he was one of the first persons that I had an experience in the public eye using the press, where I understood in a way even if it wasn't good for me, there was an element of it not being personal. And I think that's a testament to the man.

NICK OLIVERI: Me and Mark stayed in contact [after Nick left Queens of the Stone Age in 2004] – as far as we would send each other email every now and again, and I'd text him every now and again. And we started doing that more and more. But at first, I was closed off from everybody, and I wasn't trying to get ahold of him at the time, as well. Because I think there was a "Josh element" there – where we weren't getting along at the time. So, with that in mind, I think it was one of those things where he didn't want to rock the boat with Josh – it would have sounded weird if he was in contact with me, at first. But we got back to talking. I went and saw Mark play the Troubadour in LA. I also saw him with the Gutter Twins. I did go to see Queens of the Stone Age play and they put me on the list – for a show with Mastodon.

TRAVIS KELLER: Like big bro/little bro, pretty much [is how Keller described Mark's relationship with Joe Cardamone]. I think Mark saw a lot of himself in our little crew. He was always giving off "big brother vibes." He would just come and hang at the studio. It was cool to watch them work, because especially for someone from Mark's generation – to be open to different styles of music that were more modern. He was taking chances and doing things that I don't think a lot of people from his generation kind of have at their age. So, it was cool to see he was trying all these new things – and trusted Joe.

CLAY DECKER: Every Sunday or every other Sunday, he would come over the hill from the valley and meet me, and we'd go to the farmer's market right by my shop on Cahuenga. We would hang out, eat chicken, and laugh about shit.

CHRIS GOSS: I had known Wendy [Rae Fowler, Mark's first wife] for years. When he was staying with her family around Christmas time…I think it might have been the Christmas before *Bubblegum*, he called me and said he was having a great Christmas with Wendy's family. They lived down south somewhere near the shore – in the Carolinas, or something like that. And said he was enjoying a great Christmas dinner with Wendy's family. And it seemed like it was a pretty fair match-up for a while. But it was probably pretty hard for her in the long run, I would imagine. Wendy is brilliant. I'm sure she had to know what she was getting into. I've known actually two guys Wendy had married and divorced – one of them including Mark, and then another one. And they're both very intense people, and they can have a dark musical side to them.

NICK OLIVERI: I remember when I first met him, he was like, "You're in love with my wife, aren't you?" [Laughs] I was like, "Yeah, I love Wendy, she's great. I mean not like *that*, I meant, 'I love her voice'." We'd toured together with Earthlings, so I knew of her and she is very talented. Great voice and bass player. So, he was like, "You're in love with my wife!" "Yeah…but a *different* kind of love." He was married to Wendy I think for most of *Rated R*. I think when they split up was when he did *Here Comes That Weird Chill*. That was when he was staying in LA and not staying in North Carolina anymore with her. So, he started staying at that Beverly Garland, if I remember right. I hadn't spent too much time around them as a couple, but the times I did see them together, they got along great.

ALDO STRUYF: I met Wendy when I was in Joshua Tree for the *Bubblegum* album. I met her only briefly. The only thing I did with her was when I had a couple of hours off, she took me to the Joshua Tree Park, drove me around, and we had a long talk. She was really sweet, and I think Mark also really loved her. When we were on tour with the Queens of the Stone Age a year or two before, she would leave little notes in his suitcase. For his birthday, it would say, "Look in that spot in your suitcase, behind this or that. I've got a note for your birthday."

Shelley [Brien, Mark's second wife] I knew way better, because I stayed at Shelley's house when they lived together lots of times. I think she's really different from Wendy, and Shelley is also really sweet, and I think Mark loved her as much as possible. He was always really concerned with her – he called her every day. She got ill on tour in 2019 – one of the first shows. And we had to leave her in Sweden because she had to go into surgery. Mark would call her, and ask everybody who was connected to her how she's doing – every hour of the day. He was really sweet to his wife every time. They also started to make music together and he was really proud of her – that she could work programs to record music really well. She would be recording the stuff they did together for the Black Phoebe album [self-titled release from 2020]. He was really proud and in love.

CLAY DECKER: [Mark and Shelley's relationship] was like, fairytale and passionate in every aspect. They were as in love as it gets. I remember him calling me from Europe when they were on tour, and her ex-husband, Michael Barragan, was playing in his band. And Mark called me and was telling me what was going on. And I was like, "Oh, shit. That complicates a tour, I'm sure." I had already known

Shelley before they got together – she always seemed sweet. We were friends. I don't know how they first met – I just now it was on that tour that they got that close.

MATT PINFIELD: I thought it was a great relationship. Shelley is an incredible woman. I love Shelley. Shelley is smart, cool, and was great with Mark. I felt that she was really his soulmate and spirit. It's so important when you find somebody who gets exactly who you are. She loved Mark very much – that much I knew. And he loved her very much.

NICK OLIVERI: They seemed like they were meant to be. I was there on that tour [in support of *Bubblegum*] that they got together and fell in love, and I think they were very much in love with each other and were very happy. They were super in love.

ALAIN JOHANNES: Creatively, she was really good at synths, and they had a really cool set-up at the house. *Synths everywhere.* Like a really cool, hip couple. They had their creative space that they would share and sequence some crazy electronic stuff. They were together since the early 2000's – 2003 or 2004. They were pretty tight, I would say.

TRAVIS KELLER: [Mark and Shelley] seemed like they were really into each other. I just remember their make-out scene in the video [for "Stitch It Up"] was really long and I filmed it…so it was kind of uncomfortable!

JONATHAN HISCHKE: We ended up going out there [to the Stoned and Dusted show in 2019] and it was Josh Klinghoffer, Mark, myself, and Shelley – we were the carload that went out and came back from these boonies. So, we had the chance to talk and got some really funny Mark stories about things. I remember there was a moment very clearly where we were waiting to play, and seeing Mark standing there, wrapped around Shelley – like trying to keep her warm. I remember thinking that was a really sweet thing to see from somebody as non-demonstrative and kind of badass as that guy. To see that kind of humanity – and how much he obviously adored her and how much they meant to one another – was really cool.

Chapter 10
AUTHOR

Mark penned several books over the years, with his two
best-known being memoirs:
Sing Backwards and Weep and *Devil in a Coma*.

ALDO STRUYF: He wrote the book [*Sing Backwards and
Weep*] at my place here for quite a bit. He was telling me
about it the whole time, so I kind of knew already what was
in the book before it came out. But I did read it and I've also
listened to it while he was reading it himself. Sometimes
there is criticism that he's a junkie, so is it true or is not true
– "you can't trust a junkie." But I think everything in the
book – as far as I know – is true. Especially for an outsider,
it's an amazing experience to read the book. I really like it.

MEGAN JASPER: I read it right when it came out – which
was when the world shut down. Which now makes me laugh
– because I couldn't have picked a darker time to read a
darker book. *And I couldn't put it down.* But, I will say a lot
of the stuff that he had written about I already knew – but
there was so much in there that I didn't know. But it didn't
totally surprise me. It's hard to not have understood that
Mark had a lot of demons. He *clearly* carried demons with
him – you could feel that in him. I feel like Mark walked
with a lot of shame for much of his life, and you could feel
that.

But I would also say about that is to read what some
of those demons were, or where some of that stuff that you
could sense came from – was heartbreaking. The images of
him being so desperately trying to get to the next fix…it's
hard to read. When it's someone that you care about, *it's
heartbreaking.* That said, I was struck by what a great writer
he is. And I knew he was a good writer, because he was also

a really good emailer. His emails were fun to read and always made me laugh. His writing was awesome.

And I think that's one of the reasons why I couldn't put the book down. And I emailed him, saying, "No surprise you're such an awesome writer. There's a lot of stuff that was hard to read, and you did such a killer job – I loved reading your book. I hope you feel super-good and proud." And he did not respond to that email.

I called up J Mascis – because we were reading it at the same time – and he said, "I wish there was a little more 'Lanegan humor' in it." Because he could be so cutting and fucked up with his humor. You see bits of it – like when he talks about Liam Gallagher and all of that. But I totally agree with J – I almost wish he sprinkled a little more weird Lanegan humor in it.

CHARLES PETERSON: I just read his book for the first time about a month ago. I'm still reeling from it. I think it was great. I think there was definitely some unnecessary character assassination – I don't know what he was trying for there. I think he meant it, but I don't think he meant it in the same way it came off on the page. I think he was shooting for a literary type of trope that didn't work in that part of the story.

GARY LEE CONNER: I've read parts of it, but he said lots of bad shit about me – and a lot of it was because we didn't get along, because we were like a dysfunctional family. But there were two things about the book that just really upset me. One, was it had been 30 years since any of this happened, and later in the band, we got along pretty well – especially in the last two or three years, when we were just flying back and forth, and doing demos and stuff. So that was talked to him once or twice since then – in the early 2010's.

But then the other thing was when he said that all that old SST music before Epic was complete shit. And that surprised the hell out of me, because he would get *so* excited sometimes when I wrote songs. When I wrote "End of the Universe," I wrote it one night – really late – and he came over the next day, and he's sitting there listening to it, and he was scribbling on a piece of paper, and he just wrote "YES!" over and over again, because he liked it so much. I don't understand that – because why didn't he just quit? I *really* don't understand that.

And the other thing was – at some point, after he moved to Ireland – he must have had a complete change of heart about the book, because he wrote me a couple of extremely heartfelt apologies on Twitter messages. It wasn't like, "Oh, I'm sorry." It was, "I really shouldn't have said that stuff." And the thing is I don't know much about his personal life – the drug stuff that happened after the band. I've heard from some people that he definitely was not clean during those years. And if you look at his physical progression from 2015 to when he died, he was just on the way down. His face was hollow and I don't know what happened to his teeth.

Also, he did this weird interview with *Spin Magazine* from I think the spring of 2020 – right before he moved to Ireland. And he's going off about all this stuff – about electronic spying on him and people trying to get him. So, I'm thinking possibly crystal meth. I don't know for sure, but I heard from a couple of people who worked with him that maybe that was the problem. And with his history, it wouldn't surprise me at all.

SALLY BARRY: I think it's a really good thing that that happened [Mark making peace with Gary Lee before Mark's passing], because if somebody that you have that amount of history with dies and you're on bad terms, it will fuck you up for the rest of your life.

JOHN AGNELLO: I read it. I loved it. It was horrifying at times. He left out a couple of things that I could have added – like during the unreleased Screaming Trees record, when he had me drive him to some neighborhood in Seattle for some reason and drop him off. And then I realized why I was waiting for him – he was buying drugs. When he got back in the car, I tore him a new asshole, and said, "Dude, *never* get me involved in this bullshit again. Fuck you for lying to me and making me think you needed to do an errand…and you're buying drugs and I'm driving you around. *I'm involved.*"

I didn't know a lot of the stuff in the book – I didn't know his day-to-day was that harrowing. It was really disturbing. I was pleasantly surprised in the book when he didn't trash me. He trashed Mascis! He called him "cheap" or "frugal" or something – "a noted penny-pincher" or something like that. But he trashed a lot of people. He was tough on the rest of the band – he treated Gary and Van like shit. He would just beat them down – he was a tough motherfucker. But I was so lucky and happy that he treated me great.

TRAVIS KELLER: It was a great book. And I was always telling him what a great writer he was. Honestly, I was really looking forward to "part II" – all the Queens stories and all that. That's kind of a loss. The book he wrote was one of the best rock bios I've ever read. So many characters and so many twists and turns. He's a great storyteller. It feels like he's there.

Another thing about his music – it sounds different now. I guess people always say that, right? But those books are great. I was so amazed that he wrote the last book, too [*Devil in a Coma: A Memoir*] – after being in a coma. He just cranked that one out. But I love the poetry books that have come out, with Wesley Eisold [*Plague Poems* and *Year Zero: A World with No Flowers*].

MATT PINFIELD: I thought the book was absolutely incredible. It's heartbreaking in so many ways the things he'd been through. And this one just cut through me in so many ways. For me, it's got so much heart and soul in it. It's really fucked up and honest. It cut through everything – which was so indicative of the way Mark's life interweaved with his art. And the book was the same way for me. And it reminded me to keep fighting for my sobriety in my life. And I'm still going – which I know that he would be very proud to see and happy to see. It's the way I plan on living the rest of my life – it's improved *unbelievably.*

CHARLES PETERSON: A lot of that book was a revelation to me – in that I didn't realize just how far he had gone. I do realize there is some hyperbole going on. And I can give you one example – and it's a minor one – but it just sort of points out, "Yeah...*OK, Mark.*" I mean, he is exaggerating for literary purposes I think in many cases. He talks about the Reading show, and, "Oh, Bob Whitaker's foolishness, etcetera, etcetera, and then he passed out in a bed with Mark Arm, then woke up, leaving Mark Arm sleeping, and snuck out of the hotel into the night, and caught a bus back to London."

That's all bullshit. Because I have a picture of Mark sitting with Mark and others the next morning at Reading – Mark laughing away at Bob Whitaker's shenanigans that morning. So, he kind of likes to talk himself up a little bit more as "the dark prince" than I think he really was. I don't know if that's just memory stuff or if that was consciously done. There's a lot of stuff *I* don't recall properly from back then.

SALLY BARRY: It was amazing. And I know that he wrote it from a place of...I think he was just trying to exorcise a bunch of shit out of himself. And that's why it came off so harsh on some people. But see, Mark was like that, too – if Mark didn't like something, he'd pretty much tell you about it. He wasn't one to mince words – and he didn't. It was an arduous read for me. I thought he was real good to me in the book – he could have tattled on me for a bunch of shit, but he didn't. He just told nice stories about me – which I appreciated. I also have *Devil in a Coma* – which I thought was really interesting. Because, "Oh look, you're writing poetry!" [Laughs] Making poetry books – the thing he said he couldn't do. I'm going to have to go back and re-read everything at some point. But it's too soon.

JEFF FIELDER: He gave me a copy of it on that tour. It's one of my prized possessions – he signed the entire front pages, the title page and stuff. He had to write it all sideways. He wrote this little dedication to me. And it was one of the test pressings. There are only three of them – he had one, he gave one to somebody else, and he gave the third one to me. Which is really cool. I haven't read it. Because at the time, I was around him so much when he was writing it.

Lanegan started smoking cigarettes again, and before that, we would do a show and you wouldn't see him – he would just disappear. We'd never see him. Maybe every once in a while he would come out and make a sandwich or something on the bus, and then go back to his thing. We just never saw Lanegan. And once he started smoking again, he was *always* around – he was always smoking with the crew and smoking with the guys. Everybody smoked cigarettes – except for me.

So, he was always around and this shit was always on his mind. It was just story after story after story – because he was re-living all this stuff. So, if you sat in an airport for a couple of hours…I've got the "raw footage" – I heard the shit that *didn't* make it in the book. It's hardcore. I knew he was crazy, but…Jesus Christ, *really*? [Laughs] And he would tell me, "Yeah. That didn't make it in." He would sit there and write when he was home – because I stayed at his house sometimes, and he'd be on the computer all the time, writing the book.

And he'd go outside and smoke, and tell me all about this guy, that guy, this drug deal that went crazy – I heard so much of it. But now, I'm sitting here, I don't have anything going on until February [the interview took place in November] – as far as touring. So, I'm going to read the book around Christmas. It's just sitting there. Because I know he's a great writer.

CHARLES R. CROSS: I personally like his lyric book [*I Am the Wolf: Lyrics and Writings*] more than I like his two memoirs – because I think you get more of who Mark really was in that. I have some problems with his first memoir. And I talked to Mark while he was working on it – I encouraged him to write it. But part of his motivation was also money – Mark still, even being a great artist, had a hard time surviving without touring. But his memoir is unbelievably bitter. *It's fucked up.* Some of the ways he tells the stories and the meanness…a sober Mark was a much more mellower Mark than when Mark was fucked up. But Mark had a mean streak in him – particularly, the first memoir really displays that a number of times, in a way that I'm quite surprised. Most people grow old and they look back and they have a fondness thinking about their youth and the people they worked with.

And what Mark says about the other members of the Screaming Trees, number one, isn't true. Their musical contribution and their contribution to the band was far greater than he gives them credit for. And he inflates his own role and he ignores the horribleness that it was to be in a band when your lead singer was stealing your instruments and hocking them at the local pawn shop. That is not something any band should have to put up with. So, in a way, I thought the book was beautifully-written, but what he says, many of these stories are *not* true. And his views towards women are offensive to me – he talks about himself as kind of a "cocksman," and almost brags. Mark was a member of a number of twelve-step communities, and part of that is people make amends. And that book has *no* amends. Mark is still holding on to these resentments and burning people in that book. It did frankly make me wonder how well Mark was doing – because there was nothing to be gained in that.

And much of what he said about the Conner brothers just simply isn't true. And Mark wrote them – towards the end of his life – and said he was sorry, in some instances. But that's not enough to let you off, y'know? If you write the book, most kids that are interested in Mark read that and are going to think that the Conner brothers had nothing to do with the success of the Screaming Trees. And I can say – unequivocally – for the first eight years of the band, they had far more to do with the success of the band than Mark Lanegan. And he's not as kind to Barrett as he should have been. Barrett is an unbelievable drummer. And I think Barrett kept the band together in the last era – he doesn't get enough credit for that. The memoir also displayed an egotism that I think was part of Mark's issues.

GREG WERCKMAN: Where he came from and how he

was raised, it weighed on him. I remember one of the first times we hung out in Seattle, he took me for a drive. I think we were supposed to go to Sub Pop for a business thing, and he said, "We'll be late. I have to take you on 'a tour'." What he did is he took me on a tour of the lowlights of his life in Seattle. And it literally was *the worst* car ride I've ever been on in my life. We'd pull over and he'd point to underneath a bridge, and go, "I slept there for six months." "I overdosed here." "I passed out there." "I scored there." It was just like, "*Dude.*" It was brutal for me. But he was very clear-eyed about it.

That's why he needed to write that book. But I thought it was a horrible book. I know it did well – and I was proud and happy for him. He was stunned at the reception to it. *I hated it though.* Because I always thought Mark had so much to offer, and Mark's life was about life moving forward – it wasn't the past. Because he did not have a pretty past, and it painted that in that book – as much as I could read it. I never could finish it.

JOSH KLINGHOFFER: I did read it and I enjoyed it immensely. That was during this sort of "reading renaissance" for me in 2020 – when the world was particularly slow, and I was reading constantly. I went through that book in a week. I loved it. I felt like it was really *his* voice. Just a great introduction to who he was. I know for sure there was stuff left out of it, and I was kind if disheartened about how negative he was about the Screaming Trees and the early Trees. I don't know why he felt the need to take that more negative stance on his work with them or his singing. But I think as you turn the pages, it's clear he was not a "settled soul." I haven't yet read [*Devil in a Coma*]. I know I'll get to it sooner or later. I was going to reach for it before he died, but his dying, it almost seems like "the final."

JONATHAN HISCHKE: I haven't. Again, after Covid let up, I was going to read both of his books. But I was kind of shelled by his death, and didn't really want to know yet. There's one where he did an audiobook [*Sing Backwards and Weep*] – *that's* the way I want to experience that book. Maybe I'm ready now. It's funny, because I'm not usually that precious about musicians dying. And I think that year with Bowie and Prince [both passed in 2016] really changed my tune – because it was like I lost *everybody*. All my heroes left. But now that I'm having friends that are starting to leave more and more, and people I've worked with…God, it's just rough.

And that's the thing – I've been kind of turned away from that book by a few people I know, that have read it. My friendship with him was budding when that book came out, and they were kind of like, "*You may not want to read that book.* You might want to wait on that, until you feel like you know him better…because you might not want to know him much." Which, I thought was interesting – because I know he was very honest and forthright about a lot of stuff. I've heard it's a hard read, and you don't necessarily like him coming out of it – a lot of the stories. But the fact that he's so forthright is pretty remarkable.

MIKE JOHNSON: I didn't read it. I'll be honest – I got a copy and went through the index, to make sure he didn't say anything about me that was bad. [Laughs] But I didn't read it, because I heard enough about it, and I knew people who did. I was like, "I know these stories." Do you know the book by Klaus Kinski, called *Kinski Uncut*? I knew that was Mark's inspiration for that. It's Klaus Kinski's autobiography, and it's quite harsh and hard to read, in a way. I think Mark was judging himself – I think he judged himself probably *too* harshly. It was like, all the bad stuff about him and none of the good stuff, it seemed like from what I heard.

KIM THAYIL: I read selections that have been published, and I've heard from people who have brought it up to me. I know a number of people who have read it. I'm not personally into rock biographies. I read a few when I was a teenager. Rock and celebrity biographies are not important to me, but I understand that it is important as a fan. I love David Bowie, but I've never read a Bowie biography. But I've read some interviews with him. I did read a Zappa biography and a Townsend biography – but I was 18 or 19.

But I do have friends who do read whenever an article comes out about someone we know or a book comes out about someone they like or know, they'll read it and then they'll often tell me, "Did you read Mark's book?" "No, I haven't." "Oh, there's a really cool section here and a cool section here." I heard that it was maybe a little bit *too* candid and confessional at times. I'm not the kind of guy who wants to stare at someone's dirty underwear – especially someone who I've been acquainted with for decades, and I have a respect for that acquaintanceship and friendship, and wouldn't want to look at people's…I'm not that much of a voyeur.

ROBERT ROTH: I read a few excerpts enough to be horrified. I'm a big William S. Burroughs fan, and Jim Carroll was a friend of mine. And reading *Junkie* and reading *The Basketball Diaries,* they were cautionary tales for me. I loved the writing, I loved those books. But I also realized that the message in there wasn't to pursue that path. So, I lucked out and was warned off by books like *Junkie* and *The*

Basketball Diaries. Whereas some people read those books and said, "Oh, this is fuckin' cool. How do I get in on this?", I wanted in on the *writing* end of it.

MATT PINFIELD: Shortly after I got out of rehab, he sent me his book and signed it. It said, "Matt: So good to know we are both still standing, against heavy odds. Hang in there my friend and keep music real. Love, Mark."

Chapter 11
SEATTLE SINGERS

Why did the Seattle area give us so many outstanding singers circa the late '80s and early '90s?

JACK ENDINO: It goes into the whole, "Why did Seattle give us so many bands that ended up in the top-10 of the album charts?", at a time when a lot of people would have thought that rock was creatively out of juice. I don't know. It just happened. And a good band has got to have a good singer. So, without a good singer, most of these bands probably wouldn't have gone anywhere.

We had a creative environment that nourished the development of these singers, actually. People have suggested that Skin Yard do some sort of tribute or reunion show. Everyone knows I have multiple solo records as a lead singer at this point, and I can sing…but I can't sing like Ben McMillan. *It's impossible.* Aside from the fact that I couldn't do it and play my guitar parts at the same time – you just can't sing like the guy.

And who's going to sing like Lanegan? Who's going to sing like Chris Cornell? Plenty of people have *tried* to sing like Kurt Cobain, and it's usually pretty embarrassing – because I get their demos! It's like, "No. Just don't do it. Find *your own* voice." There's way too many people who've tried to sing like Layne. Again, you make a fool of yourself. *Don't do it.* So…we still have Mark Arm, who's better than ever. You've got to listen to the last few Mudhoney records – they have yet to make a bad record.

MEGAN JASPER: All of those folks grew up and came out of "punk rock days." I think when you are steeped in that mindset of DIY and just do it and create your own rules and put your best foot forward – there was really something important to individuality and not just being the "same old, same old." To be yourself and to be able to celebrate that and to figure out what that even is, and to know there doesn't have to be shame in that.

I think when you grow up in a scene or community of people, or you can tap into that way of being that felt very "punk rock," I think those people have the freedom to just figure out how their artistic expression can be true to themselves. There was something really special to that – it wasn't everything else, it didn't sound like everything else. But I can't help but wonder maybe there was something to that – maybe there was greater freedom to just explore that and not just try to mimic something else that was doing well. Punk rock was so different from that.

MIKE JOHNSON: There was a lot of great music in the Northwest at that time. There's no doubt about it. All over it. Those guys were really something else. To me, particularly Mark and Kurt. They were both these smalltown dudes who were such *monumental* talents. I guess the Trees weren't quite as mainstream in some way, or they had some strikes against them – because I could never believe it. *Everybody* worshipped the Trees. They were bigger than anybody. And somehow, all the other bands were more popular. It was very strange, in a way.

I didn't know Chris Cornell, and I didn't know Layne that well, but I'm sure that Kurt looked up to Mark the way that I did, and a lot of other people. He had a presence, and those guys were a little bit before some of the other bands. You had to see them live, too – because maybe those first few records don't quite convey how powerful they were live, the Trees. I don't have an answer as to why. But boy, it was something else – that that much great music came out of that place.

GARY LEE CONNER: I don't know, but there sure were a lot of them. You had Layne, Chris, Kurt, Eddie Vedder…I don't know, maybe it's the weather? [Laughs] But that wouldn't make sense for the Screaming Trees, because the weather in Ellensburg is different – it's much drier and it's half desert. Western Washington was much darker and dingy…and so was Seattle.

The thing is, nowadays, Seattle is this shining, gleaming tech cove. Well, back then, it was just kind of a grimy fishing city that had Boeing in it. Airplanes. I think that probably has something to do with it. And very isolated, too. I don't know about the city, but at least the bands reflected that – that something was going on. And the thing is you find out after all these years there was a lot more music going on than I knew about not being in Seattle – even in the late '70s and the early '80s. Like, the Fastbacks, they started way back in 1980. And the bands that Duff was in early on [The Fartz, 10 Minute Warning, etc.]. There were quite a few punk rock bands. It was a very low-level scene.

But even being a hundred miles away, we never heard much about it. Usually, when we went to Seattle, it was to see a big arena show, or punk bands and new wave bands would play the Paramount or Moore Theatre. And then we'd go to a record store, and then we'd go back to Ellensburg. It wasn't until after we got the band going and played club shows that we found out there was actually something else going on over there. The people in Seattle, we were total outsiders. They were like, "Who are these guys? *On SST? From Ellensburg?*" Because by the time we got to Seattle, we were experiencing touring all over the country and Europe. We didn't have much to do with Seattle. That changed – especially nowadays.

I haven't been up there for twenty-something years, but Van says everywhere he goes, people recognize him and want to buy him free drinks. I mean, some of the jobs he has gotten was because he was in Screaming Trees. And my dad, his name is Gary Lee Conner and he's 83 and in a nursing home, but he went to some doctor and he said, "Gary Lee Conner? Were you in the Screaming Trees?" He's like, "No, that's my son!" So, we're *still* famous in Seattle. [Laughs]

ROBERT ROTH: I think that there was a lot of effected quality to a lot of singing in the '80s – whether it's from the new wave side or the metal side. There was sort of this "trying to be something else." Or on the opposite end of the spectrum, it was the beginnings of indie rock, where no style, just kind of bland indie punk vocals that were non-distinct or not very good singers. You had this wide gamut of lousy singers and people who probably had taken way too many vocal lessons, and were trying too hard to be a great singer. Or to sound like Bowie, or to sound operatic if they're metal – to be the "greatest singer" and to hit the highest note.

And I think that middle lane of pure expression with a non-effected voice…maybe it was just people reacting to the heavily effected, pretentious vocals. I mean, I remember hearing about Chris Cornell's voice before I ever heard it – people talking about it and being really blown away. I think I saw them play "Beyond the Wheel" at the Central when Hiro was still in the band, and man, that was *not* the kind of music I was into at all. I was not a Queensrÿche fan at all. I was a Replacements fan. So, hearing Chris sing like that…in the old rules, it would have been pretentious – but it wasn't. It was just something new and different.

And then Kurt, my God, *what a voice*. And similar to Mark, just came from his gut and from his inner-self. It's funny, because we were talking low voices and high voices, and I think when Truly did their first EP [*Heart and Lungs*], I always wanted to be a singer like Robin Zander – I wanted to be able to hit those notes. Like Roger Daltrey. But after we made that first EP, I was like, "That is not where my voice wants to live." My voice is much more of a baritone voice. And once I got comfortable, I no longer wrote parts for myself where I had to sing that high. But when I look at guys who can sing that high with a lot of power – like Kurt or Steve Marriott or Robin Zander…even Eddie Vedder – these are like, kind of short guys. Like Daltrey, they're five something. Kurt wasn't *that* short, but it goes with the body type. And lanky guys like me are more the crooners – like Ray Davies, David Bowie, Jim Morrison, Nick Cave.

I realized that early enough to correct it and write for my voice, and not for how I wished my voice would sound…or maybe how it sounded in high school when I could actually sing Cheap Trick songs well. I found my voice and I was glad to have that parameter, where "Now I know who I am, and now I know what my voice is and will do." Mark was tall – he was taller than me. And he could hit some high notes – I'm not saying that he couldn't, but it's a different kind of voice. He definitely lived in a "deep baritone kind of world" with his voice. Which suited the music and his personality. His is very growly. I remember him mentioning that a big part of his sound was his chain smoking.

CHAD CHANNING: Because nobody really wanted to be a part of what was going on then – like radio or whatever – it seemed like we were defiant about what was going on and what was big, and just completely did our own thing. And because of that, nobody really cared. It's like, "Who cares if they like us or not. I'm doing what I'm doing, and I'm having fun while I'm doing it." And because of that, more and more people were like, "Let's just rock out and let everybody else decide."

What I'm trying to say is because nobody was looking to get really huge, and people were just doing what they wanted to do, more and more people – no matter what they sounded like – felt more comfortable about just going out and doing what they do, regardless of what anybody thought. So I guess because of that, more different kinds of voices were being heard. I think that's where you find the uniqueness from. I think *that's* where you find all these different, cool voices – because there was nobody there saying, "No. You can't do that."

Nobody listened to *just* punk rock – everybody had all kinds of music to listen to. Some of my biggest influences are '70s singer-songwriter stuff. It didn't sound like an influence on anything I was doing, but it's still there. When Nirvana was traveling around touring, we would be listening to Shocking Blue, and then next to that the Vaselines or something – just to give you an idea of the diversity.

And I think it's the part of the thing with everybody – they grew up listening to whatever they wanted to and not what was forced on them. It's like, airplay on certain radio stations is going to have a certain format, and they don't really deviate. It was a lot different in the '70s and '80s, compared to now – where just about *anything* gets airplay. You were also forcing yourself to search for other places for music, as well – that you normally wouldn't hear. We didn't really care about what people thought. We were just doing what we wanted to do.

CHARLES PETERSON: Maybe a sense of healthy competition? Or brothership? Or the bands just found the right formula at the right time and were doing their thing? It's a good question, but a hard one to answer – other than just...*fate*. The Seattle music scene, early on, we were all these crazy musicologists. When Mark Arm was still in Mr.

Epp, and we were rooming together in a basement apartment, we'd sit around and put on Black Flag, then we'd put on Brian Eno, then we'd put on Can, then we'd put on the Birthday Party, then we'd put on Tom Waits, and then we'd put on Nick Drake. We weren't like, "We're just listening to hardcore" or "We're just listening to metal" or whatever. We listened to *a lot* of different music.

SALLY BARRY: It's desolate – or at least it was. I'm in Aberdeen now. I couldn't afford to move back to Seattle – I had to move back to the east coast for several years for family stuff. But now I'm back out here in Washington State – which I missed terribly after I left. But it is desolate. And the winters are long and boring and grey and shitty. By the time I moved to Seattle – it was '93/'94 – there was already a lot going on. But I think when a lot of these people were coming up, there really wasn't a whole lot to do. There's not a lot of sun, the summers are beautiful but they're short. I think most of these [singers and musicians] were working class kids. It was a perfect place for something to brew.

JOHN AGNELLO: The weather. It's really dark, rainy, and depressing. But I think it really enhances creativity – because you've got to do *something*.

CHARLES R. CROSS: I thought you were going to ask what I'm often asked – "Why do so many people in Seattle die from heroin?" I've done a lot of work on that, and statistically, Seattle's heroin overdose per capita put it about twelfth in the nation – compared to other cities. We just had bad luck with a bunch of young men in music dying of heroin. But we have no greater number of heroin deaths than any other major metropolis – and we're behind in a number of places that don't get talked about. So, there's nothing special about Seattle in that front.

I think there's so much focus on the voices – there's a hundred other musicians behind that. And when it comes to Mark, you've got to give some credit to the Conners – who wrote those songs and wrote those lyrics. That's something that gets lost at times – that Mark as a lyricist was not always writing some of the Trees songs that people knew and loved, that he sang. Eventually, he was.

CHAD CHANNING: I could see that [that a lot of the Seattle/grunge singers from that era possessed "soul" in their voices]. It boils down to the passion you have with what you're doing. You don't have to be a soul singer to sing with soul. Great singers can come from any genre of music. And if they're passionate about it, that's going to show. And that's going to come from the soul – so whether that's soul music or punk rock, it's going to be there.

KIM THAYIL: There are a lot of factors. But I think there are a lot of great singers all around the country, in general. There definitely are singers of a similar caliber. Having the ability and talent is one thing, and then working to develop it is another thing. And then, publishing – that is the ultimate determining factor as to whether someone is heard or whether someone's work is presented to others, where people become acquainted with them. And I think having that talent, and having a particular cultural reference and taste that is shared with other musicians, provides you the opportunity to play with other musicians. And having a kind of band that has a similar vision – culturally, aesthetically – allows you to play shows with other bands.

And I think then, bands having success influences the modeling of other bands. Punk rock in general, being proficient as a singer was not an issue – it was not a requirement to be in a punk rock band. You've just got to have the lung power to scream and sustain that, and have some cool stage presence and have some degree of charisma. And write some cool lyrics and jump up there and whip it out. But having a good singer like Chris or Lanegan in the '80s might indicate to other bands, "Hey, you don't just have to scream and yell. *It's OK to sing.* There are contexts in which it's very cool."

A lot of these bands came out of the punk rock/post-hardcore thing, and within that context, there are ways in which you could sing that are both powerful, but also showed some ear and melody. And when bands do that, it inspires other bands to do something similar and they see if it works. It wouldn't have always worked – there could have been some cases where somebody might have come out singing overly-dramatic and maybe theatrical. That probably would not have worked – it probably would have invited ridicule from their peers.

But in other contexts, it's trippy and powerful – Andy Wood, Chris Cornell, or Mark Lanegan. And it influences other bands – you start to get people like Kurt Cobain and Eddie Vedder. And not every great singer in Seattle sang like that. There was also the way Chris Ballew from the Presidents of the United States of America sang – it was different. He wasn't singing in that more soulful thing. Or the way Mark Arm sings. Mark Arm is arguably one of the greatest frontmen to ever come out of Seattle. But he isn't going to croon or sing liltingly or with a melodic ear in mind – it's a different approach. But he's still a very regarded and prominent singer/frontman. So, I think that's probably part of it.

I think Lanegan had that ability to interpret not just punk rock stuff, but also, the kind of singing you might see from the Stooges or the MC5 – and the MC5 had basically a soul singer, with Rob Tyner. I know the Screaming Trees were into the MC5, and I know I was. So, when you have somebody who has that ability, you can expand the spectrum or the parameters of what kind of songs you can do. You can do these hardcore songs. "But wait, we can play in weird time signatures." "OK, we can do some really fast, quirky songs in 5/4 or 7/4." Or, "Hey, our singer can do more than just scream or yell or talk or read from a notepad. So…let's add that element to a chorus." And these give you some opportunities, and you keep expanding that and working in different elements that are possibilities that the band has. And we had a really good singer, a really good drummer, good bass player, good guitarist – so there was always more that we could do than just what everybody else was doing. And so, we would add that and expand it.

I think other bands developed their line-ups and their songs accordingly, and we inspired each other – that's kind of what happened in Seattle. So I think what happened in Seattle – amongst other things – is a certain kind of songwriting and performance worked and developed and grew and inspired and influenced, and it became a signature kind of thing. It's not to say there aren't singers with the abilities of Kurt or Chris or Eddie or Lanegan in Florida or Arizona or Minnesota. There certainly are – we know that. You've got guys like Paul Westerberg and Bob Mould in Minnesota. And of course, there's tons of people who relocate to Los Angeles and New York to try to develop their abilities as singers.

There's so many great musicians and great singers. Broadway is just *loaded* with people with perfect pitch. But what is it they're doing? If you're singing a Neil Simon or Stephen Sondheim musical, that's going to address a different audience than if you're writing your own hard rock song or writing your own folk song. So, context is a lot of it and publishing is a lot of it. But because there is a record label here that is popular and a few bands that were popular, that provided opportunities for other bands and other people's ideas and other songwriters. That whole body of talent can grow – because they're being published or making records, and people are buying the records, so, "OK. Let's make records from this other band that we really like."

It just provided all that opportunity, and Seattle kind of developed an identity – with a particular guitar sound, fronted by talented singers. These are great singers, but they're rare to find in a good band. What if Chris sang in a shitty band? You wouldn't have known who he was, because no one would have wanted to hear those songs. What if Lanegan was asked to play in some thrash metal band? Maybe it wouldn't have worked. Maybe you wouldn't have heard of him. Maybe the band would have been relegated to the bargain bin. There's a lot of things that go into it. And certainly, the artistic community had something to do with it, and the community that would share with everyone.

But it's not a once in a lifetime voice, because that would be an insult to all the people struggling away in their garages or their bedrooms or their small studios, just hoping for their break. Great guitarists are a dime a dozen – you walk into any guitar store in any city, and there's some fourteen-year-old that's going to be able to play the whole Van Halen catalog. But that doesn't mean that he's in a band, or that doesn't mean that he's writing songs that people want to hear, or that doesn't mean he has a style that is distinctly unique. There's so many factors that go into this. With publishing, you can write a book, but if it sits on your coffee table and the only person that reads it is your mom, it's not going to help you at all.

JOHN AGNELLO: It was just a fun time, because there

really weren't that many rules. And we were all comfortable around each other, and we could act the way we wanted to act. And there was no pressure.

MATT PINFIELD: It's incredible that from that era, to lose all these incredible singers and incredible forces in music. Some of the most important people *ever* – from that Pacific Northwest. And losing Mark absolutely broke my heart.

Chapter 12
MARK

The different facets of Mark Lanegan, subject by subject.

Influences

CHARLES PETERSON: I think there's Tom Waits, and a little Nick Drake – the usual suspects. I know Mark absolutely *hated* being compared to Morrison…but there's that in there, too. It's undeniable – just in his delivery and songwriting topics.

GARY LEE CONNER: I hate to say it, but definitely Morrison – because he's turning over in his grave, like, "You shouldn't say that! I don't sound like Jim Morrison!" Because that was one of the things he was really into – we used to listen to the Doors *a lot*. I think that was probably one of his main influences – the Doors. And then later on, definitely a lot of blues artists – like Lead Belly. He covered a lot of that stuff – like all the songs he did with that band that was called the Jury. But the thing is, I remember Mark saying that they didn't like that name.

JACK ENDINO: He specifically would talk about certain artists that I never listened to – until I hung out with Mark. He was the one who turned me on to the *Pink Moon* album [by Nick Drake]. He was a big fan of Tim Buckley. And also, Leonard Cohen. I didn't even know who Leonard Cohen was in 1989. So, Mark specifically told me about those three artists, and said, "You've got to listen to these guys." He was a listener and a music fan. He definitely wasn't afraid to tell you who he liked and who he was listening to.

CHARLES R. CROSS: I love Nick Cave's voice – that's

very similar to Mark's. They were compatriots. And when I spoke to Mark, he never didn't bring up Jeffrey Lee Pierce – that was "his guy."

MIKE JOHNSON: There's a lot of them. Tim Hardin I think was pretty huge with Mark. And Skip James. Jeffrey Lee Pierce is probably the biggest. Lightnin' Hopkins. Tim Buckley. Chris Bailey – the singer from the Saints. There's songs that he would do things that were little riffs that were comped from like…Ian Anderson from Jethro Tull – stuff like that, where you wouldn't think it, but you're like, "Oh yeah. That's a total *Tull-ism* right there." He had a pretty incredible, wide-ranging appetite for music.

ROBERT ROTH: Probably stuff like Nick Cave and Johnny Cash. I'm not going to say Tom Waits…I did, I didn't! [Laughs] We have mutual friends, and I know that Mark had a really good collection of R&B records and I ended up in fact with some of his records – Johnnie Taylor, O.V. Wright. These are things he sold in the late '90s period to a friend of mine. I know he had a big love of R&B, older country, and folk – Tim Hardin, the great songwriters of the '60s and '70s. He dabbled in all that stuff.

JOHN AGNELLO: He turned me on to – along with the books and the literatures – some amazing music I'd never heard before, like Rain Parade and stuff like that. I think he was influenced by that. Have you ever listened to Rain Parade? Google the song "No Easy Way Down" – that was a song he turned me on to, that blew my fucking mind.

JESSE HUGHES: One of the means I attempt to get to know people is in our world – especially singers – most people are cagey about where their influences come from.

Or, they directly lie – because they don't want anyone else to know the source. So, Mark was seemingly cagey, but I think the thing about Mark, truly, is that he could tell you that he was inspired. Like, we liked Lindsey Buckingham…how the fuck are you going to tell me you can see that? Point to a Mark Lanegan song and go, "Oh, Lindsey Buckingham." *I couldn't do it*. So, the fact that I can't do it tells me that I think Mark was in full possession of the knowledge that he was unique. And I think that's what kind of fueled his isolation. He truly was unique in a lot of ways, and maybe he over-accepted it – if that makes any sense.

MATT PINFIELD: Even though their music is different, absolutely. [In response to the question, "Do you see a similarity between Mark and David Bowie, as far as both taking on a variety of styles throughout their careers?"] I think Mark was a creative explorer, and he was so open to all different styles of music. He was immersed in it, because he loved it *so* much.

And I think that whenever he put his stamp on it and embraced something, he found a way to make it part of his creative process, and to keep evolving and at the same time, taking chances always. I think that's why people like Mark was such an important artist throughout his career. Definitely I see those comparisons to Bowie, because he was never afraid to take chances – *ever*. And he was one of a kind. That sounds like a cliché, but it's not.

MIKE JOHNSON: We used to talk about the albums that we thought were the best. Skip James: *Today*. That album was huge. Probably the first Tim Hardin album [Tim Hardin: *1*]. I think Tim Buckley: *Starsailor,* the second Saints album [*Eternally Yours*], the entirety of the Gun Club catalog.

NICK OLIVERI: He'd listen to music a lot on his headphones – rather than playing it in the back lounge. But mainly, he'd listen to old blues. He would buy CD's and then give them to me – because he would upload them into his computer. So, I have this CD collection of his. I remember Wire: *Pink Flag*, Joy Division, Robert Johnson, the Cramps. At the end of the tour, I'd have a collection of "Mark Lanegan's once played CD's." I still have all those CD's – I should pick out a few and listen to them one day. Y'know, I didn't like Joy Division when I was growing up – because it wasn't a metal band. But he got me into some of their early stuff. I didn't really get what they were doing until Mark explained it to me – that the singer [Ian Curtis] hung himself. Like an older brother would say, "You've got to check this out. *Listen to this.*"

CHARLES R. CROSS: He loved to talk blues. It was both Mark and Pickerel together who turned me on to Lee Hazlewood and Nancy Sinatra, and appreciating the Bakersfield sound. But I loved the blues, and those Robert Johnson recordings and some of those Folkways recordings, they were not commonly talked about in the '80s in Seattle. And if I talked to Mark, that's what we discussed – those records. They meant an incredible amount to him.

MEGAN JASPER: We talked a lot about George Jones, and I was listening to a ton of Charlie Rich – and I know he loved that, too.

SALLY BARRY: He liked so much different kind of stuff. It turned out surprisingly toward the end there we all realized just how much he enjoyed the electronic bands – like the more new wave stuff. I think the way he worked his influences into his own work evolved very slowly over the years as he became a little more confident. But I know he liked a really diverse catalog of music.

The usual names that come up when people are trying to pool his influences are probably not his influences at all. I know when we would go out drinking together and the jukebox came on, he really liked singing along to Roy Orbison. We both did – because it was so much fun to sing. Usually, we were so busy getting obliterated that the subject never even came up. We were just out there being assholes, like we were.

CHRIS GOSS: Johnny Cash's last record [2002's *American IV: The Man Comes Around*] effected both of us. Kind of like a stunner when you heard Johnny Cash is dying and he's gone, and then hearing that record. I remember when I got it, I was listening to it in my car, and Mark showed up at the studio, and he goes, "You're listening to the new Johnny Cash, huh?" And I said, "Yeah." And he goes, "*You look devastated.*"

GREG WERCKMAN: I remember late in Merle Haggard's career when he came out with a new record, I got it, and I was like, "The Hag is back…this is great!" And I remember sending it to Mark, and he loved it, too. And Buck Owens.

CLAY DECKER: He loved all kinds of abstract stuff – everything from Bill Laswell to…a whole range of stuff, really.

ALDO STRUYF: He was really interested in the whole Australian scene. I think the whole Seattle scene was a bit based on the Australian scene – with Cosmic Psychos and Radio Birdman. Also, when we went to Australia, he knew a lot of people there – like the drummer of the Cosmic Pyschos, Simon Bonney from Crime & the City Solution, Nick Cave. They were always at our shows. We always sent new records to each other – it could be more fingerpicking guitar, rock music, dance music, techno music…it's so wide. But I know his favorite artist was John Cale. And a guy he said he'd love to play with or do something together was Brian Eno. But I think he was really into electronic music the last year of his life.

It was always fun to be around him and especially, share music. Because I'm hooked on buying records – I've also worked in a record store for many years. We always talked about music and that was really fun. When I hear something new, I still think, "I've got to tell Mark!" And of course, I can't anymore – I miss that a lot. We were always providing each other with good music. He was the kind of guy that would go on tour, and in every city, he would go along to all the record stores that were in those different countries and cities, and would buy a bunch of stuff, especially CD's, way back – and he would put them all in his iTunes.

And then at the end of the tour, there were like 500 CD's in the room – I also shared the same room with him in the beginning. And he said, "You can have them all…or leave them for the cleaning lady." And not only music – jeans, shoes, coats, or whatever. He would buy stuff the whole time, and then he would just leave it somewhere. I could never understand it – he would spend thousands of dollars on music or clothes, and then he would just leave it, because it was impossible to carry it back home on a plane. I don't know if there's a word for it in English – that you can't help buying, like an addiction. He had that completely – every time, he bought stuff…and just left it, or hid it in the tour bus somewhere!

CHARLES R. CROSS: We both liked the writer Raymond Carver. A lot of our discussions were also literary. "Who are you reading?" Raymond Carver, Richard Ford – the kind classic American short story writers. Mark was a fan of both those writers. Raymond Carver has a poem called *Gravy*, and Mark was well-aware of that. So, gravy was what Carver got after sobering up. And Mark had some gravy in his life – and some of that was from Courtney Love's generosity [in reference to Mark crediting Love for getting him into rehab and supporting him financially for a spell in the late '90s, discussed in *Sing Backwards and Weep*].

Temper

GREG WERCKMAN: He was a battler. He fought his whole life. He was a scrapper – he would get in fistfights. But he also kind of felt he was at the bottom and he was always fighting to get out of the bottom.

JACK ENDINO: Apparently on the road, he had a bit of a temper – because the stories I would hear later from Barrett and Van, they'd start laughing hysterically, and "Remember when somebody threw a punch?" "Oh yeah! And then we threw him down the stairs! And then the cops came but we'd already left!" Just these mad stories. I'm thinking, "Wow. This is what life on the road with the Screaming Trees is?" Seemed like they got violent sometimes – either with themselves or with bouncers or with hecklers or something.

GARY LEE CONNER: He was a big talker when it came to fighting. He could corner people with words, though. I'd seen him take people down *so* badly – just by saying shit to them. I don't know why he could do that. He probably did it to us a few times. [Laughs] But I never saw a fight. We never actually "fought fought," but apparently, I remember one time he hit me in the arm. Van says I tackled him one time – but I can't remember doing that. So, we never had any real physical fights between us. And I never saw him actually get in a fight, but I always thought maybe he'd just get knocked out. Although, he was Irish, I don't know, Irish people…uh-oh, that's a racial stereotype – Irish and fighting. And drinking, well, you didn't fight unless you were drunk.

JOHN AGNELLO: Like I said, he kicked me in the nuts one night on the lower east side. That was the night he got in a fistfight with the guy from the band Surgery – that guy has passed away too, so, rest in peace – and I was one of the five people who jumped in, to try to break up this fight in a bar. And that night, I was walking to his cab, and I don't know what I said to him, but he turned around and gave me the boot to the groin. We were so drunk that I didn't notice it until the next morning when I woke up – and then it all came back to me. And then the next day, we went into work like nothing was wrong! We hugged, we hung out, and we laughed our asses off. That was a "typical Mark Lanegan scenario."

MEGAN JASPER: Mark asked us [Megan and her then-roommate, Chris Takino, who previously worked for SST Records and was friends with Mark] if one of his closest friends, Mike Johnson, could live with us. Mike was moving up from Eugene, Oregon, and Mike and Mark were super-tight. Mike ended up moving into our home – so, Mark was around in our house a lot during that time. I was living on Queen Anne, and Sebadoh was on tour.

Now, Sebadoh had Lou Barlow, and Lou and J Mascis were not speaking. And Sebadoh was becoming pretty popular – they were signed to Sub Pop, and Mike

Johnson had already joined Dinosaur Jr. as their bass player. And Mark – being Mike's best friend and loving J so much – decided that he was going to have it out for Lou Barlow. And maybe Lou annoyed him – I have no idea. But Mark – who at this point, had a lot to drink – had heard that Lou might be stopping by our house.

Now, Sebadoh's van had just been broken into, and they were playing a show at the Crocodile Café. When they came out to their van – they realized a ton of their shit had been stolen. So, they came to our house and kind of needed a space where they could just "be" and figure stuff out. *And Mark decided that he wanted to beat the shit out of Lou.* So, Chris and I were trying to contain Mark – or at least get him out of the house – but he kept going out and taunting Lou.

He didn't end up doing anything – we ended up getting Mark to leave the house. But it was one of those moments where with Mark, I was like, "Oh my God. This is either going to end without there being a huge story" – which thankfully, it did – "or it is going to end up with Lou on the floor with bigger problems than having his van broken into."

GARY LEE CONNER: I remember one time in 1992, we were in Shepherd's Bush. It was probably when we did Reading. And Urge Overkill was in town playing, and I really liked them. I can't remember if we played with them before. And they were staying close by, and [UO's singer/guitarist] Nash Kato came in, and I had no idea they had something going on bad between them. But it had to do with some girl or something. He sits down at the table and starts talking and I'm talking to him, and Mark's just like [makes low growling noise]. Then Nash starts saying, "What's wrong with your buddy? He's not saying anything." Finally, he got up and left.

And it sucked, because here's a guy from a band I

like a lot, and there's obviously something very bizarre going on between Lanegan and him – something to do with a girl they both went out with. That's the kind of thing Mark would do when he's cornered – killing you with words. There was one guy who was with Das Damen and he was their tour manager or soundguy, and he'd been the Flaming Lips' soundguy. But in the hotel room late night, he had this guy…I don't even know what he was saying to him – but it was this horribly upsetting situation, where Mark was ready to kill him. He was threatening to be physical – but he just did it all with words.

MEGAN JASPER: Chris Jacobs was a publicist at Sub Pop. And one time, Mark called him. I don't know if Mark was confusing Chris with someone else or what the situation was, but Mark asked Chris where he lived. Chris gave him the neighborhood, and said, "Why are you asking?" And Mark was like, *"You might want to watch your back."* I don't know what spurred that, but I feel like that's another thing that would happen with Mark – there were a lot of weird moments. But nothing happened to Chris.

JEAN-PHILIPPE DE GHEEST: He bought an iPad, and he asked me, "JP, do you know how this thing works?" I was like, "I don't know. Maybe you should do this…" And he was just like, *"Bah!"* – and smashed it on the ground. But I didn't witness the kind of stories I heard of when he was on tour with the Queens, or even for the *Bubblegum* tour – when he had to get out of his own bus, because he apparently smashed the bus driver in the face. So, he had to drive behind the bus, apparently.

GREG WERCKMAN: I know two times where things had to be broken up – that he was physically going to get in an altercation. Mark just didn't want the spotlight. Like, one time, it was just an over-aggressive fan. And that fan almost lost all their teeth. Mark was a really strong guy, too. I was with a small group of people having dinner – including Mark – and all of us were like, "Look man, *get away*." And Mark took it to another level. In this day and age, things got weirder and weirder, because everybody had a phone with a camera. And Mark didn't like that – he hated seeing everyone videotaping instead of watching the show when he played live.

CLAY DECKER: He's a big fellow, and he'd stand his ground.

Screaming Trees Split Up

GARY LEE CONNER: It was a surprise that he announced it on stage and didn't tell us [that the Trees were breaking up, during a performance on June 25, 2000, at Memorial Stadium in Seattle, as part of the opening of the Experience Music Project]. Because at that time, everyone was off doing their own thing. What happened after *Dust* is we'd been with the management company Q Prime – that was a big mistake. Those guys were too "big time." They wanted to be involved musically in what we were doing. The record company never cared what we were doing musically, but these guys were like, "These songs aren't good enough."

Peter Mensch and Cliff Burnstein, the Q Prime guys who managed Metallica, Def Leppard, and they got Smashing Pumpkins after us. Mark started cancelling a lot of shows in '96/'97 after Lollapalooza. They had enough, so they just dropped us. And then at the same time, we decided we wanted to get off Epic, and they let us go when we asked them to. They didn't drop us. We owed them a million bucks

– probably half of that were the videos we did. Videos were a waste of money.

So, we played a few shows in '97 – we did a west coast thing, in Seattle. And then I moved out to New York where my wife lives, and I went back to college and got my bachelor's degree. And Van had a family in the Seattle area, and Lanegan moved down to Los Angeles. I had been writing some stuff, and it was the summer of '98, my wife and I went to Las Vegas – to go to the *Star Trek Experience* thing, which was kind of lame – and I get a call from Lanegan on my answering machine. I called him, and he said, "You've got to come up to Seattle and do this demo...*right now!*" He always had a sense of urgency about everything like that.

So, instead of flying back to New York from Las Vegas, I had to fly to Seattle to do this demo – and that was part of the stuff on *Last Words.* I remember that was one of the ones that Peter Buck played on – Barrett was friends with him. So, we recorded that and we were thinking, "*Maybe we can get on a major label.*" We didn't want to be on an indie label, although we probably could have done something on Sub Pop. But also, '96 and on, the time for rock music was really waning – it wasn't like in the early 2000's, where it picked up again.

And we got together two or three times to do demos and did a few shows – we played the Roxy and the Viper Room out in LA. And then, we got that Experience Music Project show – which is now the MoPOP [Museum of Pop Culture] series. They've got one of my amps and guitars. It's like, rock n' roll doesn't belong in a museum...*but there it is.* I've always hated the Hall of Fame kind of thing. But they offered us $65,000 – which before, probably the most we got was $10,000. *$65,000 for one show.* We all probably got a few thousand dollars after all the bills. There's always bills.

[Laughs] And I had to fly out to Seattle. I didn't even know until after the show that he said that. Somebody said, "Oh…this is your last show?" And I'm like, "*What?!*" I guess I was kind of numb to it. It didn't really affect me then – it was surprising, but on the other hand it's typical that he doesn't tell us what's going on.

And also, he was the one that was always so resistant to breaking up. I know a couple of times in the book he apparently talked about telling us…I don't know the time he's talking about in '91. That was when we needed to find another drummer – we had *Uncle Anesthesia* and we didn't really know what we were going to do. So, he probably didn't even tell me about that one, because it's typical – he doesn't tell me what's going on. We spent like, 15 years wondering what was going on.

I probably spent ten years mourning the whole thing – because I was never in another band. That was *my band*, y'know? The only other bands I'd been in were the ones with Van – cover bands. And I haven't been in another band since. So, it took me about ten years before I finally got over it. Plus, the technology caught up, so I was able to do stuff at home with my computer that was much more complex – it sounds like it could be on an album. I wrote a lot of songs over those years, but my daughter was in elementary school and I was busy with that, and I was living way far away from everybody – in West Texas. I didn't even leave that town at all – until probably five years ago, because I delivered papers in the early morning, for about 15 years.

Nowadays what really makes me happy is writing songs, putting them out, and having a few people listen to them. It's pretty much exactly back to where it was before the band started – except I have a small audience, which is fine. Plus, I've got a craft – I can write songs and I know I can do them well. And I still write something I like. If I ever stop writing stuff that I like, then maybe I'll give it up. It's funny – I get the Apple Music plays for the Screaming Trees and for me, every week. And it's like, Screaming Trees: 70,000. Gary Lee Conner: 35. [Laughs] I don't care – I'm just in it for the artistic rewards nowadays. Which was what we were in it for until we got signed to Epic.

We were always so serious – so was Mark – about the music. Even though there was a lot of joking around, music was always the one thing we didn't joke around with. We wanted to do the best stuff we possibly could. But then, after getting signed to Epic, there is suddenly this enticing, "Y'know, you could make some money doing this, maybe." And in the long run, we made a little bit. Nowadays, we'd probably make maybe $10-15,000 a year. It's not enough to live on, but it's supplementary income – which is good to have. And also, just the fact that when we get money, we're actually getting rewarded for what we did – which is kind of a nice thing. It took a long time – I really didn't make much money until ten or twelve years ago. Finally paid off a publishing advance and stuff.

JACK ENDINO: There was never going to be a Screaming Trees reunion. It wasn't going to happen. It *almost* did a couple of times, but somebody always changed their mind. I can't imagine them doing it other than the money, because I think Gary Lee would have done it, and Van would have done it, but I don't think Mark wanted to do it. He never wanted to do it. He might have done it if he was hurting for money, and he would have probably held his nose. That was the sense I got – that he wouldn't do it unless he had to do it. The Conner brothers would have done it, I'm sure. Barrett would have probably gone along with it as something interesting to do. But I think Mark was probably always the catch.

GARY LEE CONNER: Mark was always pretty always against re-releasing anything…although he did go – without even telling us – sell our album *Clairvoyance* to some company in like, 2005, and put it out on CD. He gave us a little money for it – I don't think it made that much money. One of the problems is a lot of our multi-tracks, Mark had them in Seattle, and at one point, maybe pawned them. And at another point, maybe left them in a storage space that was auctioned off because he didn't pay for it – along with a car Kurt Cobain gave him.

That was a good story – in 1994, after Kurt had died, I was writing songs and Mark came by the apartment. He comes over driving this old Dodge Dart, and he's like, "Courtney gave me this car – it used to belong to Kurt. But I can't get in the trunk." And I don't know if he ever got in the trunk. I don't know what was in the trunk – but you can just imagine. [Laughs] Was it guns? Drugs? Song lyrics? What the hell could it have been? It's probably missing forever now because it was sold. Whoever bought it didn't even know it was Kurt Cobain's car.

CHARLES PETERSON: The Trees, it was also funny reading the book, I was like, "Oh yeah…the brothers!" I did quite a few sessions with the Trees, and sort of always it dissolved into the brothers having a fight, beating each other up, throwing stuff at each other, typically Gary getting all pouty and going off, Mark Pickerel trying to smile through the whole thing and pull it all together – so you could get a good photo shoot. And then Mark usually holding his head in his hands and laughing about the whole thing, walking off, and smoking cigarettes. The Screaming Trees shoots were a microcosm of the band itself – the personalities. I love them all, but it was like, "OK…when are the brothers going to explode at each other here? Oh, we made it two hours this time…"

Songwriting

JACK ENDINO: In the early Screaming Trees days, I think Gary Lee Conner would write like, 30 or 40 songs for each Screaming Trees record…and they would just go through and pick the twelve best ones and make them "band tunes." And then the next one would come up, and he'd have another 30 or 40 songs ready to go. He was very, very prolific. So, pretty hard to compete with that.

MIKE JOHNSON: For me, that started with his first record, and he mostly just wanted me to help him flesh out his songs – because he was insecure about them. So, he really had the songs done, and he wanted for me to just put an intro on this song, or how we should arrange the song. So, that was kind of a "nuts and bolts" type thing – where he already had the song. But later, we wrote songs – and it can be any type of way.

There were songs of his, like "Last One in the World" – I had the entire music already done and just sent him a tape, and he put his thing over it and that was that. And other songs on that record [*Scraps at Midnight*] or on *Field Songs*, sometimes, we'd just be sitting in a room and I'd be jamming, and he'd be like, "That! Keep doing *that*." And he would riff off of it, and come up with his own melodies and words.

The thing with him that he was so great at, I think a lot of solo stuff – and I think it was maybe out of a function of his primitive level of guitar playing – he would have these simple, hypnotic, repetitive chord progressions or riffs, and he would be able to build multiple melodies off of it. In a way that's pretty unique and powerful. There was never just one way with writing songs with him. I think when I collaborated with him, it wasn't the same as like, with Lee or Van writing with him – where they would just crank stuff out, and he'd be like "yay this" or "nay that." Because I don't know how many songs they wrote for their last two records…but it was *a lot.* And with me and him, it was more just like, sitting down and hashing something out.

ALAIN JOHANNES: The main thing is he didn't like being in the studio, so he wanted to arrive and have things really flow great, and then two or three hours later, he wanted to be singing one or two or three takes, comp the vocal, and then he could go home and be done with it for that day. That became my goal – make him happy within two or three hours. He just loved to flow fast – so there wasn't that much overthinking.

And it was so wonderful how many hundreds of times I got to sit right next to him when he recorded his vocal in the control room next to me – usually with a handheld mic – and we both wore headphones. That was a great part – to be sitting next to him and having his voice resonating in my head, while I was reading the lyric, and being the first guy to feel the impact of the stories and his voice and what it could do as a listener.

The usual way we always worked was he almost used me like an instrument. The goal was to get his vocal on it. He came with an idea – a song without an arrangement. What he'd have is he could sing it on acoustic guitar and play the chords – and sometimes just two or three chords – but he had an entire landscape in his mind that he was imagining, and he would guide me. And also, room to fill in the blanks.

NICK OLIVERI: Josh was saying at his funeral, "With songwriting, Mark would do this thing where he would hum you something" – because he didn't really play guitar, he sang – "he'd hum you a part, you'd play it on the guitar, and it would be a little bit different, and he'd say, '*That's* what I meant!'"

Old Scratch, Dark Mark, the Night Porter

JESSE HUGHES: One of his nicknames is "Old Scratch" – because he's terrifying. So, the second time I met him, was at a show Queens were playing in Arizona, and I had driven out there. I'd got there kind of late – Queens were on stage – and I got on stage just as Mark was finishing his performance. I think it was "Hanging Tree." And as he walked off stage, the dressing room door was locked, and it infuriated him so much that he kicked his foot through the door, and he looked at me and goes, "You'd better not be the one who locked it!" And I was like, "No! I swear! It wasn't me!"

He had the ability to terrify everyone in the room, and then almost without any effort, lullaby them. That's what *Bubblegum* does. *Bubblegum* is in my opinion…I don't know if Joshua would ever consider this to be true, but I almost felt like *Lullabies to Paralyze* was consciously or subconsciously inspired by what Mark does every day…*lullabies to paralyze.* That album – even though my way of masking it may be a little clever – heavily informed and directly informed *Death by Sexy* and *Heart On.* And going forward, it's one of my studio references.

GREG WERCKMAN: That's how I thought of him – he always seemed like an old guy. Way older because of his voice. Just an old, scratchy, "Get off my lawn" voice. But it really wasn't him – he'd talk to you for hours. There was one time we were in England, and Rich, Mark and I were driving around for hours, and his obsession with Shepherd's pies – we drove *all over* the United Kingdom.

There was one day where he must have eaten *eight* Shepherd's pies – wanting to test them all, to see who had the best Shepherd's pie. Or, talking about the Seattle SuperSonics. Man, to his dying day, his sadness that Seattle lost the SuperSonics – it haunted him. He would just talk about all the old Seattle SuperSonics players.

NICK OLIVERI: I heard Josh call him that, and that was the first time I heard someone call him that. The first time I ever heard him say it, we were doing *Rated R*. It might have been an old nickname, or something Josh came up with – I'm not sure. I know it fit him perfectly. He had that scratchy, raspy voice, and he was older than us. So, Old Scratch.

GREG WERCKMAN: The nickname "Dark Mark," it fit him on stage. He was a dark presence, his music was often dark, and like any of us, he had his ups and downs in life where he wasn't maybe the happiest person – but whenever I saw Mark, I would instantly smile. I would always blame Greg Dulli [for possibly coming up with the "Dark Mark" nickname], because Dulli and Mark were brothers – and they gave each other so much shit, but loved each other more than anything on earth. I wouldn't put it past him if it was something Dulli came up with…but maybe it was just a writer. Mark certainly didn't enjoy it.

JEFF FIELDER: The first time I ever was aware of "Dark Mark" was the Christmas EP that he put out, *Dark Mark Does Christmas.* I assumed that was his own nickname – along with "the Night Porter," which is from "When Your Number Isn't Up." And then "Old Scratch" was his email handle – and that's the devil. All those nicknames were pretty obvious to me…but I always thought Mark was pretty spiritual. You know how Black Sabbath, everybody always thinks they're so demonic and evil? But really, their lyrics are always warning against all the dark stuff – it was almost considered…I don't want to say "Christian," but that kind of vibe. Where it's *against* all the evil.

I always looked at Mark in the same way. Where he was so personified in his darkness and all, but if you listen closely, there was always this spiritual element to it – "On Jesus' Program," and he loved gospel music. I think he felt like there was a realm outside of this, but he didn't dare guess on what exactly it was. But I think he lived his life in a certain way that was respectful of the spirits.

I just know that there's folklore – when people talk about Lucifer, one of his names is "Old Scratch." Like, you get those old creepy drawings back in the 16th century – it dates back to that. But he definitely played that part – he was a performer in a way, that he kind of lived it. So, all those things were part of his persona.

I assumed a lot with Mark, because I didn't dare ask him about his tattoos and shit like that. But, "Did you call for the night porter?" [lyric from "When Your Number Isn't Up"] – it comes from that character in that story. It just creates an image. There might be a deeper story to it, but I think it's more about imagery and conjuring up something. [Note: In *Sing Backwards and Weep*, Mark explained that "the Night Porter" was a nickname given to him by Kurt Cobain, after Mark was able to procure and deliver drugs for him late one night] So, when you think of that, it automatically creates a world. It's so perfect.

That's what was so good about Mark – the simplicity in the poetry that would create something with just a couple in the poetry that would create something with just a couple of lines or a few words. That would create a whole world that you could live in – that was scary and warm at the same time. He kind of lived in those spaces. That's just where that stuff comes from. I don't think he labored over those type of things – I just think it was there, it was said, it was easy, and then you could live in that space. For him, it was just simple.

He didn't want to go around explaining himself – *ever*. He was very open as far as if you were to interview him and he wanted to do it, he'd answer your questions. But anything that went deeper, he'd come up with some blow-off answer. Because there's that sense of mystique that I think was important to him. Even now that he's not with us, I think it's important – he was setting that up, to where there was almost a "mythic quality" to all that stuff. Even though he would never say that – because that's borderline pretentious to set up something to make it seem like something. But he did, *anyway*.

Teeth

JONATHAN HISCHKE: I remember him telling me that he needed work on his teeth, and he was going to have to have them redone anyway. Resurfaced or redone. And Shelley – for whatever work she was doing – had insurance, I remember him saying. So, he was able to – on her insurance – get his teeth fixed. And that was one of the options – and it was paid for, and he was just like, "Yeah, I went for it. Why wouldn't I?" Like, "Of course if I could have gold teeth instead of normal teeth, why wouldn't I?"

And I thought that was hilarious – what a weirdo, y'know? I think the first time I saw him, he had a gold tooth. The second time I saw him, he had *all* gold teeth on the top. I asked him if it was fake – like something he was wearing. He said, "No. Those are them now." Just a weird character – tattoos on his knuckles, the whole thing. To the beat of his own drummer.

Tattoos

CLAY DECKER: There were just dots, basically [on Mark's knuckles] – it made it look like he had hobo hands. I didn't do those tattoos on the top of his hands. We never even talked about them – they look like Russian prison tattoos, but I know he didn't go to a Russian prison...

NICK OLIVERI: So, the Freitag 4:15 (which should be 16:15) tattoos me, Josh, Scratch, and Hutch (our soundman) all got are to remind us that life and music and events (festivals), Rock am Ring, are much bigger then we are individually and collectively. [The show took place on June 1, 2001, with "Freitag" being German for "Friday," and 4:15 being the time Queens' performance began] And it was hands down the worst show I have ever had. I mean *nothing* went right. I never gave up and kept trying, but never got there. Just kept playing and looking for the end of the set, which seemed to take a lifetime.

Josh had a broken foot and was sitting down for the whole show, and was not comfortable and was very unhappy, as well as our soundman had a bad one too, and Mark fell down the stairs (after tripping) going up them on the back of the stage. Things started bad and just kept getting worse, and finally it was over, and we all agreed to quit playing music or get tattooed on a spot that *really* hurts. So, I got mine on my ribcage. [When asked where the others got their "Freitag 4:15" tattoos, Nick replied "I think Hutch and Lanegan got it on their ribcages. Josh on his inner arm?"]

It was worse than I am stating here but, I've learned to put it past me, but, just when I think it's in the past, I look in the mirror with my shirt off and it hurts all over again! A nice reminder to stay humble and keep both feet on the ground. After all, what goes up (you know the rest).

CLAY DECKER: I tattooed him one time on his forearm. It was relatively challenging, because it was super-sensitive – because his arms were all scar tissue. And it was right on some of that scar tissue on his forearm. It was kind of cryptic – it was crossed drum sticks and a little Civil War-looking hat. This little stack of designs – four little things above each other, I can't remember what they were – on his forearm that went up. It hurt him a lot – I felt bad doing it. He always kept his arms covered anyway, so I was joking with him, "Why are we even doing this if you don't even see your own arm?"

JEFF FIELDER: He hardly ever talked about his tattoos, and he always wore long sleeves, so nobody ever got to see the tattoos on his arms. I know there were some people who got the same tattoos on their hands [as Mark], and would come to the shows and put their hands on the stage – and that always freaked him out a little bit. There was that cross on one hand, and that almost heart-like design on the other one. He had dots on this knuckles [and stars on his fingers]. He even wrote a song about it – it was called "Knuckles" – but it never got recorded. We opened with it on the last tour. It was only about 30 seconds long.

The Good Old Days

CHAD CHANNING: Most of the time, for the Screaming Trees shows, it was with the whole band – with Kurt and Krist – we'd go see a show. It would be more or less hanging out and chatting. It wasn't a whole lot [of shows that Nirvana played with the Screaming Trees]. Maybe two or three.

When things started rolling, we just started playing

all kinds of places. Every band was playing everywhere.

JOHN AGNELLO: A lot of the favorite moments were just me and him – one on one. In crowds he could be somewhat controversial and a little thorny. But, one on one or in the studio with the band members, he was great. I just loved hanging with him. Also – this is not controversial in any way – I will be honest and say there was a physical thing with him, too. Like, we hugged a lot. There was a lot of touching. Considering he was a big, burly, caveman motherfucker from the Northwest – he wasn't shy about his feelings. We didn't kiss or anything, but we hugged *a lot.* And I feel like he had that soft spot in his heart, where he just wasn't a big, burly, Northwest shit-kicker. I loved seeing that. Not a lot of people saw that, but I did.

MIKE JOHNSON: [An interview and performance of "House a Home" on MTV's *120 Minutes*, in March 1994] was another one of those things where we were all in the same town. Because I was in New York doing Dinosaur Jr. stuff, and Mark was like, "We've got this *120 Minutes* thing. Well…we'll get J to do it." I'm playing J's guitar, and got J to play rhythm. That was pretty cool – it worked out pretty well.

JONATHAN HISCHKE: A lot of his stories that I heard [on the car ride to the Stoned and Dusted show], had a knowing, little nudge of his prior days – of being a mess. Of being a drug addict. And going through all the things he did. I remember when we were waiting to go to the gig, we were at Dave Catching's house – he was having a barbecue with a bunch of people. Mark was staying to himself – because that's the way he rolled. But I remember I was sitting outside with him, and Josh had shown up at the gate around Dave's property – which was locked.

So, Josh was walking around the other side of this chain-linked, barbed wire fence. And I remember Mark saying something when Josh got in. Josh was like, "Oh man, I thought I was going to have to scale that barbed wire fence." And Mark said, "Yeah…you don't want to do that. I had to do that at one point." And I go, "How come?" He said, "There was something on the other side of the fence that I needed to get back. I had to throw something over the fence and then answer some questions, and then I had to go get that thing – because I needed it. *And it was expensive.*"

JOHN AGNELLO: Also, "bowling night in Ballard," while we were doing some of the solo records. It was always so much fun – Mark was really into bowling, I was really into bowling, Tad from the band Tad would bowl, we'd have people from Mudhoney. We called it "grunge bowling" – it was hilarious. And they all had these amazing ways of high-fiving each other for strikes and spares. These silly little things they would do – that I *still* do.

MIKE JOHNSON: Mark was in increasingly poor condition at that point [as to why there was no tour in support of *Whiskey for the Holy Ghost*]. *Really bad.* We did the Johnny Cash shows [in 1995] – but that's after *Whiskey.* That's all we did. He was going to do the CMJ Festival [which Robert Roth discussed in chapter 5], and he called me. At that point, he was in *really* bad shape. I wasn't doing that great as well, and that's actually when things completely split apart between him and I.

He was like, "We're going to practice over at the Soundgarden space." I go over there, and he's got these guys who I hadn't ever played with, and he's telling me to learn these Screaming Trees songs. I'm like, "What the hell?"

Then he goes in the bathroom for an hour and a half – he's smoking crack and he won't come out. And I'm like, "*Dude.*" I just split. I was like, "No. I'm done. I'm not doing this." And he was extremely pissed. That was that – until he went to rehab, and we made the third album [*Scraps at Midnight*] after that.

MEGAN JASPER: There was a time when Mark was not doing well – he was peaking with some of the drug stuff. My mom was visiting, and my mom wanted to come up to Sub Pop and say hello to people. So, when we got on the elevator, Mark was on the elevator with his then-manager, Danny Baird. The four of us went up to the top floor of Sub Pop, and we said hello. I was *shocked* by Mark's appearance – he was so rail-thin and he had a cane.

And when my mom got off the elevator, she said, "Who were those men?" And I said, "Well, the one with the cane was Mark Lanegan." She had met Mark before – because she would visit quite a bit. She said, "That was not Mark Lanegan…that was an old man." And I said, "He looks like an old man right now…but that's Mark Lanegan." And she just went, *"Jesus Christ."*

JESSE HUGHES: One time I got a phone call from him – after I'd first met him. And I don't even know how he got my number. And he goes, "Here's what I need you to do, kid. Get a videotape, open it up, and I need you go get me a couple of eight-balls, stick it in there, and then you're going to put an address on it." I'm like "Uh…OK." "Don't fuck around, hurry up! Did you do it yet?" And I'm like, "Um…*probably not.*" I rarely ever wanted to share my drugs – because that would be the end of them for me.

But being Josh's best friend is a blessing and a curse – when we were making *Death by Sexy*, inside, I wanted someone to be on the record because of *me*. And not in a spiteful way or a jealous way – but just in a "I want to contribute, too" way. And Mark decided to be on that record because, think about it, *he liked Eagles of Death Metal*. We're a fun band. You're not going to tell me Mark Lanegan is a "fun band guy," y'know what I mean? But he did it, and that was one of the first moments where I really felt like I was "one of the gang." And that was a difficult sensation to achieve for me, because I knew how I got here. I no longer felt like I was in Josh's shadow – I felt like I had it made in the shade.

CHARLES PETERSON: As far as solo, probably the most noteworthy solo photo shoot that we did was the one in '93, where I dragged him down to Georgetown in Seattle, and posed him in my '67 Buick and did the "rearview mirror shot" [later used as the front cover image of *Has God Seen My Shadow?*]. I had this '67 Skylark, and I thought, "Let's get Mark…" – again, he doesn't like having his picture taken.

I think part of it is his eyes are just a little bit close set, so he always wanted it from one side of his head or the other. Just trying to get him to a situation where he's comfortable. So, I thought, "Let's sit him in my car." We also went to the Hat n' Boots Truck Stop and shot some stuff. But typical Mark – he just sat in the car. And then I have a picture of him actually from the side, lighting another cigarette with his cigarette – because he would sit there through photo shoots just chain-smoke and chain-smoke. That was his thing.

He mentioned in his book at Reading when we were walking around, and he tripped on a tent wire and went in mud. And I did actually have my camera on me – he says I'd left it – but I did have it, and went to pull it out, and he's like, "*No fucking way*." He said it while all the while laughing. Beyond all the crazy shit that he talks about in that book, he was a somewhat vain person, in that way – as we all are, to a degree. He wanted to put across this certain image. He wasn't the Mudhoney guys – let's just put it that way.

I took him down to Little Saigon [while shooting photos for *Scraps at Midnight*], and I just thought, "There's something about this little, scrappy area. We can find plenty on the street there and in the shops." We just had a really good time. My favorite picture of him from that day is standing in front of this one shop, where on one side, there's this little Chinese or Vietnamese granny holding her purse with sunglasses on, and a scowl on her face. And Mark stood next to her. It looked so much like she would just beat his ass! Just loved doing stuff like that with him.

Definitely the side mirror on the '67 Buick [is Charles' favorite photo he took of Mark]. It also was kind of a tour de force in the dark room making that too, because the exposure between his face and the mirror, and then all the place outside, it just makes for tons of dodging, burning, and work to get that right – whether it's in the dark room or on a scan. I love that one. From *Scraps at Midnight*, there's one where we're just drinking coffee in a café, and he's smoking – that I really love, too.

JOHN AGNELLO: *Field Songs* was the last time we actually worked together. But then when he was in Queens of the Stone Age and they were playing in New York City, he put me on the list – me and my wife, Sharon. This is back in 2005 or 2006. We hunt out backstage after the show, and he hugged us. The best thing he said to Sharon – "I think you've heard a lot of crazy stories about me." And she just smiled and was like, "Oh no, Mark. John only speaks about you glowingly." He kind of chuckled and they kept talking, and then on the way home, she was like, "*Did I do OK?*"

We always stayed really close and there was always a love between us. In a way, I almost felt relieved not to have to work with him – because he could be a little bit of a handful. And the guys he ended up working with, I think they were more like "band members" too, so it was a better fit for him. Because I'm not really a musician. Alain Johannes is a really good fit for Mark – because of the way they work together.

CHRIS GOSS: I did do some backing vocals on *Blues Funeral.* So, we were still amicable [post-*Bubblegum*]. Obviously, I'd see him a lot through association with Queens of the Stone Age and all the other musicians. And I think we did some shows, too – we did a few benefits in the early-mid 2000's. At Pappy & Harriet's, I think there were a couple of them in the desert, where we did Mark's music. And that was a pleasure – especially when we would do "One Hundred Days." It was kind of his answer to my song "One Hundred Years." And I sang back-ups on that song. On the *Bubblegum* record, he was very proud of that piece of music.

And "When Your Number Isn't Up" was one of the highpoints of *Bubblegum.* There's some songs on that, that are just absolutely stunning and haunting – that I'm very proud to have been a part of. It's a very mixed memory. There's a sadness in connection with Mark. Also, the joy of being able to work with someone of that ilk of talent. He was *incredibly* talented.

JACK ENDINO: I was very happy with my own work on his first two solo records. And of course, I would have been happy to work with him some more – but it didn't happen. But he did alright as a solo artist – he kept going, and developed a fanbase. I don't really know if he was making money at it. I don't really know if *anybody* makes money in music anymore.

But it seemed like he had developed a following worldwide…a "worldwide cult following," if you will. I mean, I can only compare it to Nick Cave, maybe. Maybe not a lot of major label success with the stuff he was doing, but there were definitely people waiting to hear whatever his next record was going to be. I met them in multiple countries – people who were Mark Lanegan fans.

MEGAN JASPER: I was laid off from Sub Pop, and I went on tour with Dinosaur Jr. – they were touring with My Bloody Valentine. It was a super-fun tour, and in New York, the show was great – we were there for a couple of nights. And the Screaming Trees were in New York, working on the *Sweet Oblivion* record. I think Rod Doak – who was the Screaming Trees' tour manager in the early days – was the tour manager for the Dinosaur Jr. tour. Rod and J and everyone got in touch with the Trees, and I remember we were hanging out. I think Mark must have come into the hotel room – I was sharing a hotel room with Rod on that tour.

I remember getting into the elevator, and we were going down to the lobby. Mark was kind of fucked up. I had come straight from the show – I had a leather jacket on, and I had cash because I was working the merch table on that tour. I had *thousands* of dollars in cash in my pockets – but I wanted to hand it off directly to Rod. I didn't want to just leave it anywhere. So, I kept it on me. And Mark – who obviously, had been on a million tours – knew how it

So, we're in the elevator, and it starts as a joke, where he asks me how much money I have on me. And I just didn't say anything – I think I just made a shitty comment. And then, he was like, "No, *seriously*" – and he tried to get in my pocket. And I was like "Oh my God…*you motherfucker.*" So, I grab my coat and try to bundle it in front of me and try to hold my elbows in front of the pockets – so that he can't get to them. But then, he becomes *super* persistent. And somehow, I end up falling in the elevator – so I'm on the floor, trying to be in the fetal position, so he can't get the money out of my pockets. Because at this point, I'm thinking, "Oh shit. He's going to take this money." And it's *my job* to deliver this money at the end of a show.

And then, all of a sudden, the elevator doors open, and Mark is on top of me – trying to get the money out of my coat. I am grateful that the doors are open and there are a bunch of fancy people waiting to get on the elevator – who look mortified at the scene. Lanegan has a moment of *"Oh shit,"* and he fuckin' bails. So, I walk out into the lobby. But I didn't want to go outside – because I didn't know where Lanegan went. I waited until I saw J or Rod or someone else, got rid of the money, and then ended up just hanging out with them.

And then, later – I want to say it was 7:00 in the morning or something – the hotel phone rings. I answer it, and it's Mark. And Mark says, "Hey…just want to say I'm sorry." And then I hear a woman's voice saying, *"What are you doing?"* It's like, this whole evening is just like a book and he's in the next chapter right now. It was one of those moments where every once in a blue moon, we would make jokes about that – years later.

But it's kind of a funny Mark story, because it kind of sums up how fucked up he could be, but also, there really is such a wonderful, decent person behind it. And at that time, *he needed money.* I didn't know at that time how fucked up he was – I didn't know how bad. But in all of the darkness, there was really a lot of decency and light, as well.

And I love that that it ended with an apology – while he's in his next "dark zone."

Underrated?

JEFF FIELDER: He was just underrated in general. I never understood that. I think he's underrated in the United States – and he knew that. He would talk about that all the time – because we would play in the States for two weeks. Seattle, LA, Portland. Go to the other side – New York, Boston, Philadelphia. In the middle – maybe Chicago, maybe Detroit. And that's it. It would take a couple of weeks. And then the last few tours, his new manager decided we needed to go after this whole "metal audience." So, we were all of a sudden playing on these metal festivals. That was a new thing for us – this was the summer of 2019, on these last tours.

In the States, audiences didn't really know what to make of us. We would have the regular "Mark Lanegan people" show up – that are generally into the Screaming Trees. That was the biggest thing – it was like a nostalgia thing for the people in the States. A lot of Soundgarden t-shirts – that kind of thing.

Whereas all over Europe – and particularly in Italy and France – it's a big deal. Mark was famous for his own merits, and people liked his new material – not for the nostalgia of the Screaming Trees. There was still some of that – but not like in the States. It was *all* that in the States – that's all it was. And the audiences were relatively young in Europe. And the festivals there are much open-ended – you can see all kinds of cool music.

And the people there appreciate it on a different level. It's not this "separate deal." Hip-hop, metal, and whatever the genres were, were all mixed together – and you could see all kinds of cool shit. In the summers, it was just festival after festival there. All over Europe and Australia. People came to see Mark, and once we got kinda good at it, people knew the band and were excited to see the band. And we were pretty personable – me and Aldo would be hanging around, and everybody would want to come hang out. It was a really cool thing.

GREG WERCKMAN: To me, one of the most underrated rock singers of all-time.

Chapter 13
LAST WORDS

"When was the last time you spoke to or saw Mark?"

CHARLES PETERSON: It was many, many years ago. Maybe the last time I saw him was when I took photos for *Scraps at Midnight*. I think I saw him once at a dinner party after that. But that was the last time we *really* hung out together – for an extended period of time. And that was great, because I remember him showing up, and thinking, "Oh God...what am I going to get today?" And he was super-healthy looking. Clean. Funny. He was like, "You want to go shoot all day? Let's go all day. Do whatever you want." It was a fun experience.

JACK ENDINO: I think it's possible that I might have gone by the merch table at one of his Seattle shows in the last 20 years, and perhaps said a brief hello. But other than that, I had some email interaction with him when Barrett and I were mixing *Last Words* – which was 1997-1999 recordings that the Screaming Trees made. Barrett and I finished it, we mixed it, and he put it out through his label [Sunyata Records]. They're pretty good songs – it's a decent Screaming Trees record.

And I had some email interactions with Mark during the course of mixing those songs. Of course, he wasn't here – it was just Barrett and I. And we would run the mixes by Gary Lee and Van, just saying, "Hey, what do you think?" And Mark really excoriated me for having his vocals up too loud in the mix. He said, "Turn me the fuck down! What do you think you're doing?" It was kind of funny. I was like, "Really? But...your singing is great!" It was the same old thing again – kind of "self-cancellation."

CHRIS GOSS: It had to be at least five years ago. It may have been backstage somewhere – I think that's where it was. I didn't think he looked that well at the time.

JESSE HUGHES: I saw him at Rancho de la Luna. I just started dating Tuesday [Cross] – and I think this is possibly why I will always love the man – he took me aside and said, "Hang on to this one, motherfucker. I know it will be hard, but she loves you." And when Mark Lanegan said that to me…nobody could have told me that – no matter how sincere they were – and would it have had the impact it had when he said it. Because it was so far out of leftfield and not the thing he ever says to anyone. It's also the moment that I felt like he actually thought of me as a friend.

JOHN AGNELLO: I saw him in Lausanne. He was headlining, we went to the show, the kids [a band featuring Swiss snowboarder Pat Burgener] waited downstairs while I went to the dressing room, and we stood in the dressing room for an hour catching up. He thanked me for being so helpful and patient with him – we hugged a bunch and we laughed a bunch. It was just a wonderful night. And then the kids drove me back to where I was staying, working on this record. And that was it.

JEAN-PHILIPPE DE GHEEST: The last correspondence with him was when he sent me an email back in 2018. We had just come back from a summer tour in Europe. During that tour, something happened between the two of us – there was something that "broke" in a way, in the relationship. He was this "boss," and he could be very tough. So, at some point, I couldn't take it anymore, and I would just stay very stone faced. I came back home, and was like, *"This is it."* But he sent me an email before I had the chance to send him an email – just thanking me for the great time we spent together and that I was a great musician. I know he also wanted to go musically in another path. So, that was the last correspondence.

ROBERT ROTH: The last time I saw him, I was actually playing at the Sub Pop store [at Sea-Tac Airport] at one of those day gigs, and I saw him coming up, and I think I was playing "Killing Moon" by Echo and the Bunnymen. He comes up and he had a cane, and he walked up slowly with this big shit-eating grin on his face. I just stopped mid-song and we hugged and talked. That would have been 2018/2019.

CHARLES R. CROSS: He did a show at the Showbox – and I can't remember the date of it – and we talked. That's pre-Covid. I didn't go to the Timber Festival that Mark was at [on July 19, 2019] – which was his last Seattle appearance. I wanted to go to that…but part of my own love and appreciation of Mark's music was that Mark's music is "late at night/dark club." It is *not* a music where the vibe is a meadow in the woods on a sunny day. It seemed like the wrong venue for him. So, I did not go to that. But the pictures I saw and the people I know who talked to him said he wasn't doing great.

MEGAN JASPER: This is one of my favorite email exchanges with him – it was before he moved to Ireland. He made some comment about people streaming music and what a horrible listening experience it is. Which, I fully understand. And then he said that he couldn't understand his place in it. I wrote back and said, "It's funny to hear you say that, because I actually can *totally* see your place in it. I think you're one of the artists who could benefit immensely from having your music available on streaming services."

"I think it's harder for new bands coming in than for an established artist like yourself. I think you have a lot to gain – as far as people being able to better access your music. When you're in town next, if you want to talk about this, I can break down a bunch of the streaming stuff and tell you why I don't think you have anything to worry about." Ultimately, he said, "I would love that. It would be good to hear and maybe it will make me think of it a different way." But, we never ended up having that conversation.

NICK OLIVERI: I had an issue and I had to get ahold of him through email. This was right when the lockdowns happened. Our friend, Steve Hanford – "Thee Slayer Hippy," who was Poison Idea's drummer – had passed, and I had some recordings I was doing with Steve, and wanted to finish them, because he would have wanted them finished. We finished this little hardcore 45 [Dead End America's *Crush the Machine*], and I know Mark was his good friend, so the last time I talked to Mark, I was asking him to write liner notes for Steve's last project. So, he did.

MATT PINFIELD: Before he left [for Ireland], Mark invited me over, and we hung out in his studio the whole day. And I always loved Mark, because Mark was just so fucking real. And that was the connection that we had – he knew how much my love for music was real and pure. We spent a whole day talking about music and life over at his studio.

TRAVIS KELLER: I hadn't talked to him in a little bit. I was talking to him through Joe, because Joe had gone over to Ireland with his brother Shawn to film some of the last videos – for the Skeleton Joe record. But I guess it was probably six months before he died. It had been a couple of months – I felt bad.

MIKE JOHNSON: I saw somewhere online about his Covid ordeal out of the blue, and I was like, *"What the fuck?"* I emailed him. I'd read that he had been in a coma and was out and was OK. So, I wrote him an email, and said, "Hey man, I just heard about this. I just want you to know I'm glad that you made it out, that you're kicking." I just wanted to tell him I loved him and was glad he was alive. And he wrote back, and was like, "Hey man, thanks for writing." And he told me he had moved to Ireland, and told me he was glad to get out of the US and stuff like that. We went back and forth a little bit, and that was that.

SALLY BARRY: The last time I was in contact with him, I was really expecting he would still be here. What happened was in late April of 2021, I hadn't talked to him in a long time. And I hadn't seen him in a long time. But we were passing regards through friends – like the way I met him. If I knew one of my friends was going to be near him, I'd say, "Hey, give Mark a hug for me." Every once in a while, I'd get a message from somebody on Facebook or Twitter, saying, "I saw Mark and he sends his love."

After the book came out, there was an immense amount of backlash – which was reaching into my personal life, because at the time the book came out, Van Conner and I were in a relationship. So, I had to hear about it a lot – because Van was really bent out of shape about that. I know there was some drama around Mark's treatment of Lee in that book. And I was hearing about it and hearing about it. I was like, "Well, shit…this is a good time for me to check in and say hi to Mark." So, I wrote to him in early April, and I didn't hear back for a few weeks.

And then I got a long email back from him, saying

that he had just gotten out of the hospital, and telling me about the Covid and he as in a coma and the dialysis. He was like, "So you see, I really don't give a shit about any of this petty shit – because life is just too short, and you never know what's going to happen." And I was like, "Oh my God, I'm so glad you're OK." And he was like, "Take good care of yourself, take good care of Van." And the way he described it to me, it was brutal. And then later, in the book [*Devil in a Coma*] he tells the whole thing.

Months later, Van told me that he and Mark had kind of reached out to each other and just dropped the whole thing – kind of made up. And I was really happy about that. Because I really cared about both of them a lot. I wrote back to Mark, saying, "I'm so happy that you and Van are talking to each other again." And he was like, "Yeah, that was a nice surprise. It makes me happy, too." The last messages I have from him, I said, "I love you, man," and he said, "I love you, too. I always have, I always will."

JEFF FIELDER: I do remember thinking on that last tour, "*This could end at any time.*" Because he's just such a hard dude. I never met anybody like that. I don't know if I necessarily took him for granted or his whole scene for granted – just because I was so close to it. I don't think I did. But, at the same time…I don't know. I thought about it often, "I don't know if he'll make it through another year." Although he was just so fuckin' hardcore. On the other hand, he might live to be a hundred years old. Just this stone mountain.

When he got Covid, I was one of maybe…twelve people who knew about it, and told, "Do *not* say anything about this." So, I was really reluctant to talk about it – even after the book came out. When we got the call about him getting Covid and getting the bad shit, we'd get updates every day, and it was like, "Well, he made it through another night. But there's *no way* he's making it through the next three days." And then…he'd make it through the next three days. And getting all these updates all the time. And then he was in a coma and all this stuff, and came out of it. The last time I really talked to him was after he came out of the coma. I could tell he was smoking.

Everybody was asking me about Lanegan all the time before he died, and I was like, "Mark's going to do Mark. If I'm in there somewhere, then that would be great. *But he's going to do what he's going to do.*" And he was definitely moving into an electronic…he liked electronic music, but he also liked the fact that he could do it with just him and Shelley, and maybe one other guy. Keep it really sparse and not have to have a band. I think he would always go back and forth. He was a true artist, man.

ALAIN JOHANNES: We had a long conversation on January 7th and then he sent me sketches for songs. February 3rd is the last time we texted each other. He definitely had an album's worth of material already planned. Because originally when he moved out of LA, he was heading to Portugal. And then something happened and he just stayed in Ireland – in Killarney for a while, to weather that craziness that happened. The eventual idea was for him to move and hang out in Portugal. The idea then was to go ahead and meet up in Portugal [during July 2022] – with amazing friends and musicians there and studios, and we were going to make the record out there.

ALDO STRUYF: Mark came to Belgium a few days before he died. The guitarist, Jeff Fielder, quit the band at the end of the last tour – in 2019. So, Mark asked me to find a new guitarist. I had found a great guitar player to join the band

[Geoffrey Burton]. Because of Covid and Mark was sick and recovering, we couldn't go out and play. Finally, he was feeling a bit better. So, the first thing I did was go to Ireland in January and visit him.

And he was really pleased – because not those many Americans came over, except for Joe Cardamone, I think. We spent a couple of days in Ireland, went shopping and walked around – it's a beautiful area where they lived, Killarney. And then I told him, "I have a new guitarist. Let's start, and come to Belgium in a couple of days, and we can do a rehearsal with the new guitarist. If you like him he stays, if you don't like him he goes."

Mark came in mid-February to my place and stayed with Shelley in my house. We did the rehearsal [Aldo recalls the following songs being played: "The Gravedigger's Song," "Night Flight to Kabul," "Hit the City," "Come to Me," "This Game of Love," "Nocturne," "Beehive," and "Death's Head Tattoo"], and he was really pleased about the new guitarist.

We were going to play the whole summer. With shorter sets – festival sets are not as long as club sets. So, that would've been easier for him if he had the strength. We noticed at that one rehearsal, he didn't have the same strength as he used to have singing. He was getting there…but it wasn't the same. If we waited a few months more – towards July and August – he would have been in shape to sing an hour set.

We listened to music [after the rehearsal], because I've got lots of records. The last thing he made me listen to was Robbie Basho: *Visions of the Country* – a finger-picking guy. Mark told me a story about him, that lots of people were really jealous of him because he could play such difficult guitar picking music and sing along with it. He was playing music from his iTunes, I was playing music, and then he said, "OK. I'm going to go back to Ireland." And then four or five days later…I heard he died.

Chapter 14
1964-2022

*Reaction to the news of Mark's passing at the age of 57
(on February 22, 2022).*

CHARLES R. CROSS: Everybody expected Mark to be dead in the '90s. And every year of his life, he felt was an absolute miracle – he and I talked about that several times. So, the fact that he lived to the point that he did…but in a way, it ends up being a surprise, because you excepted that he had outlived all his demons – and had beaten the devil. So, in a way, his death at the time it came was even more shocking than it would have been at another point. I don't know how complicated years of smoking made his capacity to get Covid – and his bad journey, with it was. I'm certainly sure those things did not help. But nothing prepares you for a voice as unique as his to be gone from your ears forever. So, in a way, it does end up being pretty shocking – that he's gone.

ALDO STRUYF: It was the opposite of what I expected, because he was feeling better and better and better. I couldn't believe it.

GARY LEE CONNER: The day he died, it was weird – because it was 2/22/22, and I remember a day before, people saying, "Bad shit is going to happen tomorrow, because it's all 'twos'." I was like, *"Yeah, right."* And then I got a call from Van and Mark Pickerel, and they were like, "Mark died." The very last thing I heard from him was on Halloween, he put out the song from Dark Mark and Skeleton Joe, "Living Dead." And I Twittered him, saying, "That was an awesome song." And he said, "Thanks a lot, man" or something like that. And we heard about him having

Covid and getting over it, so I thought, "He got through that. Maybe he'll outlive us all." I think Van was thinking the same thing. And Van had been through some real horrible health problems over Christmas – which he's still dealing with now. [Note: Sadly, Van would pass away from pneumonia on January 17, 2023, at the age of 55 – shortly after this interview took place]

Gus Brandt – who was Mark's manager, and an old friend from the old days – called Mark Pickerel and told him before any of it had got out in the press. Thank God, because that would have been a horrible thing to read on Facebook. We had a talk about it, and we were like, Mark did treat us bad sometimes and we maybe didn't get along with him, but we wanted to remember all the good things about him and not all the horrible things that people say. Just remember all the good times. There's no reason to hold a grudge against him. Because we had our thing and we did it and we're proud of it…I guess he was. That's the thing – "Everything you guys did was shit, what I did was amazing" – in the book. Although he derided himself a lot in the book, too – it kind of makes it OK.

The one thing that was real horrible about the book – that I found out later – was he asked everyone else and cleared it with them. He tried to clear it with Van but couldn't get ahold of him. He never even attempted to ask me if it was OK if he wrote that shit. I don't know if I would have said, "Yeah, that's cool." Anyway, that day we got Steve Fisk on the phone with us, and also Jack Endino – guys we worked with. And holy shit, I couldn't believe how much regular press there was about it. It was weird. But I mean, I can't even imagine what is must have been like when Chris Cornell died, and the band was on tour doing shows, and you get up in the morning, and…*Chris is dead.* And then all of a sudden, your entire world is turned upside down. This was more like…your long-lost brother or something like that. It's definitely really sad that he's gone. Every time someone posts a picture of his grave on Facebook, it's sad.

ALAIN JOHANNES: I was actually at my stepson's wedding in Cincinnati – Natasha's son, that I raised since he was a little boy. I was just kind of hanging out and my phone was vibrating, and I didn't look at it. I went outside and I saw I missed a call from Greg Dulli, Josh Homme, and Rich Machin – all within four minutes of each other. *I knew exactly what that meant.* Out of all the things he survived and all the craziness in his life, it was still shocking to everybody. He survived almost a three-week coma from Covid. Who does that? Who gets up from that? Once he made it from there, we thought, "OK. It's all good." It was *very* shocking.

ALDO STRUYF: I found out from Greg Dulli – he called me. They had this message on Twitter – I don't have Twitter, so I don't know when Shelley and Rich put it on the internet. But Greg Dulli called me, and at the same time, Sean Wheeler called me, who was also a really good friend of Mark's – they always went to see basketball together. He was crying and heartbroken.

JOHN AGNELLO: The day I found out he passed away, I cried and I walked in the kitchen. My wife was like, "What are you doing?" And I said, "I've got to have a shot of whiskey for Mark." And I literally had a shot in my *Whiskey for the Holy Ghost* shot glass that he gave me years ago – when the record came out.

JEAN-PHILIPPE DE GHEEST: I was in my kitchen, and I received a message from a friend. But she just sent me a link of Belgium media. I clicked on the link…and I was totally in shock. I was really touched – I had just lost my son before, so I was like, "Oh no, *not this.*"

GREG WERCKMAN: Rich called me. It came as a surprise because I wasn't ready for it, but the fact that he died young did not come as a surprise. I was sad, but I think I was angrier. My emotion for that first month was anger – more than it was sadness. And then I think I was able to ease into sadness.

MIKE JOHNSON: It shocked me. It affected me deeply. He and I weren't close for a while, but he was like a brother to me. I couldn't believe it…I *still* can't. I can't stand it. I just don't want him to be gone. As difficult as my friendship with him might have been…I don't know what the words are. I just wish he wasn't gone.

CHARLES PETERSON: It did definitely come as a surprise. Especially, it was unfortunate after his whole Covid thing. I was in Hawaii with my family at the time. It was like, "Fuck…*another one*. When is this going to end?" It's unfortunate. I'm assuming it was probably complications from long Covid. It's hard – all those drugs, they really do a number on your system too, I think. Their long term effect on your organs and everything.

NICK OLIVERI: Yeah, I was surprised – I wasn't expecting it to happen when it happened. I think he had been going through so much stuff, I figured if he pulled out of that, he was going to be alright. It was unexpected, but considering how – at moments – he lived his life, he lived nine lives. *At least.* It was bound to happen sooner or later. But I think he was pretty young to go.

JOSH KLINGHOFFER: Lanegan died the day I was playing Benaroya Hall in Seattle with Eddie Vedder – with his solo band. Those guys [Eddie and Mark] didn't have a big connection, but they hung out a couple of times from just being in Seattle, and my interest with Lanegan began with that *Singles Soundtrack*. And just to be in that town on the day he died was pretty crazy. We didn't so much talk about his music. I think when we saw each other that day, I told him a little bit about that show I played with him and my little experience with him.

And then he was like, "I didn't know him very well, but there were definitely a couple of times where we wound up at the same place back in those early days, and we went to some other house, and we just wound up drinking all night…or had a couple of really great hangs." But that was it. I don't think he had seen him in a long time, and I don't know how closely Ed followed his solo music. But honestly, I think Eddie would probably like a lot of it. I could totally see Eddie being taken with *Ballad of the Broken Seas*, *Whiskey for the Holy Ghost,* and *The Winding Sheet.*

It kind of did come as a surprise – even though he led one of the more unhealthy lives out of anyone that I listen to musically. And I don't know where he was with drugs. I'd always hear, "Oh yeah, Lanegan's been clean for three years," and then the next time I heard his name, "Oh man, I don't think the guy has slept for a month." And then sometimes you'd hear that information was out of date. In that sense, you would never be surprised when someone like that dies, because he could be doing all sorts of unhealthy or dangerous things.

But because of how much I feel like he actually wanted to live and wanted to get to the bottom of what was going on in that soul of his – even though there was probably part of him that has been trying to kill the pain for his entire life. But I know there was this other very powerful force in him, that was trying to stay alive. Obviously there was if the guy was writing books, and wrote about his experience with Covid. I really can't say where he was at mentally at the end or what was going on, but I do feel like he had a drive to live. So yes, in that sense it was surprising. He was stubborn in that way – for as long as he could, he wanted to say "Fuck you" to the forces that were trying to kill him.

GARY LEE CONNER: I have no idea how he died – I don't know if he died from the Covid thing, if he died from a heart attack…I just know he woke up dead, like they say.

ALDO STRUYF: I always thought it was because of the flight to Belgium. Because he was sitting for such a long time and recovering from Covid, and I hear when you fly, if you have a blood clot in your leg, it starts floating towards your lungs or something. I always thought it was that – but I'm not sure. I don't know if there was an autopsy. He wasn't walking around and moving for months after Covid, and people tell me that something like that happens. And because of the flight maybe…I was the one who said, "Come on over to Belgium and let's start rehearsing." He was totally with me on that, so I don't blame myself. But I have no idea.

ALAIN JOHANNES: I would imagine that it would be some sort of circulatory or cardiac arrest. He had just taken a flight – maybe the flying. I can't imagine what being in a Covid coma would do to you – all that time. He traveled, and maybe he shouldn't have.

NICK OLIVERI: Not sure. But it could be a number of things. 1. There was damage done over the years. 2. There's drugs, of course. 3. He also highly believed in a vaccine that is totally and completely in its experimental phase. 4. Life caught up to him. Again, I look at it like this, Lanegan is gone and he ain't coming back. My friend is dead and to me, it doesn't matter how he died – I've got zero judgment about it. I'm sad either way, so I don't need to be told how he died and never have asked. I miss him.

CLAY DECKER: I have my conclusions, and my conclusions are probably not the politically correct conclusions. But I know that Mark was sober when he died. And I also know that Mark got triple-vaccinated. And my dad died right after getting vaccinated – I talked to Mark long distance from Hawaii at the time I was going through it. Mark was telling me about this brain fog going on and all this other stuff. I only talked to him once after he got out of the coma.

He was going to do what he was going to do – no matter what I told him about my thoughts on the vaccine. He just wanted to play music, so he was going to do what it took – and get vaccinated. My conclusions are – and I'm pretty confident in them – is that he getting triple-vaccinated is what killed him. Because I know he was sober at the time and he wasn't getting high at the time that he died. I think it's a tragedy that he had such a history – a very open one – about using, that that's a conclusion so many people came to. Including close friends of his. But I feel differently, personally.

JEFF FIELDER: Nobody knows [the cause of Mark's death]. Shelley knows and nobody else will ever know – I can guarantee you. And everybody's theories and shit – they don't mean nothing. Because there's just no telling. My theory is he didn't like being home…not that he didn't like being home, he didn't like being stuck. I'll tell you man, when we had that conversation about me stepping away from the massive, hardcore touring, he told me, "I'm a lifer with this shit."

His whole thing was make a record, go out, and push that bus *everywhere*. So, I think two years of not doing that, while reflecting on his life so much – just because he became a writer. He said, "Thank God I got this book deal before all this shit went down, because otherwise, what the fuck am I going to do?" I mean, you couldn't really record. He had a little kind of home set-up, but really, it's just him and Shelley. They can do *some* stuff. The music thing just wasn't happening.

He didn't think – and I agreed with him – that there would ever be touring again. There was a point in early 2021, where it was like, "This shit is just *done*. It's not going to happen anymore." After they put all the restrictions on getting in and out of the UK and all of that stuff. It was almost like engineered to fuck up musicians. Especially after all of the other shit – Spotify and them completely de-monetizing music as a profession. The only thing you had left was touring and merchandise. You take that away and there's nothing left.

I just don't think he was good at sitting there – because you can get into television, these godforsaken internet rabbitholes...everybody on some level has been affected by this garbage. Because it's just like, everybody picks which one they want to go down, and they just get lost in it. And then reality almost doesn't matter anymore, because everybody is so not on the same page and far from it. And nobody's immune to it. It's just like the concerts were the one thing that we had that could bring all these people together, all these cultures.

We played in every country in the whole world – and it was eye-opening. That was what it was all about – these different audiences all the time. It really personified for me how together everybody is. Then you take that away and you take all of the travel away, and you make it such a pain in the ass. I just think that he sat there for long enough, and just as the world changed the way it did…I could be making it up, but I think I saw some quote from him somewhere, it's like, "This world isn't made for me anymore." And it's kind of not. Because he was such his own guy, and he said his own very concrete opinions about things – and certainly, about art and music. All of the things that people care about now are the things that were the nemesis of all that shit. It was just like, "Man, *fuck it.*"

Early on, when we were driving around, he'd pick me up from the airport and we'd go somewhere – just drive around in his big old black car. He never talked about this kind of shit, and I forget how it came up – this is early on – he was talking about Layne Staley. And I'm a big fan – out of all that stuff, Alice in Chains was *my band.* During that whole time that stuff was going down, I was in high school and I lived here. So, he talks about Layne a little bit, he talks about Kurt, and he's like, "They were my best friends, man. Junkie friends. All my friends are dead now." And I was like, "But you made it through this somehow. Here you are." And he slowed the car down and stared at me. He says, "*Our time is coming, my friend.*" [Laughs] And then we pulled up, and he let me out – I'll never forget that.

JACK ENDINO: It was a nasty surprise, because it was known that he had had a pretty bad time with Covid – being in the hospital and being on a ventilator. I heard all kinds of stories – I don't know what is actually true. But apparently, Covid went really bad for him – or at least the medical treatment of it went really bad for him. But he had gotten through it, and was back at home getting better…and he died. So, that was a big punch in the stomach, really. Because you're thinking, "Damn, this guy is like a cockroach – you can't kill him! Layne's gone, Kurt's gone, Chris Cornell's gone, we've still got Mark Lanegan." And for that matter, [Skin Yard's] Ben McMillian was gone, as well.

That interview I did with Krist and Kim with Rick Beato a little while ago ["In the Room with Nirvana and Soundgarden: The Krist Novoselic, Kim Thayil and Jack Endino Interview," posted to YouTube on August 25, 2022] – we are all in the "there will be no band reunions club," because all of our bands have no singers. Now, there *really* will be no Screaming Trees reunion – same story. And you've got to hand it to Alice in Chains for being able to continue – it's not easy to do that. It's really hard to replace a singer and have any sort of continuing career. Van Halen notwithstanding, it's rare. OK, AC/DC. *It's hard.*

MEGAN JASPER: When someone shows you they can endure, it's almost like you expect them to endure. And as weird as it sounds, I felt super-surprised by his passing. His death just made me really, really sad. Sad to know that there wouldn't be more experiences and conversations with him. And then, I felt incredible gratitude to be able to access all of the art he left behind. And, to have some *really* awesome memories of him.

JEFF FIELDER: Was I surprised? No, not really. But you're shocked, anyhow. It's still happening – the flooding of memories. In fact, it wasn't until really recently I watched an entire show that we did – the two of us. There's a pretty good show that we did in Olympia [at the Capitol Theater, on May 5, 2018] that's on YouTube – it's just black and white, one shot. The entire gig. It's about an hour and a half, and I watched the entire thing – and all the memories and all the things came up. That was kind of my first real, proper mourning of Mark.

ROBERT ROTH: It was kind of hard to believe – it didn't seem quite real and I just was looking forward to getting to talk to him again. I was excited he had a budding literary career going on – something that I would like to do some day. And I was glad to see one of us taking steps in that direction and being well-received. I figured Mark was aging well as an artist and continuing to do interesting things. So, all have been robbed in that sense. It's a huge loss to everybody. I would have loved to have talked to him again or seen him. Just so tragic. It's been such a tragic time in the world for so many reasons. That really coincided with what has been a dark time in a lot of ways.

JESSE HUGHES: I was a little aware of what was going on in his life. It's not the first time I've seen when someone is on the "long slow goodbye" – if you know what I mean. I was shocked…but it's one of those things where, of course it's initially surprising, but it wasn't surprising at all. He seemed bound for it. And I think that's a good term to describe Mark – the path that he was on he seemed *bound* to. Unable to pull up and avoid the hills. But that's what kamikazes never do.

CHAD CHANNING: It was sad because he was such a unique individual. I'm sure he would have probably written a lot of good stuff – given all the stuff he was going through. I'm glad he was able to get his book out – that was pretty cool. But given his health situation, and just knowing about his years with extensive using and drinking, it wasn't really like a shocker.

SALLY BARRY: You never expect somebody who just beat Covid's ass to die like that very shortly afterwards. But that's the thing – the amount of strain he'd put on his body over the years, and then getting that sick, I'm sure nothing good could come of it. But there's this big sense of relief when you find out somebody beat something like that and is home and is out of the hospital and is talking about working again. You're still in the thing where you're like, "Wow. *That was close.*"

When I found out…it was like not even a shock, it was like getting hit in the head with a fuckin' bat. It was like, "I just talked to him a couple of months ago and he was OK." But you know what? That shit happens. And it happens a lot. I mean, we're older now, so it's happening more and more – because a lot of us did a lot of hard living, and the world is getting harder to live in.

JOHN AGNELLO: I was horrified that he was gone and that I was never going to see him again. Never hear his voice again or get a text from him. It hit me *really* hard. But I wasn't really shocked. I had a feeling something was going not well, because of his illness and the whole thing of him getting stuck in Ireland I thought was weird. To me, the whole thing was like, "This is not good. This is not going to end well." I just had that feeling.

CHRIS GOSS: With Mark, it was always a surprise, because he survived so much. It's like the Memphis Belle bomber in World War II, where it did all these missions but came back and made the last mission. It was full of bullet holes, but it made it. Mark was like the Memphis Belle, like, "This plane *cannot* be shot down." Of course, in the back of everyone's mind when someone was that heavy of a personality and a drug user, you get used to them outsmarting it. You think, "He'll get away with it again." But I'm not sure what killed him.

We know drugs killed Scott Weiland, but in Mark's case, I think everyone is confused – as to whether it was the accumulative effect, like Bowie having a heart attack in 2004, years after he stopped doing cocaine. This long-term damage. So, I would suspect it's something like that. But surprised? Almost. It's a strange one, because he had lived through so much, that it's almost like Keith Richards. If you heard that Keith Richards passed tonight, would it be a surprise? It probably would be, because he has made it through so much. And yet, it wouldn't be – because he's made it through so much. It's a tough one, man. Apparently, his number was up, unfortunately.

KIM THAYIL: I've talked to many people about that, and many people said the same thing – that it was sad and it was unfortunate. There's some element of surprise. Whenever it happens it's a surprise, but I don't think anyone saw it as being unexpected. I think people generally felt that he had dodged a few bullets over the course of his life. Many people say things to that effect.

Everyone I've talked to who knew Mark said that considering everything else, he had a long, productive life. It could have been longer and it could have produced more. And I am sad for records and songs we can't hear from him. I'm very sad for not being able to see him and hear him sing again. I think generally, people understood certainly wrestling with his demons, but for many years, emerging as the victor. He definitely won a lot of those battles.

GARY LEE CONNER: Another weird thing is we weren't invited to the funeral…or it was a memorial [at Hollywood Forever, which is also where Mark's grave is located]. I really don't understand. I mean, I wouldn't have gone – I can't travel. That was just like, "OK. Why wouldn't we be invited to the funeral?" Maybe he left instructions not to invite us to his funeral, but I don't think he was thinking about dying at the time. He might have been a few months earlier when we had had Covid.

JOSH KLINGHOFFER: Two or three days before his funeral, I get this email from Rich from Soulsavers, and it's basically like, "Hey Josh, I just saw your version of 'Revival' and it made me cry. And I was wondering if you would like to join us at Lanegan's funeral. Lanegan really spoke highly of you."

JEFF FIELDER: I was supposed to perform at the funeral, and I got Covid two days before I was to leave. That was heartbreaking – it was terrible. So, I couldn't go. And I got pretty sick. I never cancelled my flight or anything – there was nothing I could really do. So, that day I was watching the updates – "Now boarding," "Doors closing," blah blah blah. Those guys sent me the videos in real time, so I was able to watch the memorial videos. But I was supposed to sing – I was going to be the only performer and we had it all worked out.

I was going to do "Low," and I was going to do "Can't Catch the Train" – which is a Soulsavers tune that we used to do, the two of us. At first I was just going to do *just* "Can't Catch the Train," but it was really short – it was only like a minute and a half long. And I was like, "Eh, I should do one more." And then I just started playing "Low." I used to sing a lot with Mark, so it wasn't unusual for me to sing. And I knew all the words to everything. So, I could have done any of them. But everybody is like, "Oh, 'Strange Religion'." I was like, "*It's too obvious.*" But, it didn't happen.

TRAVIS KELLER: It was a lot of people and it was at Hollywood Forever. A bunch of people spoke. It was a cool afternoon – he would have been stoked. Where he is buried, he is literally right over from Burt Reynolds! He would have thought that was funny – that he's buried right there.

JOSH KLINGHOFFER: It was such a shame that he wasn't there for this. But just the level of respect that all of these notable people had for this guy, everyone was such a loving fan of his that was there. So, it was a great show of true love for these people – Dulli and Josh – and everyone dealing with emotion like that, it was just kind of nice to see that realness. And I think because of who Lanegan was and what he was, you wouldn't expect anything different.

He really touched a lot of people, and it's really such an oxymoron, because he was such a troubled person, who I think probably had such a hard time with emotion in a way – throughout his entire life. And what little I knew of him at the end, you can clearly see through the hells that he'd been through, it wasn't all for nothing – he definitely grew as a person. As much as it probably hurt other people along the way, and as much as it hurt him and was painful and hard for him, he definitely was metamorphosizing, I think.

But the memorial service was a real testament I think to how much of a genuine person he was, and a good person – beneath all the fucked up things I'm sure he did, and the fact that he was basically living like a crazed criminal for many years. But the memorial service really honestly showed that everyone was there to remember and memorialize someone who had one of the biggest hearts that anyone of them knew. For me, who was very peripherally involved in these people's lives, I just loved seeing that kind of honest show of emotion.

And they played some of his most amazing songs: "When Your Number Isn't Up," "One Hundred Days," "Hiraeth" – which they played the video for, I think it's the last real video of him. It's pretty moving, especially to see it at his memorial service – and they played this song of him and Duke Garwood, "Feast to Famine." One of my favorite vocal performances – and I didn't really know this song until this service. And I've probably listened to it 500 times since then. And then everyone walked over to the gravesite, they put the ashes in the ground, and all these people who he meant a lot to, one by one put a little bit of dirt on the urn that contained the ashes of Mark Lanegan. And then they put the headstone on right away [which reads: HERE LIES THE NIGHT PORTER, MARK LANEGAN, NOV. 25 1964-FEB. 22, 2022].

It's such a fucked thing to be honored about, but in a way as a cultural figure and all the different projects and just being a tortured person who had this amazing artistic ability, that he couldn't even explain or control, the fact that we had this meaningful connection toward the end of his life…and then I threw dirt on the ashes at his memorial was one of the more sad but poetic things I've ever experienced. I just couldn't believe that someone that I thought about for going on 30 years, and was lucky enough to have a little bit of a human experience with him, and then I lost it. And I guess I never really experienced it before – where I felt like I knew someone more than I truly did, by measure of time. And now, *I'm at his funeral.*

MIKE JOHNSON: I think about him all the time. And I think about jokes that only he would find funny. I thought he was going to die, but back in the '90s – I never thought he would die lately. It just really shocked me.

Chapter 15
REMEMBERED

"How would you like Mark to be remembered?"

GARY LEE CONNER: As somebody who was really serious about making great music. And somebody who had one of the best voices ever in rock. I know over the years he sang different styles of music and tried to push his own music into different areas, too – something we didn't do so much with the Screaming Trees. And also, somebody who just had a mean side…because of his flawed early life. I don't know if he wrote much about his early life in the book, but there was a really horrible divorce. Small town, I think both his parents were having affairs and they were both teachers. It was like a 10-15,000 person town. I can see why he wanted to get out of there – because it was such a stigma of that whole thing.

But he had a really nice, caring side to him, that was unfortunately pushed out of the way a lot of times by his mean side. And the mean side came from he really had a lot of insecurities I think, unfortunately. Everyone does, but it definitely drove his drug problem and screwed up a lot of his life. But the main thing is his music, and that he had just as much a good side as a bad side.

SALLY BARRY: I would like Mark to be remembered as a good friend to his friends – because that's who he was. He was so generous with himself. And if he was your friend, he'd really do anything for you. And I'd also like him to be remembered as a great talent. Because he was. There's a difference between being an artist and being a rock star. I'd like him to be remembered as a really important artist – because I think he was. And a *true* artist – right down to the core. And funny as hell. Mark's sense of humor was kind of dry. Mark and I used to crack each other up – non-stop. Just kind of subtle and dry, and slightly lacking filter.

JONATHAN HISCHKE: He's absolutely one of my favorite singers. He touches something in me that no one else does as consistently as he does. It's not like he's the only person who makes me feel like I'm right there with him, and have this intimate kind of feeling – there's a woman named Carla Bozulich that does that too, pretty consistently for me. There are a lot of people who do it sometimes, but don't do it other times. And Mark I feel does it every time.

It's a special gift to hear him sing whenever you get a chance to hear him sing. He's absolutely in my top few favorite singers – and has been for a long time. It's really a sad loss. In a way, it's shocking he made it as far into life as he did. It sounds like he had a lot of opportunities to have left us – and somehow, beat the odds. But also, I would have enjoyed it if he was just kind of like that old comfy sweater or coat you put on. I was hoping he would be like Willie Nelson or Iggy Pop or one of these people that maintained all the way – were a comfortable thing for the ages.

He put out enough stuff – there's plenty I haven't heard, so there will always be something more to hear. And it definitely rewards on repeated listens, too. Which is another thing – a lot of the recordings seem simple and it seems off the cuff, and they probably are, but there's enough things happening around these subtleties in the instrumentation and in the playing and in his phrasing. Sometimes, his phrasing would go a little longer than it seemed like it should.

I remember learning those songs, and there would be kind of strange turnarounds. I remember being thrown off while trying to learn it. But it's just part of that overall, imperfect, human feeling that his music has. It's not overdone, it's not overcooked, it's not overthought, it's not spiffed up and shiny. It's always kind of gritty and kind of an off the cuff feeling. And I love that.

JEFF FIELDER: He's one of the true greats. We take this shit real seriously, man. It's tough now, because everything is so fuckin' haywire – I don't see a way out of it. There's very little introspection, very little *calm* introspection. I don't know if that happens anymore – it's hard for me to tell. Because you get this barrage of shit. And the more people stay home and are isolated, the more barraged with shit they get. And now it's starting to manifest itself into real life. It's a bummer. And I don't know what it's like in Europe, because I haven't been back there since this has all really picked up steam. But Lanegan was an artist in the sense of that – there needs to be a stillness to it, a thoughtfulness to this stuff.

　　　　Don't get me wrong, there was a lot of hard rockin' going on, and he wanted to be a rock singer. But I think that what people remember him by mostly is this kind of elegance to his music. And the artistry. And just his general presence. It was real – it's not fake. Gene Simmons goes home and takes off the make-up. *Mark lived his life like this.* He was just real. And he didn't care what people thought. He didn't care what you thought he should be doing. Everybody's like, "Oh, you should be doing *this* and *this*" – he just didn't give a fuck about any of that shit. He was completely self-motivated – him and Shelley. But Mark in particular – just by himself, knew what he wanted to have it be like, and that was it. Rarely he gave a shit about what other people thought.

CHARLES R. CROSS: I'd like him to be remembered for the first couple of solo albums. He loved doing those records and he was as proud of those records as anything he'd done in his life. I loved the Charles Peterson picture that was shot for the cover of *The Rocket* – where Mark is looking in the round sideview mirror. That's the way that I think of Mark – is like that. I saw Mark laugh and I made him laugh, but life was not a lot of smiles for Mark – even on his best day. I look at Kurt and Layne...or even more, Andy Wood – Mark was darker than them all.

I don't know that Mark's death is darker, but Mark's life was darker than any of those people. I was surprised in his memoir, I thought there would be more joy that he would show us – that he hadn't displayed. Every single person who asks me, "Should I read that book?" I say, "No. Don't. Remember him with the music." And everyone that does, calls me up and says, "Jesus Fucking Christ. *That was dark.*" When it comes to Mark Lanegan, there are many things that you are better off *not* knowing.

JOHN AGNELLO: He was funny as shit if you really got to know him. He was a great guy. He had a big heart. He was a massive talent – one of the best singers I've ever heard, when he was on his game. But I really did love his smile – the way he'd smile and we'd laugh together. His heart was wonderful. I know he was tough, I know he could be a cocksucker to people, but man, I saw things about him that I don't think enough people saw.

ROBERT ROTH: As a committed true artist. Absolutely committed to what he did, and would follow it to the nth degree. Very admirable. Having worked with him when it was probably when he was hitting rock bottom personally, it was so great to have twenty-something years of great work after that period. There should have been another twenty or thirty more.

KIM THAYIL: I'd like him to be remembered certainly by his body of work – and as he would like to be remembered, as his partners creatively would like him to be remembered, as his partners romantically would like him to be remembered. To be remembered not just as one of the great singers from this period of time and this geography – from any geography, really – but as one of the great singers in terms of contemporary folk music. And when I say "folk music," I mean incorporating rock, blues, country-western, all that. I think music by and for the people. He spoke to enough people in his music and his lyrics, and I think he certainly should be remembered for that work.

JESSE HUGHES: As one of the great artists and legitimate troubadours of our time. And of all-time. He truly deserves his place in the pantheon of rock n' roll gods – because he delivered something that most artists can never do and want to do more than anything, and that's give us a complete, exactly wonderful, and perfect record like *Bubblegum.* I'm glad you're writing this book, because I don't ever want him to in any way to be remembered as "the person who believed in the TV behind the TV." Because he wasn't.

CHAD CHANNING: A really solid singer-songwriter. Somebody who wrote really great music. I look upon him very fondly. I think of Mark as a very talented man and I would hope that's what people remember him as. Everybody goes through hard times in their life, and it's just kind of the way life is. But…always remember the good.

CHARLES PETERSON: I think it's important to remember his sense of humor. And I think in relationship in to all the musicians who have passed – or just the Seattle music scene in general – that sort of humor and insouciance is kind of gotten lost in the myth, tragedies, and all that. As dark and disturbing as Mark's book is, it's also very funny in parts. And that's how I'd like to remember him most.

JOSH KLINGHOFFER: I get the impression that he was just a good person. Maybe contrary to even what he would like to be remembered as. I think – even though there are probably loads of people who he fucked over or was terrible to – he should be remembered as someone who had, in spite of itself, a good heart.

ALDO STRUYF: He's one of the best singers of his generation – that's for sure. An amazing poet with a fantastic voice. And also a character. If people met Mark, they would never forget it. If Mark talked to you or had a conversation with you, I think you will *always* remember it. You're blown away by seeing him, in a way.

JEAN-PHILIPPE DE GHEEST: As one of the biggest voices of the century. As a real poet – in the sense that he was kind of a tortured person. In that way, he was like this magician that a poet can be – even if you are tortured and you don't really know where you go, but you can make other people find their way in life. That's how he did it – through his songs. And he was really able to move something in other people's hearts.

NICK OLIVERI: One of the best singers ever. And an infectious laugh. A good smile on his face – he'd make you laugh. He was a good friend – if I had a problem and didn't know who I could turn to, either through an email or text, I could go, "Hey dude, this is happening to me right now…what do I do?" He'd go, "Oh, that's happened to me…" – he would know something. I knew I could trust him with pretty much anything. He was a trustworthy, great guy. A good friend to have, Mark Lanegan.

ALAIN JOHANNES: I'd like him to be remembered in the pantheon of all the greats. To me, he's to be remembered in the Rock and Roll Hall of Fame – all the great singers and songwriters and the great musical minds. Up there with everyone else – with Chris, Kurt, Dylan, Cohen.

       He deserves to be remembered as a really huge and important part of musical history and American music history. And I think generations will discover him. I know that he's not as visible or talked about because his music requires more subtlety in character and perception and artistry when you listen. It's multi-layered and the depth is tremendous. *It's not a casual thing to listen to Mark.*

CLAY DECKER: I want Mark to be remembered as one of the most genuine people ever. He didn't hide anything. He was shameless and did not have judgement on anyone. He was an amazing person. I miss him immeasurably. I've lost a lot of friends in this lifetime, but he was probably the closest one I lost.

GREG WERCKMAN: *He was a good dude.* I just miss him. He was one of those people that I would look forward to hearing from or seeing.

MATT PINFIELD: I'd like Mark to be remembered as one of the most important, unique, and gifted singers and lyricists of his generation. He was *so* absolutely special. Lyrically and vocally, he was one of a kind. He was one of the most brutally honest lyricists and guttural/visceral vocalists of that generation.

MIKE JOHNSON: As the greatest singer of his generation. As a great artist. I think there's a reason why he kept going and kept working and kept putting stuff out – he obviously wanted to leave a mark. That's how I would want him to be remembered – as the important artist that he was. Because he was.

TRAVIS KELLER: He was one of the greats. He was one of the best to ever do it. And one of the coolest and nicest. Man, he was just always so good to me. I was always shocked that he liked me – *because he's Mark Lanegan.*

MEGAN JASPER: As a wiseass. And, really one of the greatest vocalists of our time – and songwriters. His voice was defining. And I think his records are some of the best that came out of the Pacific Northwest. Some of the best that came out of our time – my time – for sure.

JOHN AGNELLO: I've been doing this for almost 40 years now, and he's still my favorite singer I've ever worked with – even with all the bullshit.

JACK ENDINO: The best singer that ever came out of Seattle.

CHRIS GOSS: One of the great American poets of the century. *Period.*

Chapter 16:
MY INTERVIEW WITH MARK

HEAVY CONSEQUENCE – December 15, 2021

Mark Lanegan on His New Book, His Near-Death Experience With COVID, Grunge's Place in Rock History

"Whatever I had it attacks places where there was trauma in the body previous times"

By Greg Prato

One of rock's great voices was nearly silenced earlier this year, when Mark Lanegan endured a horrific battle with COVID – which left him in a three-week coma (among other ailments/residual effects) and an extended hospital stay. And his agonizing journey is documented in the singer's latest book, *Devil in a Coma.*

Lanegan is the former frontman of Screaming Trees and an erstwhile member of Queens of the Stone Age. While he mostly records with his solo band these days, he sometimes ventures out for cool collaborations like his recent Dark Mark vs. Skeleton Joe project with The Icarus Line's Joe Cardamone.

Intense reading from beginning to end, *Devil in a Coma* also inserts bits of Lanegan's poetry between his recollections. The vocalist/poet/author spoke with *Heavy Consequence* from his home in Ireland (where he's been living for over a year) shortly before the release of *Devil in a Coma*, which just arrived in the UK via the publisher White Rabbit.

Not only did Lanegan discuss the book, he also shared his thoughts on the vaccine, past musical projects, and future plans.

On how he is currently doing health-wise

A million times better – I finally turned the corner. But it took a really long time. It was crazy. There's some residuals. Whatever I had it attacks places where there was trauma in the body previous times. And I had a number of accidents over the course of my life. I have a chronically fucked up knee which still gives me some pain. That was one of the strange things about the thing – it went for any place where you were injured or had something happen before.

On losing his hearing for a spell

That was from the virus. I just woke up one day totally deaf. It came back after I came out of the coma.

On his stance on the vaccine

I couldn't get it quick enough after I got out of the hospital. Anything that would potentially prevent this from happening, I'm all for it. I previously said I'd be the last one to get it and I'd wait and see how it treated everybody else. I was a bit weary of it – like a lot of people. But a hardcore kick to the balls like I got changed my attitude on it.

On getting COVID just as the vaccine was being made available to the public

Y'know, I probably wouldn't have gotten it – even if it was available beforehand. Like I said, I was one of those knuckleheads who was weary of it. But I learned my lesson. I'll be the first one to get a booster shot when it's available [in Ireland].

On at what point did he decide to write this book

I started writing it when I was in the hospital – on my phone. Really, just from sheer boredom and trying to get my head squared away after three weeks in a coma. It takes a while to get your focus and thoughts the way they were previously.

On if his desire to create music has returned

Yeah, it has. I'm working with somebody, but I usually don't like to talk about that shit until it's done, because I've made mistakes about talking about shit that didn't come to fruition.

On his time with Queens of the Stone Age

I loved it. A great band – still is. Josh [Homme] is one of my closest friends, and the other guys were totally cool.

On his time with Screaming Trees

It's kind of like looking back at grade school. I definitely have fond memories and it's really how I learned to sing – through trial and error, with those guys.

On if he thinks grunge was the last great movement within rock music

No, I don't. It's still hard for me to look at it as a movement. I think that's something that's created by the outside world – not by the guys that were really doing it. It's not something that was contrived or cooked up around the campfire somewhere. It just happened organically. It's hard for me to comment, because there's always great new music and there probably always will be – as long as the sun keeps shining.

On if Soundgarden and Alice in Chains should be in the Rock and Roll Hall of Fame

I personally don't think a lot of the Hall of Fame. I think it's a financial thing. If it was really about true innovators and great bands, the Gun Club would be in there, Roky Erickson would have been in there before he passed away. It is what it is. It's BS, in my opinion.

On how living in Ireland compares to living in the US

Where I'm at, it's largely rural. It's like horse country. That's kind of where I grew up – in North Carolina for a period of time, in a similar kind of environment. Physically, it's really beautiful – much like a lot of places in the US. And people are people wherever you go.

On what his typical day is like now

I spend my time writing and working on music. Dabble with some drawing. Hang out with my wife.

On his future plans

I've got a book coming out sometime next year. It's another book of poetry with Wes Eisold – of Cold Cave fame. We did one a couple of years ago [*Plague Poems*]. And I plan on making music.

SOURCES

All of the interviews were conducted exclusively for this book, except for the Heavy Consequence interview with Mark, and the following quotes by Nick Oliveri:

Songfacts (August 4, 2022): "We had another...song something else."
Songfacts (October 4, 2022): "Josh is really...the band special."
Songfacts (October 4, 2022): "The video was...a fun day."
Songfacts (October 4, 2022): "I think it...I played on."
Songfacts (October 4, 2022): "Josh was saying...what I meant!"

OTHER BOOKS BY GREG PRATO

Music

A Devil on One Shoulder and an Angel on the Other: The Story of Shannon Hoon and Blind Melon

Touched by Magic: The Tommy Bolin Story

Grunge Is Dead: The Oral History of Seattle Rock Music

No Schlock...Just Rock! (A Journalistic Journey: 2003-2008)

MTV Ruled the World: The Early Years of Music Video

The Eric Carr Story

Too High to Die: Meet the Meat Puppets

The Faith No More & Mr. Bungle Companion

Overlooked/Underappreciated: 354 Recordings That Demand Your Attention

Over the Electric Grapevine: Insight into Primus and the World of Les Claypool

Punk! Hardcore! Reggae! PMA! Bad Brains!

Iron Maiden: '80 '81

Survival of the Fittest: Heavy Metal in the 1990s

Scott Weiland: Memories of a Rock Star

German Metal Machine: Scorpions in the '70s

The Other Side of Rainbow

Shredders!: The Oral History of Speed Guitar (And More)

The Yacht Rock Book: The Oral History of the Soft, Smooth Sounds of the 60s, 70s, and 80s

100 Things Pearl Jam Fans Should Know & Do Before They Die

The 100 Greatest Rock Bassists

Long Live Queen: Rock Royalty Discuss Freddie, Brian, John & Roger

King's X: The Oral History

Facts on Tracks: Stories Behind 100 Rock Classics

Dark Black and Blue: The Soundgarden Story

Take It Off: Kiss Truly Unmasked

A Rockin' Rollin' Man: Bon Scott Remembered

Avatar of the Electric Guitar: The Genius of Jimi Hendrix

BONZO: 30 Rock Drummers Remember the Legendary John Bonham

John Winston Ono Lennon

Shannon

Iconic Guitar Gear

A+ Albums: The Stories Behind 50 Rock Classics (Vol. I), 1970-1982

A+ Albums: The Stories Behind 50 Rock Classics (Vol. II), 1982-2000

Sports

Sack Exchange: The Definitive Oral History of the 1980s New York Jets

Dynasty: The Oral History of the New York Islanders, 1972-1984

Just Out of Reach: The 1980s New York Yankees

The Seventh Year Stretch: New York Mets, 1977-1983

Butt Fumbles, Fake Spikes, Mud Bowls & Heidi Games: The Top 100 Debacles of the New York Jets

Made in United States
Orlando, FL
19 November 2023

39188076R00176